THIS JOURNEY WE TRAVEL

By

Tom Paterson

ISBN: 9781983243233

DEDICATION

To all my family and friends.
Thanks for sharing fabulous time together. When life has its problems, it's then
your truest friends are by your side.
I thank you all from my heart. You are the truest friends.

CONTENTS

ACKNOWLEDGMENTS

I want to thank Mina McGuigan, Rintu and Jeff who were NLP Scotland, for what NLP and psychology gave me; Rintu Basu (my NLP mentor in language) and Jeff Goodwin.

Open University for helping me bring out the talent I have, alongside other folk who have experienced disadvantages – either they weren't good enough at school to obtain certain highers for university courses or had some experience in life like mine.

Ann Low for introducing swimming teaching and coaching. I excel at swim teaching and coaching for bringing out people's potential.

Invictus

by William Ernest Henley

Out of the night that covers me,
Black as the Pit from pole to pole,
I thank whatever gods may be
For my unconquerable soul.

In the fell clutch of circumstance
I have not winced nor cried aloud.
Under the bludgeonings of chance
My head is bloody, but unbowed.

Beyond this place of wrath and tears
Looms but the Horror of the shade,
And yet the menace of the years
Finds, and shall find, me unafraid.

It matters not how strait the gate,
How charged with punishments the scroll,
I am the master of my fate:
I am the captain of my soul.

This poem was created by William Ernest Henley, an English poet, born 1849. At the age of twelve, Ernest was diagnosed with tubercular arthritis. One of his feet needed to be amputated and the other needed surgery because of the disease that was eating away at his bones. From this, Ernest wrote a lot about inner strength and perseverance. We travel paths of strength and drive in dealing with loss from health or misfortunes. His most popular poem was considered 'Invictus' (1875). This poem was recited by Nelson Mandela while he was in Robben Island Prison. William Ernest Henley passed away from tuberculosis on July 11, 1903. There is a disabled athletic competition called 'The Invictus games'; contestants get to that stage because they never give in. Through my injury, with its changes and loss, I never gave in.

INTRODUCTION

At some point, there are events that manifest themselves into loss in your life, which we all experience to some degree, although some people deny this confrontation and persist in hoping it will eventually go away.

Returning from climbing, my car skidded on ice and hit a tree. I experienced many broken bones and a traumatic brain injury (TBI) which put me into a coma. The after-effects predominantly affected my speech. It was defined as dysarthria (known to some as 'foreign accent syndrome'). Overall I couldn't walk with my right hip joint messed up, my speech was poor, and my left side was only working at a minimum. Being left-handed, I had to relearn how to write sentences without causing confusion in the reader in how and what I wrote. A big problem was that my memory was frustratingly affected.

I nearly lost my life. I was left with tatters of what I was before: I lost my job, my wife, my prized home, being with my sons full-time; I lost my driving licence, ability to climb and so on. I was a lost, crumpled entity compared to who I was. I even had to relearn how to make a cup of tea and toast from the beginning again, with adaptation. The isolation of unexpected differences beckoned me to follow this lonely path. This added to the 'cross I had to bear' loss I experienced.

This story is about how I dealt with these losses, changed those obstacles with determination, and never gave up. These difficulties made me learn about myself and what life's really about.

Through this head injury I had, I experienced vast loss, yet coming to terms with these differences, I found personal qualities that I was

1

never aware of before. I saw things in a different light; a new day was to dawn its light.

I found myself achieving gifted, powerful results through the challenges I experienced. Some achievements I had to re-accomplish may be small to some folk, but they were massive to me in spite of the limitations that I was now burdened with.

A saying comes to mind: 'What you think is what you become.' This is a core life lesson I discovered. Instead of wallowing in self-pity, I focused on improvement in some way – any way. It's all down to your perception. Besides hearing other folks' versions, your version is the ultimate line in deciding your fate. The words you use can affect your result. If you say it's so difficult, it will be so difficult. If you say it's easy and you can achieve this in some way, you open up the possibilities in your mind to achieve this.

Whether you experience an accident, or an event, a change of lifestyle, even the process of your old life, my experience emphasises the stages of change and shows how to gain more control and direction through flexibility and determination. My personal journey has its funny times: humour can lighten up a bleak situation. This is one of the key parts of learning to see a funnier side of life.

CHAPTER 1

Building A Dream

All men dream, but not equally, those that dream by night in the dusty recesses of their minds, wake in the day to find that it was vanity; but the dreamers of the day are dangerous men, for they may act upon their dreams with open eyes, to make it possible.

– T. E. Lawrence, *Seven Pillars of Wisdom*

Sitting cross-legged underneath the Mir Lidol in the glorious vista of the breathtaking Pyrenees mountains, I find myself casting my thoughts back on how far my journey has taken me so far – not just the physical space I now occupy, but the vast emotional and physical distance between what I was then and what I am now with this journey I am taking.

I let my thoughts drift to the mystic times I had climbing on mountain peaks of astounding natural beauty, that continued after reading countless climbing adventure books to broaden the passion I had for further adventure on mountains of dreams. The enthusiastic oneness, without fail, has never left me, even to this day.

My journey begins with my life story and my wife from a previous journey I had.

My wife Tania and I had been together since we were fifteen. We had two young boys. We lived in what could be described from my view, as our dream home. A home made by long, hard hours of working through such enduring times, building on the dream of what we deserved and aimed for. We finally made this family setting in a house that was in just the right position for schools, shopping and a vista that filled my heart with pride. The views displayed wonders of the gift of living in this area of Scotland, such a beautiful country.

This house offered a breathtaking scene over the broadening vista of the Firth of Clyde, an astounding angle of the Island of Cumbrae, with the end peninsula of the bays of the Isle of Bute and the sea casting a following on the contours of the rugged coast. This natural ruggedness of a distant-looking, unkept land blended with the smoothness of the ever-changing sea in the opening panorama of the Firth of Clyde, giving scenic pleasure that bathed your eyes.

Most importantly was the magical grandeur of the mountainous peaks of Arran in the Firth of Clyde, often capped with a dusting of snow up high in the hub of winter: 'the mini Highlands', as Arran is commonly known. With these vistas, the distant speck of the edges of Kintyre seen on a clear day added to the finale of these beautiful Clyde views.

This bounty of pleasures displayed various shipping activities mainly to Greenock. In its day, Greenock and Port Glasgow was once busy, booming with ship building and cargo deliveries for Scotland. The constant routine of ferry journeys to their ports and sailing boats roaming freely to destinations in the Clyde completed this amazing pleasure for your eyes.

On the other side of the dream house, the enchanting panoramic view from the attic bedroom looked to the fairly steep, rising hills that displayed the outcast of sullen crags high up at the top of the raised landscape, 350 metres high. I spent regular time climbing on the crags, getting lost in flowing movements of freedom on these rocks.

Let me introduce you to the start of a long, passionate love affair I have had for hills, mountains crags and cliff faces, where nature is free of man-made interference and exists in its truest form. This was the playground that kept my excitement pulsing, which gave me a drive for living. I climbed, losing my passing thoughts, being in tune with the smooth rhythm of physical climbing manoeuvres. This rock and I sang the same song. To be at one with the rocks and the presence of truest nature, is one of the highest forms of oneness I can explain in this world. I climbed by myself without being 'roped up': I would climb freestyle. This was the ultimate experience for me. One miscalculation and I would fall to serious injury or death. My focus was a necessity to keep me on the rock. I had to be in tune with the rock and my physical self. I got lost in the dangerous, intense, rhythmic flow of climbing. I was awe inspired.

I regularly was contented with how lucky we were to live here. Yes, it was difficult and hard travelling to work in Glasgow every day with long working hours, yet the effort of this gave me the gift of living in a beautiful seaside town. Here we were building this life we aimed for. In my life then, I had a sense we were finally reaching our aim of personal contentment.

To broaden my horizons, I progressed with the step of setting up a business that would be a reward for all the effort that I had put into the hairdressing industry. This in itself would bring on fresh, new problems, but that has to be expected in day-to-day living. Hairdressing in fact was how I worked at that point.

I ploughed on to get this far with hairdressing which conjured up a few plausible ventures to choose from. Pressure of fulfilling my work dreams grew and grew its encompassing presence in my day-to-day living. Without having this ready to go ahead to make it a reality, I put immense pressure on myself and it haunted me, having the career opportunities and not using them. How was I to earn my reward?

When I eventually left school at sixteen, I couldn't wait to get out the door. I didn't know what I wanted to do except for being a mechanic (I'd helped my dad sort out his car all the time since I was very young). At that stage, I was holding a torch. Later I took an engine out when I was twelve. Getting work in this field didn't work out and it came to a dead end. There was no employment in this field that came my way, or I never saw the opportunities that were available. Then, there was my cousin Robert who was training to be a hairdresser. Hairdressing seemed to suit him with his gothic/indie image. It wasn't the 'done' thing and not having to do the 'humdrum' of normal work' appealed to me in in that period of time. Hairdressing's connection with art made it an acceptable angle for work.

I went for an interview as a trainee hairdresser locally and got the job. I was still just sixteen. On the Friday I said goodbye with glee to formal education and started work as a trainee hairdresser on the Monday. I found working with my hands natural to me and it was creative with shapes and forms. This seemed just right for me. I found the gift of outputting creativity through my hands. I without doubt got the creative part from my mum, who was an art teacher. Painting didn't really appeal to me, yet hairdressing seemed to produce creativity through shape and form that I had interest for. There are so many forms of creativity other than art. Shapes textures, words, conversation, and physical activity like sports or dancing and so on, display this creativity.

With the training lessons I got in the salon, I was also to go to a college that covered the accepted national standards of hairdressing.

This was the start of unleashing the most important part of my way of life: I had a new discovery – actually liking education, with something I actually enjoyed and had a great interest in. I was not just scraping through by the skin of my teeth, as I had previously done at school. I now discovered study that had a purpose. This was the very start of the education that I would continue to gain to this day.

This hairdressing assistant's job was in the town in which I grew up. Over a couple of years, I worked at two different hairdressers in Largs and after this, a big company in Glasgow. With this initial training, I was 'pushed in at the deep end', performing on stage at a number of hair shows which built my confidence greatly. I was carrying out hairstyles on stage. It was a brilliant experience, only I wanted more on that level. I was drawn by 'performance adrenalin'.

I needed more challenge to make the most of what I felt really comfy with. I began to be aware I could make a difference. After a few years, on the off-chance I applied to a few big famous companies in hairdressing that were worth chasing after.

I actually got an interview with one Glasgow-based international salon. For the interview, I arranged for a friend who I knew from school to be a model for me. Claire was originally from the Isle of Barra and I had known her for years. In the interview, I cut her hair in a trendy style that was not everyday normality. Then in talking to a director, I was asked some interview questions.

I actually got that job as a stylist based in Glasgow in that fashionable salon, which was regularly involved in the Alternative Hair Show in London then. I was ecstatic. This seemed a dream come true. My dream had started to form the way I wanted it to. Even if I was only there for a few months, it would look great on my CV. I felt I was recognised. With this, after lots of hard work, I could over time take my relationship with my childhood sweetheart Tania closer. That would have been a continuing crescendo for us in being together. We had been together, side by side, and supported each other.

At this salon, it took all my effort to fit in with this image, trying to prove myself in the city's trendy hairdressing ways. This was long hours with long train journeys too. It took all my time up. I initially lived off tips I got to get by and always had change kindling my pocket, as the wages at first covered my train fares. With hard effort over time, I worked my way up the hairdressing levels in this company. Then I progressed as a stock controller, supervisor, assistant manager, manager and trainer.

After eight years of rising up the ranks and feeling fantastic from achieving this with exceedingly long hours, I took ownership of my hairdressing and management styles. The Rainbow Room worked exactly the same way I did and we fitted our way of working like a glove. I always felt different, as if I had some purpose in the world, and at this time it suited me perfectly. They had fabulous business skills that allowed me to develop both with myself and working with people. I was so in tune with where they were coming from. I gained positional promotions and my final job role oversaw training. I became the Rainbow Room training director. I gained the position of art director through graft and a passionate devotion to hairstyling. Over the years I gained over a dozen awards for my achievements within the Rainbow Room at their yearly congresses. I definitely was on the same level as the way the company was going. Our paths were heading in the same direction. This made me feel like I worked hard, was worthwhile, and that I had a purpose. I was so enjoying life. I was living with passion.

This was me. I couldn't imagine anything else that would give me a closer match. Achieving something I felt was just right for me, my creativity and passion for working with my hands was at its peak, as well as communicating with people, which was another love of mine.

Then, my heart was set towards an offering of a franchise salon with the Rainbow Room.

My wife was progressing up the scale with her own work. Having been a care manager for years, her interest in going her own way towards nursing like her mum grew stronger and kept calling her to follow it through.

Yet there was more confusion for myself. I was in turmoil with the choice of following the increasing complexity of training and development which I loved, or going for an actual franchise and running my own salon under the Rainbow Room wing. What was going to be my chosen direction? This decision haunted me with heavy, dragging chains. Which path should I follow: furthering my delivery training and developing through their training school, or a franchise salon with the Rainbow Room? I was torn between these two, both having their advantages and burdens.

Having learned a substantial amount of necessary knowledge through running the training and being known within the hairdressing field, this was a good start to my plan, in case I chose to take the training route. With the years I devoted to hairdressing training and respect within the company, this seemed a big opportunity to open up a training academy. It posed a battle against going for a franchise salon and this became a stronger and stronger option, leaving me confronted with such confusion. Training had become more of a reality for me, which I loved the most. It was me. I had actually designed a system with the experience I had gained through training and development, and I was fully qualified in training.

My future was now becoming clearer in its own way. Slogging through long, hard hours, it seemed as if I was on the last straight for success on another scale, having my hands in many pots.

I was fully alive, thriving in the pressures of hairdressing success in such a competitive field. I had a beautiful wife, had found work that suited to me to the ground, a love for an outdoor life with its share of adrenalin extremities, and my kids, whom I love. For me, the jigsaw seemed to be starting to fit into place. This was my career and life dream.

Back home, the two boys we had were only a year and a half between them.

My first born was Euan, in 1997. The most joyous, brilliant experience is contributing to giving life to a child entering into the world. I felt I was on top of the world. The biggest glow I will ever experience was my first born coming into the world. Seeing him for the very first time, he was born, love in itself: the first sight of him can't be justified by words alone. It was the whole entity of being. It was the most unique experience, bringing another into this world.

A year and a half later, my second boy, Adam, was born in 1999. Another full, life-changing moment, the same as the first time. For me, those were the highest peaks in my life journey. Again, having such pleasurable, unforgettable moments was the core gift of all. I experienced immeasurable love for my kids. It was similar yet so different to the last time I brought a child into the world. Having the experience beforehand didn't seem to dull the extreme loving pleasure this gave me. It was the ultimate experience of bringing new life.

To be the other half in producing life is the most fantastic gift of all to me. Nothing comes even slightly close to this.

Their eyes told of the unlimited, immeasurable love they and I both have. This will remain with me, so clear, always.

From then on, one more day, a day older, bigger and becoming astute, every day I lived to share was so special. This in itself filled my sense of accomplishment and also where I settled in society.

This society I lived in dictated both my upbringing and what was accepted in terms of how relationships fit in, as if you have a purpose and belong to this community. Work gives a sense of status and standing with people, which can show the effort you have put in. We all live in what society dictates. Being human, we strive for social belonging. With hindsight of trying to fit in with this social image, I had accomplished this as far as my role would dictate. I was living my dream.

CHAPTER 2

The Vigour of Climbing

That fine line between bravery and stupidity is endlessly debated – the difference really doesn't matter.

– World War II British Air Force pilot

One of the passions I discovered was adventure in the hills and in the mountains. It has imprinted Scotland with tales of many adventures, from me and the classic outdoor stories of my heroes that live on. I found such mountainous peaks and crags that were away from the pollution of mankind.

Venturing into the open wilderness found in the remoteness of the hills gave me the purest refreshment; an experience of being free and part of this beauty.

Getting away from the humdrum complications of life, I would find myself escaping up north for hill walking, or climbing. I'd be there amongst the glory of the constant variation in weather and the seasons. This leaves an imprint on you, an impression of different stories and actual memories that recall such adventures with glorified passion.

When I had a good selection of mountain destinations travelled with hillwalking, I then took this further, for the greater addiction of climbing. This gave access to mainly inaccessible sights, to venture in these environments in a different way. It also took me to newly found peaks. This at times was by far greater in my personal journey.

The drier conditions were more suitable for mountain rock climbing. I would travel once or twice a month up north to different mountains and crags with a collection of my fellow climber friends.

This climbing got me drawn to the flow that only rock climbing gives. This was my way of being away from all normalities and relying on my focus and physical ability. Complete practice danced with my improving climbing style. With this, I then built my compendium of climbing experience along with the ongoing gain of expensive equipment and specialised clothes that I now yearned for in this obsession.

This followed suit to the ever-expanding dreams I had of peaks and mountains, making them more possible. Out of all the accomplishments I wanted in the world, these innermost goals were now becoming feasible.

I rehearsed with regular practice that sharpened up my ability just a little better every time. It made me focus on the big picture of testing my ability to the maximum. I love pushing myself towards what I am aiming for. This practice gave me heightened focus. This in itself built a mixture of needed experience, to serve me well in the future.

Winter climbing was then brought into play, taking a step further from what rock climbing alone could offer. Different technique, conditions and attitude affect the ways a climb can be achieved: an extravaganza of technical conditions that displayed beautiful and sinister results. The difference in technical format made all climbs uniquely special to me.

Through the week, one evening, I climbed at an indoor wall in Glasgow after work to keep the practice consistent. I also climbed the local crags on other evenings. I would climb at these crags without a rope, giving way to a smooth flow solely relying on my movements. With this 'free climbing', I often climbed with crampons and axes at times. Winter climbing seemed to suit me better and I liked the winter adventures this offered.

I was always oblivious to the hassles of life with the focused concentration climbing gave me. It was a peace of mind, focus and action that were found only in climbing. It forced me to become attuned to my senses inside and out, for results. I got used to the routes on the crags: they became second nature to me. I remember some routes with vivid clarity; movements of technical skill happened without any conscious thought.

With this extent of climbing, I pushed my extremities to their highest capability. Nothing in comparison was a problem then. It put things into perspective.

An error in climbing can be very serious, even fatal. The mind comes into top form with such physical extremities and precision movements. This was physical and mental concentration that worked me to my limits, strengthening my focus.

With winter climbing, the moves seemed easier for me and the techniques suited my approach. I seemed to have the best adhesion in the ice and rock compared to the intricate detail of summer rock climbing. I love the cold, crispy conditions winter climbs offer. Snowfall and the seasonal change were my ultimate favourites. This was my Disneyland. The low rise of sunlight in the shortened day and the pace required to achieve the route before it got dark, added even more adrenalin appeal to me.

I spent years summiting hills and mountains in Scotland, only to have an increasing desire to do more.

My introduction to rock climbing was on a holiday to the awe-inspiring state of Alaska with my wife and brother-in-law, to see their uncle with his family who lived in Anchorage. Alaska's beauty blew me away. It made my heart sink. I fell in love with this place. It was similar to Scotland, yet by far more remote, colder, dramatic and extreme in size with immensely taller and jaggier peaks. I felt most comfy in this faraway destination.

At an indoor climbing wall in Anchorage, I then had my first introduction to rock climbing. This was so exciting, prising my way up the wall to what seemed like very high heights in the building. Though I was scared of heights at that time, it disappeared from this point on. I climbed my first route and got the buzz of accomplishment that would never leave me.

On returning from Alaska, Tania's brother and I went for a lesson about climbing outside on rock faces known as crags. It was different, not having the exact footing and handholds available when you needed them. I liked it better than the inside wall. Again, this gave excitement, as my imagination exploded with thoughts of what we could do with climbing outdoors now.

One day after, we went to the crags above Largs, to put into practice what we had learned. We practised putting in gear and rope techniques. Then I cyced up where I wanted to attempt my first climbing route. I prepared with adrenalin pumping and went for it. I climbed this route, placing the rope devices needed for protection on my way up.

Finally, I completed and led my first route: I lost my climbing virginity. What an amazing achievement for me at that time. I felt vibrancy rush in; truly alive like I had never felt before. It filled me with such a sense of accomplishment despite possible danger. We went regularly when the weather permitted us to venture up on the hills and further still to different crags of Scotland.

A while later, at a DIY shop in a town near where we lived, I met someone I knew from school who was working there. It was good to see Kenny. We talked, pondering on normal formal topics, and then discovered our mutual love for climbing. This led to us meeting up at the Largs crags one evening.

This was the start of a good climbing buddying-up, and also a great friendship.

I climbed with him a few times and now and then I met up with one of his other climbing pals. The three of us turned into a good team: full of humour, adventure and drive. We all had this drive for climbing. Years of continual climbing gave experience and fond memories of climbs that will never leave me.

We all were drawn to adventure from reading the mass of expedition books, which helped drive our climbing dreams. This set us on course to do things we could only dream of. We started with the sprawling, rugged beauty found at our back door in Scotland. We planned trips to the French Alps. Next, the majestic Himalayas, South America, the Antarctic and North America: it seemed endless. There are so many climbing goals to strive for.

We climbed from crags to mountains, summer and winter. It was exciting. With different people's styles of climbing, this broadened my experience of climbing to rope work and securing rope protection. There was a spell of finishing my work on Saturday and directly driving up the A9 to Avimore to meet up with Kenny, Gary and one other person so there were two climbing teams. We had an early rise and headed up to a part of the Cairngorms called Coire an t-Sneachda. This area had good winter climbs: getting there involved a snowy walk in, then we climbed the chosen routes. After the climbs, we walked out to the cars and drove all the way home. They were long, tiring days. For me, this was a good way of lifting the tension from my too-busy job.

Getting to this level was an addictive buzz. Only at that point, when it hastened the possibility and the lure of distant challenges, did adventure come into play. It was becoming real.

These times of climbing proved a match for me. I had spent a life trying different hobbies and sports, yet nothing clicked. I then discovered my love of mountain activities. I had found the physical exercise I was looking for. I physically experienced being in the mountains, and I physically experienced the flow of climbing. This was a strong belonging I had that I could experience only with the outdoors and crags. My heart would fill and the hassles of the day would be lost with this wonderous experience of going to the hills and mountains.

CHAPTER 3

'Wee Car Bump'

There is only true courage when first there is genuine fear.
– Dr David Livingstone

Coming up to the end of a good year of climbing, the weather produced an exceptionally cold front early on in the winter season. It delivered a spell of weather conditions primed for winter climbs. It gave a good frost with a heavy fall of snow on the mountains. They were brilliant and crisp, ideal for winter climbing particularly. The low sun kept these conditions pristine.

These wintry conditions were exciting in the time before the New Year. Mainly, the weather produces better conditions for winter climbs in Scotland from January to April. The weather in Scotland, unfortunately, is also temperamental. It can display north-easterly cold from the Arctic, giving cold and dry conditions, or south-westerly warmer and wet conditions from the Pacific to deal with. It gives such contrasting conditions to adapt to.

I was busy with my work. This was the busiest time of the year in hairdressing with people getting ready for Christmas festivities.

At home, I had lots of Christmas activities and family gatherings on the go as well.

I made arrangements with Gary to do a climb before New Year and take advantage of the weather conditions. It was exhilarating to finish the year with a winter climb.

We were to go up early in the morning. I was to pick him up in Glasgow and we were to go on and do a route on Ben an Dothaidh, a route I had done before with Kenny earlier, yet sections would be on better form for winter climbing under these conditions.

I don't remember a thing about that particular day. I have no doubt that this is my way of protecting myself by blanking this part completely out of my mind. The climb was done well, so I was told: it was as good as we anticipated. That, I can't recall, or the swift descent down the mountain, as it was getting dark very early. We met some climbing friends going for a short hill climb. There were words passed briefly as we wanted to get down to the car and they wanted to borrow as much fading light as possible, then the return to make the most of the day.

On our swift return, the weather became even colder as I drove my reliable new Vectra past Crianlarich, on the way to Tarbet. The thin road was continually winding and clung to the edge of the cold water of the looming Loch Lomond.

There was fresh snow on the road that covered over an ice patch. As I approached one particular section, so I was told, the ice was hidden by the fresh snow. Unaware of the treacherous conditions, my reliable Vectra skidded on a turn verging to the right and got lost in an uncontrollable motion. The car lost purchase over that winding road only to confront the trees at the other side. On my side, the car collided with one of these looming trees. The front window smashed as the tree came in to meet me like an unwelcomed gatecrasher. It crushed my door. I love nature but I am not a tree hugger, like I interpreted hippies to be. This tree came in to meet the car with dramatic force.

BHAM!

From this moment on, my life would never be the same again.

From that point, my life was completely transformed, good or bad. What I had known up to this point had died.

This life had come to an end. Life as I knew it, was no more.

This life, built up with such effort, had breathed its last breath. It had died.

The tree forced its way in to smash my pelvis in six places, ribs snapped, and with the immense crushing impact my head suffered the main trauma, giving injury to both of my temples. A scattering of broken glass from the windows showered me with surface cuts to my wrists and hands. I also lost one of my front teeth with the severe thud to my head.

'A wee shoogle' is a small shake in Scottish dialect. This is what I called my accident to take away the seriousness and stop pigeonholing scenarios of people's interpretations of head injuries. People normally made assumptions about the conditions based on what knowledge they had or what they presumed the symptoms would be. It was how they constructed those symptoms. This blew the horn of always dealing with stereotyping resulting from suffering a head injury (traumatic brain injury – TBI).

I fell into deep unconsciousness. Fortunately, the car behind us was driven by a male nurse and he helped until the ambulance arrived. Gary had a shake-up.

I was taken to the nearest hospital, the Vale of Leaven, where they made an assessment of me and I was taken straight to the Southern General which specialised in the treatment of head injuries.

I was in a bad way. My throat was sliced open to help me breathe with aid (a tracheostomy). With these traumatic injuries, the seriousness of what my body endured, I inevitably drifted into a coma for an unknown time, if I was to come back at all. A big sleep, as I called it.

With the pace of my lifestyle, it was going at 100 miles an hour day in and out. My 'self' was demanding time out. This in itself was an extreme way to get a rest, not even bothering to hit the proverbial snooze button. It looked like I needed to recharge and rebalance my life in some way. I was going too fast.

Tania was told by the police who came to the door of our house. That must have been one of the most horrific things that could ever happen, to be told that your husband was in a car accident and was just hanging in there. She had to tell our oldest son in a way that at his age, he would take it in. He was listening in the background. With friends of mine in the police, Euan concluded it might be one of his dad's friends. Tania told him at the front door in a panic-stricken state. At that point, her life had fallen apart.

From that point Tania's life was to change completely, both out of our control. 'Fate' had condemned us to this dramatic change.

My wife got hospital accommodation near the Southern General for her and the boys to visit me. Her family and my family would come up to see me and assist in getting me out of the severe danger I was in. It was just like what is seen in movies; the only sign of life was my slight breathing. She and our boys saw me daily with hope I would pull through. I can only guess that my pure will and the sense of love kept me going. This, I assume, was keeping me fighting in this battle.

To this day, the pain, the shock, the catastrophe they experienced seeing me in a coma, wired up to machines with my major wounds, brings me deep, agonisingly sorrowful pain, knowing what my loved ones had to go through. I would never have wanted to give this kind of pain to anyone in any form, never mind to close family.

It fills my heart with tearful regret to have caused immense, horrific suffering to the people I loved.

My coma lasted for six weeks. It was torturous for my wife and both our families, not knowing how long I would be in a coma for, or if I would awaken at all.

It's not at all like what folk presume from an inexperienced view of coming out of a coma. The common image of coming out of a coma is waking freshly the next day after a night's sleep, never mind six weeks of being in a suspended coma, not ready yet for the normality of the day looming ahead. My wife and family who saw me, did not know what would happen. If I came to, how many disabilities would I have? The impending anxiety must have been the worst scenario. They just had to wait, mainly my wife. Her anxiety would have been overwhelming with all the effort she had to give with organising the boys, our home, her work and wondering what our relationship would be like if I came to. This was all presuming maximum change forced upon her life.

After six weeks of my wife and family hanging on, paused, waiting for me to awaken, I came to awareness very slowly. I was told later I followed this with a waking coma. I was not lying flat, as if sleeping, but propped up, contained in my inner world with a blank haze in my eyes.

The days and dreaming nights became one and confusion seemed to melt together with uncertainty as to what was real or imagined from inside my mind through dreams. What was a dream and what actually happened, as if there was no difference. The normal structure of a day had disappeared with the upheaval of such traumatic injury. This didn't help with the effects of the brain injury.

Becoming more aware of events happening, this mixture of reality to dreaming was still there to an extent. It dragged its heavy, laden chains through the onslaught of my recovery.

Time was confusing, in doubt of what had actually happened and what was an invention of my dream world. There was no format as to what could be done or not.

I now saw outside the box of normality of the social world that I had constructed. This was a different way of supposedly living my dream: this had built up, presuming it had to be done, and in a certain way.

Feeling on a lonely path, I doubted the effects this injury had bestowed upon me. With acceptance of not following the average path of my culture due to the dramatic events of my accident, I stood up and showed my difference with defiance. I was injured and wasn't going to let this unknown get the better of me. Whatever my fate would be, I'd enjoy life fully whatever it turned out to be, as opposed to just surviving. I was still here. I had survived maybe by chance, or for some reason unknown to me.

It was like being on another level in this world. This level, only a few had ever experienced. This could only be explained as a spiritual experience. It's experiencing life in a different context, on a different level. In a way, I was thinking differently to the supposed ways you are brought up to think. I now lived outside this so-called box of how society dictates you should be. This in itself was complete confusion and fear of the unknown. I experienced it as not trying to fit a square peg into a round hole while also trying to fit in. My way of being didn't fit into life as I had made it before.

I didn't die and I now had a chance to live life the way I could under any circumstances. This is my life. I'm still here. This time, it was part two: a second chance at life now. I was given a chance to go through a different door to change my life.

My thinking process was that although things seemed to be on another planet, it was like coming home from a wandering, relaxed dream that gave new ideas and possibilities. The events that happened, were they constructed by reality, or were they from a dream that seemed real? The image of the two blended and became one. Could, will, or did they happen?

If life is a colourful sensation, this was adding new shades and tones to the world we know.

Eventually, during the waking time I became more compos mentis in what I was experiencing. Through this experience, the mixture of reality and imagination, I began to notice what things were actually real or imagined. It brought on my awareness of reality. I could feel myself on this level, for the first time to this extent. You can't learn this. Unfortunately you have to experience going to the very edge to see and sense things differently; that is not the normal way of the world. Culture sets out what is good and what is frowned upon. I now discovered the 'real world', without the influence of society. I could see and feel things which would have been missed before. This was a new beginning of experiencing life in new ways, only at this stage, I had not been told of anyone who had ever experienced this: I was alone, stuck on my stranded island, not knowing if I would be ever found. Would this be the way, such loneliness, till my curtain fell?

My physical injuries brought a severe loss through not being able to walk. My speech was very poor, if not incomprehensible. I was unaware of this at first. Only in talking, and the quizzing replies from others, told me something was majorly wrong. It created a worryingly twisted gut feeling that this was not normal. What made it worse was missing a front tooth that chose to leave me at the accident. My speech was static and slurred, as if I was drunk. What I was thinking and said didn't come out the same way and wasn't understood.

What made it worse was that I couldn't rely as a second choice on writing my thoughts down – my function in my left hand was a complete pitiful minimum. That's pretty hard if you're left handed, as I am.

I was experiencing similar symptoms to someone who had a stroke down one side. An occasional lone drool from the left corner of my mouth told this tale. It was as if my left side wasn't functioning.

Overall, I had problems – big, bloody problems.

Communication was not happening the way I wanted, bringing on frustration with the expressions I got from other people who comforted me like a child. In some way it was like I was a young kid, which was belittling who I actually was. I was trapped and imprisoned inside with no escape at this stage.

I frantically searched, scraping at the ways of communication I knew. They were of no use to me now, at that point. I was forced to discover new ways of expressing communication to get myself heard, different to what I was used to before. It was like going against a very strong tide and not going anywhere, only being pushed back.

I could remember, quite vividly, people who came to see me, including the medical professionals. Firstly, my family came to see me every day. The others who came were climbing friends, people from my work, my cousins and friends I have known for years. They consisted of basically my wife's mum, Jerry and her brother David, my mum, my sister, and brother-in-law Raymond. Those who meant most to me were by my side daily: my wife with my two boys.

The staff from my work who came to see me in the prison-like confines of a hospital room, saw the extreme difference in me from before, at work. There were two girls who came in that were trainers in the Buchannan Street salon. One of the girls used to work with me, Heather.

Being my first Rainbow Room assistant, she meant a great deal to me. Spending so much time getting her through her training and seeing her working with my clients in my salon, we got along so well. We matched in our nature and sensitivity, where she would appeal to my clients. When she was qualified, she was sent to Buchannan Street salon where she became a trainer. We sang the same song. I was fond of her like a big brother to his little sister. She had done me proud. For all the time in hairdressing, she could see creative potential that rose from her sensitive nature. We were alike.

The other girl she was with was a trainer who had a smile that always left you with complete happiness from her glorious nature. She was a complete pleasure to know.

With all these visiting people I was so glad to see, this brought on the reality of where I was.

I had lost my life. What I knew of life at that point, was deceased. Full confusion of the unknown was at its fullest. What was going to be physically lost or healed? What was the loss of my functioning? What couldn't I do anymore, or was a loss due to the physical injuries? Could I work again? How would this be with my family roles? The confusion between dream and reality haunted me. What did I dream? What did I experience? Confusion made me experience solitude. This solitude would always be there from then on, sometimes worrying, sometimes sweeping me with treacherous anxiety. In a strange way, this loneliness always kept me company in the constant battle to fit in again and have a purpose.

CHAPTER 4

Tour de Hospitals: Discovering Loss

There is only one step from the sublime to the ridiculous.
– Napoleon Bonaparte

My First Therapy Visits

My first visitor I got was Jane from Headway. She came to see me at the Southern General hospital. This gave me the impression that it was a very formal visit. There was an atmosphere of formality like a teacher-pupil scenario. I picked up the formality, which wasn't hard to miss. I felt like I was being assessed, from the way she visited.

She ran the Ayr division of Headway, the organisation for people who have head injuries. These head injuries can be from accidents, attacks, strokes, haemorrhages and many other brain function related conditions. With external or internal problems that cause injury to the brain, part of the mind dies in relation to what damaged occurred. Sometimes, over time, brain functions can find ways to bypass the injury to find another route to the function, sometimes not. The mind's 'plasticity' can regenerate functioning to create the best and most efficient way for you. This makes the brain in my view, the most amazing thing in our universe, with its capability.

The episode of seeing Jane for the first time was great as I loved the newness of meeting someone. I always loved this, although it was painful letting her see me this way. She put on a face of not showing concern at all, although seeing folk with head injuries is her job. It was good to see her and also be alive, yet I still had the shock of nearly 'pushing up daisies'.

After the meeting with Jane from Headway, I saw a speech therapist. The work she started covering with me was basic, almost material you would give a young child.

I thought, *This is bloody toddler stuff. No way do I need this help. She must have got me mixed up with someone else.* The therapist presumably came out of her way to see me and I politely showed I was pleased. The crushing blow was, I actually struggled with these toddler exercises. This physically shocked me and put a huge dent in the reality of my injury. Apart from being imprisoned in a bed and not being able to walk, I discovered the loss of what was so important to me: I loved communicating with others. A person of my ability should breeze through these exercises which seemed to be for young kids, yet I struggled. This was a huge emotional blow for me. In my head I was saying the reply, but physically I had problems saying the words out loud. What I produced to the world didn't sound the same as what I was saying in my head. My words weren't being produced as I made them. This frightening shock made me feel robbed of something so precious to me. I tried in desperation to find a quick solution.

No matter what's happened with the speech difficulties, I am a trainer, for God's sake. I will find my way through this. These were losses I encountered, and there were more still to burden my supposed second life that stand out with their weary presence. This theory loaned itself to future challenges and adjustments made through the toil of relearning. Still, I was to adjust to my injuries: I was to learn to cope in a different way, if I could.

The ways that I needed help and begged attention grew to a vast, mountainous amount, not just my speech.

The next day I saw the occupational therapist. The same thing again, I experienced. I found the exercises seemed so basically bloody easy and it cut me with frustration inside that I struggled frantically with these too. Physical exercise has always been a priority to me, yet with these pathetically easy exercises, I struggled, not even completing these menial tasks. With all the discoveries of parts of me that I didn't even think about, I couldn't do them anymore. Embarrassingly I fumbled my way through what could only be described as infant exercises. Now not being able to stand was an absolutely crushing blow to me. Walking was stolen from me. This drastically affected my passion for the outdoors. I was always on my feet with either work or hills and mountains. The shocking blow of such a traumatic loss began the process of bereavement for my old life.

At this point, my aim was to minimise the feeling of panic from struggling with such easy things, for my family. I refused to appear as a weak little victim encompassing the 'poor little old me' pose.

The way my wife and family went out of their way for me, I felt the unwelcome sensation that they were not talking to me as an adult; they were talking to me like a child, or a geriatric. I was being forced into my loss of life, being replaced with another identity I didn't want. I didn't want it to be presumed that my mentality was that of a young kid. I remember being young and going through these stages of growing up and didn't want to experience this again. More than anything, what haunted me was the way folk presumed my mentality. This was so scary and felt so surreal. I was knocked off the pedestal that I worked so hard to achieve. I said repeatedly to myself, 'Hang tight, this will be over soon. Then I can walk away.' Of all the times I had to be strong to get over challenges in life, this haunted me with its immense burden. With all this entails, I didn't want to be going backwards. This time, I would be struggling hard with even basic tasks, never mind complicated ones.

This caused such bitter annoyance and infuriating frustration for me. For all the pain I put them through, I let this petty annoyance go by, not hurting them anymore. Being backed into a corner, I commanded myself in a military fashion to get through this opponent. I didn't hang on to the pitiful annoyance of 'poor old me' mode, I forced myself to do something to get results. I was to gain any results, no matter what. It was closer to a solution, as opposed to doing nothing and not seeing progress. I was getting closer to a solution. I was to plough on.

I started to get back into a sort of routine as soon as I could. I became disassociated from the situation I was in, very similar to the stories I read about the holocaust in terms of the methods of survival that these people were resigned to.

I furthered this by imagining the events I was experiencing in the hospital were like programmes I would watch on television: a medical drama was on and I was an actor. I was the patient just for a while, a way of escaping reality by playing the role. It made me move away from my emotions towards the situation and made them less dramatic. This took 'self-drama' out of the situation and I could play this game I found myself in. The nurses were so helpful and professional. I saw this from my own background of working with people and noticed strong professionalism in their work.

Visiting Friends

The decision to put me in a high dependency ward was made and I was transferred from the Southern General to the hospital in Ayrshire, due to that 'all impending' postal address of mine. I was in North Ayrshire and the closest Ayrshire hospital was Crosshouse on the outskirts of the town of Kilmarnock.

A delivery by ambulance was arranged and in my wheelchair, I went in the back of the van, looking towards where we were driving.

Going by road seemed an unusual way to go, and I didn't recognise where we were going. My head was in a delicate condition and there were a lot of new sights for me to process. It felt like we had been on the journey for a whole day and I was shattered. The input of information from this previously known route seemed too fast to process. Travelling never bothered me until now. I felt travel sickness for the first time, being in the back, as I had always driven since I was seventeen. This was such a strange looming sensation of haunting unpleasantness. All the moving sights and sensations, I found it near impossible to focus on a point around me that was continually changing, whereas with driving, you are focused on the road in front.

That was a journey bound in such horrifying experiences: I still had major problems with my physical health. I yearned to forget this burden.

We arrived and I awakened to find out where I was to go, and more importantly, what part of the hospital I would be taken to.

In the ward, I was given my own room. This was just like the television programmes I watched about hospitals.

The situation in this hospital seemed as if I was in a dream, or like a television programme that was surreal. There were distortions I made with this way of coping. I still got confused between dreaming and reality. What was real, imagined, or constructed by myself? It all blended together. Normally you create your reality based on what is accepted and you go along with it. This way our society dictates how you should act and be. After all, what is reality if not only an assumption that is presumed by me and other people? Although there was this unwritten pressure to conform, it gave me insight that made me think 'outside the box' of the accepted rules in society. I saw things differently and refused to succumb to unspoken presumption. My senses found different information that my attention could process outside of normality, from seeing things from a new position. Seeing the world in a different way, with my defiant self, was the start of experiencing life in a different, new way.

Another aspect of life that changed was my sleep. It was all over the clock and my cognition was obviously poor; this sleeping disarray didn't help my thinking at all. With my head injury I still found it hard to tell the difference between dreams and reality, along with the vague disarray of my body clock. I slept a lot, although it was all over the place and not structured. With not being able to walk, having very poor communication and my left arm protesting with any grip or minimum co-ordination, sleeping confusion didn't help. Yes, this monumental path I was on began to grow into a new direction in life. In a way, from my old dreams with climbing and exploration, this was the expedition I dreamt of, although this didn't involve climbing some extreme peak, or some wild unknown piece of land. This was greater. Danger and uncertainty was present; that gave me the ultimate challenge to stretch my limits and capabilities to their ultimate potential. Losing what I had before, my life was turned upside down. With my physical injuries, this was an overwhelming change in life. Again, I was using a metaphor, this time an expedition to escape from reality.

At this stage, there was so much information for me to process. It drained me and it left me exhausted, sleeping for a soothing recovery rest and waking only for a few hours at a time. There was distortion from the outside world to my inside world, yet I was still the same person. This was confusing at times.

I thankfully started having visiting guests again, this time in the Crosshouse hospital. I was so grateful for their attention, the feeling of so much effort from my wife, our families, yet I felt embarrassed for them to see me in this feeble, broken way, although I had an abundant wealth of excitement to see them again.

From my family, my cousin Robert came visiting. He was like a brother to me. He was the male of closest age to me in my family and I always looked up to him. On my father's side, he only had one sister, therefore she was his mum. Our family wasn't big. There were three cousins I had on his side, two boys and a girl. David is a lot older than me, Robert four years older, and Maryanne is three years older. There is only a few days' difference between my sister and her. They grew up together. She was my other sister. Maryanne is now married and lives in Athens, Greece, with Vangelis. They met on Kos working at bars. They got together and opened a bar in Santorini, the most beautiful island in Greece, in my opinion. Thera was the main town up in the cliffs with a view of the high bay with sunsets creating tones of beauty. This island had a famous black sand beach further down. Santorini is one of the most romantic locations with breathtaking views that are commonly used to represent Greece to the rest of the world.

I spent holidays seeing her working in Greece. The time my wife and I visited Maryanne holds some good memories for me of the fantastical cultural change. This first time I brought my scissors to cut Maryanne's hair. I ended up cutting others who worked in other bars that afternoon. Time went on and what I expected to end with one haircut, ended up being six. By going into the bars they worked at, I got free drinks. I even got into night clubs for free. For the week I was there, I didn't pay for any drinks, for the both of us. It was just like the Aztec South Americans having a society that didn't use money (a task for a task). I gave them something and they gave back in other ways, rather than with money.

Later, I got to know Vangelis better when they came to live in Largs before they actually opened up this bar in Santorini. His

Greekness compared to myself being Scottish always made good humour for us. We had all shared good laughs together and I looked forward to meeting him again.

He always made a point when having a drink that we had to perform the Greek tradition of saying 'yamas' (cheers). Robert, my other cousin, combined a Scottish traditional saying with Vangelis's saying – 'Yamas ya bas!' This was a humorous combination of the duality of these two cultures.

Robert's humour worked well with this and we used this saying for years after. In growing up, his music taste influenced me: The Stranglers, Souxie and the Banshees and other indie bands. He way made a huge impression on me. The indie music, his clothes and the way he acted being so different, appealed to my cry for identity. This lifestyle was individual. I found it seemed perfect for expression when I was young. I enjoyed the individualism.

He was also best man at my wedding. With a kilt on, he still stood out with his long hair.

Then, he lived with a girl I went to school with. She was in my class. I was friendly with her going through school. She came to visit me in hospital. It was wonderful to see her, as she was someone that knew me who wasn't family. She was of a great, gentle nature. I had never seen her with any form of aggression. Dee making an effort to visit meant a lot to me.

I tried to give my best appearance to them on their separate visits. They both came to see me at different times, as Robert and Dee had just split up and it was a delicate, looming situation. Nothing mentioned about them coming to see me to the other. It's lucky they didn't turn up at the same time to see me. That would have been a lot of emotional turmoil for me.

For myself, I was making the highest effort, although at times when there were very obvious problems with things like my speech, I quietened down, only responding in tried and tested ways. Saying, "Yup," and head nods were favourite ones I used, thinking this would cover up my new physical, imprisoning problems. Nothing tried, nothing gained was what pathetically went through my mind while not making an effort to improve my speech.

I soon was moved to the ground floor, only this was a room

without a bed. I obtained a few bangs trying to walk from being stuck in my bed and banged my head again. I despised not being able to walk. This was the greatest loss of all at this point. I had no recollection as to how these bashes got there, but no way was it comparable to the head bashing I got from my 'wee car bump'.

I loathed the fact I couldn't walk. I was told I kept trying to stand up and walk, falling over every time. I loathed with pure revulsion having to rely on that bloody wheelchair. I was driven, with full determination, to get my legs walking again.

They were forced to take my hospital bed away for my own safety and I was in a safer position on the floor with mattresses, sheets and pillows. It was just like camping. This brought me joy, something that was important to me from my outdoor pastimes. I was more comfy in this camping style. This in itself was a step closer, back to the outdoor life that seemed feasible again, in some way.

I reckoned I was the only person I know who supposedly camped in hospital. If they had a Scouts badge for camping at a hospital, I would be the proud owner of one. Doing something that was different was a calling for me. This in its crudeness suited me, with a different approach not following the normal regimented way of life. My persona was so pleased with this.

I spent time with the speech, occupational and physiotherapists. I was making very slight improvements. Very little though they were, Everest isn't climbed in one big footstep, it takes thousands of small steps to reach the summit. It was daunting to lose so much and relearn things you don't even give a second glance to until they are gone or severely damaged. This could be described as experiencing bereavement for my life as I knew it, leaving the panic of trying to scratch some sort of identity out of such a loss and the complex confusion this brought while working out to what extent I was damaged. It left me with few ways to solve this, if it could be solved. Nobody can say whether you will regain what you had before, what has died and can't be replaced, in relation to what was I like before my wee car crash. Did I have problems in areas I wasn't really aware of and subliminally I avoided it and they blended into the background? When the damage was that severe, I forcefully dragged myself to 'wake up and smell the coffee'. This is now. This is the reality.

The work they were giving me was for early injury symptoms. With having a head injury, some people acquire a mixture of ways in which their speech delivery is affected. Some have only a slight temporary difference, others have to restart from an early age again. I was in that category, having to learn tones and pronunciation of certain words. There were words that didn't come out the same.

They were deciding which exercises would help me best at this stage and sussing out how bad my symptoms were.

The hospital grounds, I got to know. I was taken out regularly in that dreaded wheelchair. I just love being outdoors instead of being stuck inside. That was torture in itself. It was like being imprisoned, being enclosed by four walls. I was back outside again, although the difference in me now, foretold which ways I would enjoy open space.

I was getting to the stage where I had done as much as I could and was looking for more, experiencing inner frustration to make a dent in my recovery. I was looking further into conversations and how I could improve them at the stage I was at. Through practice with the speech therapist, I could hear which areas weren't good and needed work. It was the only way to tell which sounds I was slurring and what I could scrape by with; another step in being heard and understood. With speech, we can hear what we have said to keep us on track. That was one part of my speech damage I had to adjust to – hearing what I was saying to the outside world. I later found out that my voice being this way was called dysarthria.

My communication was so limited with the accumulation of after-effects from my 'wee car bump'. Inside, I'd visualised the event. When it came to me telling others, it just didn't come out right, letting them know I experienced a disability with producing words. This is where other problems aired themselves, in their perception of the brutal extent of my injuries, seeing me and hearing my attempts to talk.

My outside communication was poorly picked up, resulting in continual misunderstandings with what I said or how I replied. I merely minimised what I was saying to give less confusion over what I was trying to communicate. This was giving me such frustration and annoyance: I was experiencing it at its peak now. It was not people trying to understand me, and not being faced with such difficulty, but the lack of contact that had always been a very large part of my work and life. I was feeling as if I was completely alone and no one understood me. This was a lonely place.

A Takeaway

One night in the Crosshouse hospital, I got the most astounding treat from Tania. She arranged, through her organisation ability, to bring me in an actual Chinese carry-out meal that was approved by the staff nurses. The thought of doing something that would actively help me came to her, and she immediately put it into action.

I was actually in hospital, getting a Chinese takeaway. This was different to the daily monotony of simple hospital food.

A wonderful taste explosion: this was heaven against the burden of life changing events I had experienced. Such a privilege I was given, with the monotony of being fed from a tube for weeks at a time beforehand. It's some way to lose weight, although this was not really specifically my intention. It felt like being back to a normal existence, that we'd had a meal out as a reward for the hard work we done. I looked for a television to watch a DVD on while enjoying this treat, as I normally would have done at home. I regularly had this treat after I got paid, or went out for a meal monthly. It was a rewarding feeling then, of hitting targets, and this was a sensational treat I experienced just when I needed it the most.

My mind was occupied with useful sensations that were triggering those good memories. The memories seemed so clear, with the emotional uplift.

I was doing what they offered in terms of medical help as well as I could. I got to the stage where I was in need of more stimulation again. The dreaming of my own world lessened and reality of the world out there was becoming more important.

The high-dependency unit at Crosshouse had served its purpose well in bringing me back to camping and a Chinese takeaway. I was ready for the next stage.

My next planned hospital tour was for me to move to the Astley

Ainslie rehabilitation hospital in Edinburgh to give me specific help.

I got organised for the long journey through there, which was by far longer than the journey I experienced down from Glasgow. This time with the power of learned experience, I was given travel sickness tablets from my mum to stop the feeling I got from the Southern General journey to Crosshouse. I just closed my eyes. That helped this time on my far, distant trip to Edinburgh.

I was excited about staying in Edinburgh, a place I always looked upon as having an exciting, unique style of its own. From the west coast to Edinburgh, this fulfilled a weird sort of long-term want for me. I was actually going to stay there for a while.

Astley Ainslie

This inevitable turnabout for me, with my physical injuries and the effects from this head injury, created confusion in my life – part two. I got the needed bonus of support from Tania's family and my own. They always gave me positivity. In time, the positive consistency was a way of life for them. Family support and seeing my wife with my boys, was vital for me during the hard slog of being imprisoned in my mind. My wife went completely out of her way to see me just about every weekend in Edinburgh. Having to organise two very young boys and herself, the upkeep of the house and staying at her friend Alison's, was monumental, and bound her to harsh reality and the immense amount of suffering she had.

It was such a tremendous shock and change of lifestyle for her, and I was so thankful for her support. This made the difference for me, in not feeling alone, to such an extreme I could never explain with words.

Her friend, who moved to Edinburgh, came regularly to visit me through the week. Ali and Billy, her partner, gave me their presence daily which put the structure and support of normality back into my day. The help and friendship I got mainly from Ali through the week was precious to me. Ali was Tania's friend from way back in school all through the academy, although I lived near her and got her home from school at times.

They both came to see me every week separately, even with their busy schedules of work.

Ali brought her kids as well. It was so pleasurable to see her kids. The girls were of different ages. They were seven and four years old, displaying different personalities, which is said to be common with two kids from the same family. With the support Ali gave me, the frequent help when I needed it, just seeing someone from the outside world, her kindness will always be with me.

I had a drive from then on that I would return the kind support she gave me in some way, even if she is not aware of how much help she was to me: her loving presence gave me support through the isolation I was experiencing. I will never forget the kindness she showed. Knowing her from way back at school, I never would have believed then that I would find out her real strength as a person in this way. To see this in such a way, is about as close to seeing the truth of someone you can get.

As well as visits from her, I was privileged to have continual visits from different people so well sorted out by Tania, family, friends and climbing friends. I was so thankful for her organisation, as our family from both sides came to visit me. Only now looking back do I see how extremely beneficial it was.

A visit from her brother and his friends was such a big compliment to me, for them to come all that distance to see me. The cost of travelling to Edinburgh was a task in itself. I guess it was an adventure for them, and then tracking down the hospital after getting to Edinburgh an adventure written itself. Also my sister and my brother-in-law (Raymond) with their girls who made me laugh at funny descriptions of the difference between east coast and west coast. In the west, we are offered salt and vinegar when buying chips. On the east coast, they offer salt and sauce. My brother-in-law was always so funny. He could have been a stand-up comedian, if he wanted.

Even my bosses from the Rainbow Room came to visit me in the Astley Ainslie. I felt so bad in a way: guilty of leaving them in a position of not having a training director because of my accident. How selfish could I be? I had devoted time to and created the training system for candidates of my own accord. They came with their baby too, which showed the support they had for me. That touched me. They went out of their way to see me.

My other boss in the internal verification process came to see me from Cheynes located in Edinburgh. It was good to see him as well. With all that contact from my work life, I felt a sense of pride in what I had done. I must have been good at what I did to get this kind of support. With all my hard work and a focused aim, maybe that helped.

One of my clients came to see me after visiting her son in Edinburgh. That produced an awareness that I must have been good at my work for her to come and see me. The action of her making the effort to see me, proved my self-worth. Also, I got lots of cards from clients, some I could easily recall and had 'good times' doing their hair and enjoyed their personalities. Only very few I had a problem remembering. It was great for people to take time to pay attention to me, and made me aware of how much I was in their lives. At this time, I didn't feel alone as well.

In hindsight, I had a good friendly relationship with my clients. I was a sort of friend as well as a stylist to them. It was easy to remember them. My memory loss was a big symptom of this cursed head injury. In some cases, the loss of memory was small. In others, a lot becomes grey and faded, leaving no pronounced sights in your mind, making it blank. There was no hint of something the memory might have been to suggest possibilities – the memory path was lost. This affects short-term memory. It had lost its way of finding categories to assist with recall. Yes, long-term memory comes back, pronounced memories when you don't consciously think of having to remember. It's the processing that affects short-term memory. Memory can be constructed and after lots of repetition, it then becomes habit. It becomes long-term memory that is found by a cue to recall it, although head injuries can affect any area of the mind. Some folk can lose parts of their personality: it's so disturbing what this kind of injury causes. Some lose themselves. There is a loss in their life with the dramatic upset this causes, yet technically it is not the injury, but its effects that cause the person's loss. You can be cast away from society as the public are unfamiliar with this kind of injury. This causes loneliness and unusual behaviour due to not being on the same page as others. It pushed me away from others at times and produced anxiety of not fitting in that haunted and disturbed me.

I also got an immense bounty of cards from my staff at work. What my staff wrote emotionally touched me. I became aware, through this, of how much my staff thought of me. I had a deep understanding of each one of them. It can be called sensitivity, but I try to avoid using such terminology which can be presumed as being weak. This was the case especially coming from the west coast of Scotland in the midst of a shipping industry.

I perceived the loss my staff must be experiencing. I had thoroughly enjoyed my work with a passion. I loved working with people and I gave it all that I had. That part of my life had died and I was desperately struggling to hold on to it in some way.

Coming back to the weekly schedule at the Astley Ainslie, I had visits to occupational therapy. There were times I was in their mock kitchen: I made basic foods for mere survival that we all need to know, for my own independence. Sometimes, I gave a stumbling effort, due to my left hand being static and slow. My left arm being limited in movement affected my co-ordination. Passive frustration loomed when I had to rely on this left hand. It was worth it though. In the end, I got the successful result of beans, toast, and a cup of tea. It was very basic food and I had actually made it myself. I wasn't so incapable after all. I felt proud that I could achieve this all by myself, despite how small it was. This basic food making, I took for granted. I actually had made it, as if I had passed my first self-survival stage and I was waiting for a medal, or a gold star you would receive at primary school.

Guidance from my OT therapist with new adaptations I had to make in co-ordination while making food was beginning to not feel so unusual.

This was an event worth gold. I was over the first milestone in occupational therapy. For all I had been through and the condition I was in, this was sheer amazement to me. I couldn't wait to tell my wife and family. I was on the road to looking after myself again.

While getting my physical self functioning, I was sent weekly to go to the pool for aqua therapy to get back into swimming in the Astley Ainslie grounds. I never considered how swimming was to influence me later on. I grew up going swimming and loved it: I had gone to the pool regularly for weekly visits when I was young and my brief encounter with the swimming club. Even from childhood, I defied following an expected group, which can appear quite selfish. I just found it hard to conform to normality.

At that point, I could not consider what swimming would do for my health and fitness. I just focused on the basic movements with my new way of doing certain strokes, to achieve some basic form of swimming, never mind flexing my joints and gaining more movement. Even getting out of the wheelchair to the bed took such an effort to learn. Sheer repetition was going to help; looking at the detail of certain events. This would serve me well in later life.

There were a few patients going to therapy at the pool from the ward. We got a minibus to take us to the hydrotherapy pool just down the small twisting road in the Astley Ainslie grounds.

We got dropped off and changed to go in the water. Taking my clothes off was reasonably straight forward and back into the wheelchair with my trunks on, though this was a new sensation with normal activities taken for granted.

There was a crane or winch to lower us patients into the water. When it was my turn, it produced feelings of being a burden, having so many people that I had to rely on. I loathed this.

I couldn't straighten my right leg even with a lot of effort to sort this. This was a major crutch to me. I adapted myself to movements that suited the limitation I had. I hadn't done anywhere near as much activity as what I was used to with my arms in the last few months. I was exhausted. Activity with my whole body was exercise I was used to; I was pushing myself so hard. My arms were functioning okay, though due to the strain my left arm needed strengthening up.

Swimming gave me insight on how to resume fitness as well as walking exercises. I didn't know how long I would be bound to the sticks before walking myself and this expanded my knowledge of self-improvement and the flexibility swimming would give me.

At certain times, it was hard to swim again, especially at the beginning of the sessions. It was momentous to achieve a very small breadth by myself. Having a float helped at first. It sort of reminded me of the magical float tanks at my work that I used to use for relaxation. As time ticked away, I was getting used to being able to float and more swimming was done.

After swimming, getting changed again was hard. Peeling off the trunks, that was sort of okay. I could dress myself, only I still needed someone to tie my laces, if I didn't have slip-on shoes. That was embarrassing. Having to wait to get your shoes tied was like being a young kid again. That feeling of relying on others began to loom over, haunting me again.

From my time at physiotherapy, I could eventually start using big support sticks. Although my walking was pitifully slow, I was on my feet again, even for a wee while. Back to my bed – yes, bed, I was allowed to have a bed at this hospital. The Astley Ainslie gave me a bed, as I already had the BB badge of camping in hospital. Having a bed was strange. I would find camping some other way, only in my dreams. I was given a classic climbing book on a famous climb on the north face of the Eiger that ended in tragedy. I could only read it one page at a time. I read that book slowly, yet found I could take it in better, rather than just skimming the pages fast, and my short-term memory would reap its weary reward. In a way, it had its advantages, this slow reading and taking in what the book was covering. It was an epic story and I longed to see this mountain, 'The Eiger' one day.

I was then getting good reports back from my therapists and I was out of my wheelchair at times. This was coming to the end of my time at Astley Ainslie. Yes, there was lots of caring and help, although there was also the feeling of imprisonment, of being closed in and greatly limited that seemed unreal, like watching a film about imprisonment. It can never be understood unless you have felt the loss through a similar experience. What took away this looming loss? I continued to act out the main role in this story. Instead of being downed by emotional clutter, I made it interesting and fun; through this I gained some control and owned the experience. Yes, make it fun. I could control this. I was a director planning the scenes.

If I couldn't walk again after all this hard effort I gave, I was going to be a wheelchair athlete and make the most out of myself, turning this into an active life. I had something to offer this world and if my restrictions were going to be the same, I would make the most of it.

From the engulfing relearning I had to do, my attention was on things that I could do or I struggled with now. I was not consumed so much as before with needing to know the very basics to fit into society.

By now, my mind was used to stimulation all the time. So much was missed and now I was aware of it. I was sensitised, with new, fresh-looking eyes.

When learning was not required to such an extent, I went on to other activities to keep my mind busy. This was to be a pattern from now on, of stimulating my mind to a high degree. I always had a drive for learning and self-improvement. This world is full of fascination, and I see it in a different way now. I'm like a kid with a new toy. So much privilege I had with a second chance in life. There's so much out there and such a short time to take in and experience it.

The date when I was to be released was eventually told to my wife and me. I was actually going home. My so-called six-month imprisonment was coming to an end. My hospital sentence was coming to an end after six whole months of full-time treatment, unaware that my full imprisonment would consist of a grand total of four hospitals later.

Homeward Bound

The excitement and sheer relief to be back at home with my wife and my boys was difficult to explain with words alone. Finally I was coming home to get away from my confinements. I was taking a vast step forward on the immense, mountainous journey of my recovery, although it was scary to be left on my own with no guidance. Would I ever, ever get to the summit?

Arriving home, the steep steps up to the house were brilliant to see, yet I held on to the railing for grim death, so as not to fall so close to the front door of my freedom. This day I had longed for and I wasn't going to blow it to be taken back to my trappings in that hospitalised prison.

An explosion of excited butterflies were in flight inside me, as I stepped through the door. I seemed to let go of a burden and now I had less limitations to hold me back on my journey of recovery. The relief was tremendous. To get through all of this was such a struggle, going against the tide from the high position I had gained, to the lowest I was now left with. From my life as I knew it, and hard slog of becoming what was presumed of me, to now, I lost it all and was at a new beginning of untold direction and aim. What I could do now or not was unknown, even to an extent professionally. They did not know what I could or couldn't do before, so they couldn't measure. It was scary. I was given the chance to live again only with fresh eyes now. What was I going to do with this second attempt at life?

From then, when I planned to go out, I'd walk out of the house using my sticks. Using sticks was a brilliant swap, not having to be bound to that bloody wheelchair. I had knowledge of how to take care of myself: cooking, dressing, basic co-ordination, and I could now even tie my own shoelaces again. It was a struggle for my fingers to tie knots. I felt a big sigh of relief on eventually getting to this stage, being home and not having someone over my shoulder telling me what to do. It was like being a kid again, losing the rights and respect you gained from age and experience.

To get to this stage followed numerous improvements; one being tying my laces, another was adaptation with my left-hand actions. It was still weak and slow in comparison to how I was, yet improving daily even in very small ways. Regular exercise first thing in the morning faithfully done to help my hands and to walk again, worked wonders. I did the same with speaking daily to add to the routine. Sheer continual practice was what I needed. Now I had the structure of exercises to work on, to give me a target I could work towards regularly. This was my competitive nature coming to life again, yet not with others, only improving myself.

Co-ordination techniques were to be done also, like games. I didn't have time to waste on feelings of I can't or can. I just knew what to do now and put it into action.

Gaining small achievements daily made me feel good; after all, this was performed without hesitation. I wasn't going to let this get the better of me. I spent time experiencing the feeling of accomplishment; no matter how small it was, I was getting better. This set me up for the day I would eventually get out of this awful predicament I found myself in.

There is a general medical prediction – what doesn't return after two years, they say is lost. I didn't accept this. I felt deep inside myself that this wasn't permanent loss. The things I lost may return, or I would find an alternative to accomplish the task or aim.

I was seeing improvement in my mind's eye; with my thoughts I visually created what I wanted with a strong positive drive. It mainly came from a need for survival; maybe it was something I had learned in life through turning things around with climbing, or was it part of my initial self, striving for improvements I would eventually develop? I wanted achievement at any level, through visions of myself making it happen.

When I went over the hurdle of a subject that had proved a challenge, it put the rest out of balance, highlighting other problems. I treated this as an expedition. I was to summit my mountain, if I ever could. This vision in itself brought my attention to other needed improvements that were within my grasp, no matter what scale they had. Were they possible or were they 'pie in the sky'?

I was left to my own devices as Tania was looking after the kids, doing things by herself and going to her work, because I would slow things down just trying to get by. I felt more alone, not like at my spells at the hospitals. This was total isolation, being stuck with my own company that wasn't performing as it had done before. I was very weary of my own company: I felt this loneliness haunt me, and it drew its fearfully heavy chains. This sharpened up my effort to recover from this blackened area looming its haunting self over me. It seemed to become a living process that fortunately lessened my burden from the emotional upheaval I had experienced. I so wanted this to disappear and felt so guilty for putting my wife through so much pain. Therefore, I didn't bring what I was experiencing while recovering to my wife's attention, even with all the afflictions I had.

I picked up that this would be an additional burden on top of her life-changing turmoil. This was the way things were. I didn't want to burden her anymore and give her another problem to add to the rest. It couldn't be changed and I just had to get on with it. I took on the responsibility of my injury. It was my fault. With all the other parts of me that weren't working, this added to the big pile of broken portions. Nonetheless, there was no point in feeling sorry for myself,

I would just get on with it and leave the relationship between myself and my wife to sort itself out.

I became an outpatient in Irvine Ayrshire Central (another hospital for my collection). An ambulance picked me up when I went to the centre twice a week in the mornings. At first, the ambulance man came up the steep outdoor steps of my house to help me down. I had strong determination to bloody do it on my own. He went in front of me and let me get on with it. With the effort I put in, I got there with great focus. Because I was usually the first the ambulance picked up, I got the choice of seats. I picked the closest seat to the front. I'd learned from my previous ambulance experiences to keep a close view of the forthcoming road as if I was actually driving. Too much caught my attention if I was sitting at the back of the ambulance. I was looking all over the place, instead of just looking, like when I drove before. There are so many sights that can be missed when driving. I could now see them, but it was making me dizzy and flushing with an oncoming panic. That was the downside: I wasn't used to seeing so much, never mind with the dominance of a recent head injury. I couldn't deal with it at this stage. I surely wasn't used to this. It had its effects with different distances and I had trouble working the proportions out, as my co-ordination at this time wasn't happy.

The Douglas Grant Centre at Ayrshire Central was a good-sized building with a friendly atmosphere. I had appointments through the morning of the same categories I had in the Astley Ainslie. I always started off with speech therapy.

The speech therapist gave me homework to add to my pile.

The main challenge to me was that I could not exactly hear the precise sound of my own vocal tones. Distinctive differences in pronunciation were called for so I could produce a difference in the sound that I was actually saying. Repetition of phrases and sayings were what I needed to get this ball rolling. Not pronouncing the exact tones of certain words that I spoke made those words sound unusual – I sounded like a foreign person. Some words were pronounced differently, as foreign people do with particular English words depending on where they are from. From the physical tones they use to express certain phrases in other languages, some words sound different, as the tones in English aren't used in their home country's language. I had acquired the same difficulty as them. I physically struggled with saying certain phrases. I had lost the ability to speak English fluently. With my so-called 'foreign accent syndrome', there was no distinct similarity with a particular country, it just sounded not of this country's way of talking. It still felt confusing, not being able to control what was in my mind and physically say it to the outside world. It just didn't come out right.

Then, there was physiotherapy. It was always fabulous for making improvements happen, and especially for an active, physical challenge. This was my main concern for improvement – getting me to use my legs again. Doing physiotherapy was similar to what I knew through climbing in terms of aims and achievements. Because of this, I had the utmost drive to go to physiotherapy. I followed a set of exercises that helped my walking strength and coordination with my legs, which needed strengthening up. I loved any form of physical exercise. I couldn't do what I did before by any standards, due to being so previously fit and active, but I made the best of what I could do and could work to improve. This, again, was very similar to any sport or athletics for improvement and therefore I developed another way to view this episode, as the procedures of an athlete recovering. This was a big help for me in getting through the monumental physical barrier that weighed me down with its cumbersome, heavy chains, slowing down my progress.

I was determined to stop using the sticks. Convinced and determined, I was not taking on board any form of doubt. I would be walking again without any burden from these bloody walking sticks. I was going to walk somehow. It was time to move on.

I was shadowed from the beginning with the knowledge that with head injuries, you don't know how well you'll recover, due to the unclear recovery process of a single person and their injury, their fitness and what they were before. Vagueness was the only collective theme, that's if you would recover at all. How many ways can you adapt to get results in different ways and get things done? With this practical research I resolved to focus on improving. It was suited to me as an excuse to do any form of physical exercise, although this was a drastic way of getting fit.

I became detached from reality again, in a different way, through defining what I could or couldn't do in comparison to what I was before. The image of what I was like would always haunt me through over-exaggerations of my ability then. Sometimes I drifted away in the possibility of performing tasks I knew like the back of my hand, yet I couldn't do these menial tasks. There was no order to what I could do anymore, even poorly. It seemed so random and hard to work out. This promoted anxiety that haunted me for the rest of my life. By using the format for improving sports performance, this was something I could work with. It gave me something to focus on: something positive. That gave me a way to progress, only focusing on achievement. This would be in my control. I used my senses more internally in relation to what was happening to me. This was the greatest satisfaction for me. My ability to pick up different forms of information was prominent. This brought forward new forms of information that normally were missed. I could feel the sensations of what was happening both internally and externally in the outside world.

I bought a fitness ball for home exercises. The physiotherapist showed me exercises on the ball at the centre and I would use it at home in my morning practices.

I wanted to prove I could get sensational results, as if achieving my potential in sports. I might have lost what I could do before, but this I could do and prove my worth in another way. This wasn't going to beat me, I would turn this around. The motivation was driven by what could only be described as horrific, life-changing pain and loss, with the dramatic stress I had caused my wife. My aim was to get back to where I was before. Having experienced so much loss, I was desperate for something to identify with: not with the disabilities I had, but as a person. Having a disability is not the way I saw myself. At home, people's reactions to me had turned. Instead of supporting me in my position in society, they had to deal with a broken version. I was all alone with folk not knowing how to handle talking to me. Talking to me required such a delicate manner. I felt robbed of what I was. It was a very important part of me, communicating with others. This was a huge part of my identity. I had gained a good social position through pushing myself and now, it was as if it was stolen away from me and I was left last, like the unpopular kid at school, to be chosen by two groups in the class.

At the physiotherapy sessions, I was using the treadmill to walk. I had been taking spells walking and holding on, and talking with my therapist. I was to do the treadmill just walking and not even holding the bars. I had done so at what could be seen as a low speed for ten minutes – all me.

I was finally walking again all by myself and not holding on.

This was a long-awaited, exciting high for me. I eventually found some other means of accomplishment through adaptations, in my own way. This was a monumental transformation that was real improvement. This was where I began to integrate methods I used from then on. It was a monumental life lesson I had learned. It was a big step forward on my expedition of self-improvement.

My physiotherapist went to the effort of pulling my OT therapist away from her work to see me walking again all by myself eventually. The compliment from Alison, my occupational therapist, was a tremendous pat on the back for me with such recognition from her. All the effort I was putting in and all the hard, consistent work I was doing, was finally being noticed.

My physiotherapist shared joyous complimentary comments with me over what I had done.

"That's fantastic," I said syntactically, full of pride. "I can walk. I CAN ACTUALLY WALK AGAIN." After long months of being kept back, generating frustration, with the haunting element of possibly being bound to a wheelchair for the rest of my life, compliments she gave me picked up the triumphant, blasting joy I had. She must have sensed more than her role requirements dictated in terms of how much of a huge, enthralling achievement this was for me.

"Now can you show me how to run?" I said with a smile on my face and a sparkle in my eyes. Jokingly I delivered this with a positively serious intention. I looked for a reply, taking this further to its boundary. This way I would know what I could or couldn't do.

Her expression showed complete shock. Her chin hit the ground. Never had she worked with the likes of me before. Her focus was more on the physical aspects of things that I could do now after so much work, so she diverted from this proposed subject.

"One day, I'll meet you up the hills," she said back to me. I very happily agreed.

One day I'd go back up the hills and one day I would run again. Soon, I'd teach myself by running along the prom in Largs, which I did.

At occupational therapy, Alison's personality and drive kept my positivity high. She gave me such a lift towards living and the purpose I was aiming for. She was an absolutely brilliant therapist. She left an inspiring impression on me. When I knew I was going to OT, the other OT therapists and the patients there were also fun to be with. She was great at her job, or was it just who she was in her nature? Maybe it was a blend of these making her such a good person. I played co-ordination games on the computer and board games. It was like when I was young, going down the amusement arcades to play video games. I played them a lot and got very good at a few games down there, like most people who had done the same.

It was ten pence a game then, and that could last me a long time. I was doing the same with the computer and board games at OT. To develop the techniques needed, the strategies of how to follow them through to completion, was the fundamental key I had learned.

Going to see Alison at occupational therapy got me interested in baking. This was good for the hand exercises I required. The exercise I enjoyed the most for hands was kneading mixture when making bread. There's so much tension in the dough, that it's perfect for this. This was the start of me building my hand muscles up again. From climbing, my hands and fingers were very strong and I missed how strong they had been. I used to make bread at home twice a week. I thoroughly enjoy making bread. Baking to exercise my hand, the resulting feeling of achievement built up my self-esteem again. The aroma of freshly made bread was inspiring and the pleasure of eating the fresh bread was so rewarding. Knowing the effort it took, was a reward in itself. The fresh, sweet smell of baked bread was worth it, let alone what help it was for my hands.

With my visits to psychology at the Douglas Grant Centre, I met three therapists. They were two females and one male. One woman ran this department. She was relaxed, yet the formality was always on her shoulders. She showed signs of vast knowledge of a high position within the organisation in her mind, which gave her a formulaic, professional approach.

The other woman, roughly my age, had a smile that shone with happiness. She was pleasant on my eyes. Her personality showed her excitement and love of psychology: subtle and intelligent.

This was the time I was properly introduced to the awareness that seemed to have appeared since my accident.

This surely worked with my sensitivity. I could pick things up, which was very confusing at first – it seemed I could pick up things that were normally missed before. We all pick up on things, are given meanings and unspoken information, only now I was more attuned to unseen information to compensate for what I had lost.

She was new to this role and this newness shone through in her delivery. She was learning how to teach a group of people covering a psychological rehabilitation technique. This can mainly be learned through the experience of actually 'walking the talk'. There was a difference between theory and practicality. Yes, sometimes the theory was accurate, yet it didn't suit some people's full understanding. A person with experience and hearing different versions from friends and other patients, is in their own way accurate, yet the science argues that knowledge is gained through experience from research. This leads me to say that experience which is 'hands-on experiential knowledge' shines with more sincerity. Yet a combination of the two angles of psychology and 'hands-on' is recommended. This takes on the advantages from both sides.

I was attracted to her in an unusual way. My thoughts felt stupid as she was one of my therapists. I got caught up in that overshadowing old adage of being attracted to your therapist. It was similar to having a crush on a teacher when at school. I left it alone and couldn't discuss this with anyone. In experiencing my array of problems, this was becoming familiar ground, although I didn't have a liking to such isolation flooded with unsure worries.

Having your own time to get your life sorted has its benefits, yet all the time promotes the disadvantages of going into your own world, with all the resulting negative effects from only having your view of the situation.

This is not reality, as far as your perception of events goes. With the imbalance in my life through all this massive turmoil, I found this attraction to the therapist a form of escaping from reality, with its presumed safety and security.

I was being stupid, as a part of me kept saying. Another part was let down and this added to the emotional scars I had accumulated.

This was yet another challenge I was to add to my expedition, to the ever-steepening mountain of mine called Mount Recovery.

Back home, there had been distance between myself and Tania ever since I got home from hospital. This was a major loss to me, as I felt so alone. The team we had seemed lost and I needed the support and friendship. Maybe it was the way I didn't communicate to her, just getting on and not wallowing in tasks I couldn't do: I couldn't wallow in what was lost. That, to me, was completely defeating. The distance was increasing. I couldn't work out why this was. It was constant agony. I can only guess that I had this attraction to the therapist as I needed support, and it didn't seem real in any way.

Although having your husband close to death is a major ordeal for anyone. When Tania was young, she was very close to her dad. One day, they went out on the Clyde on a boat. The boat capsized and she lost her dad. She was trapped under the boat. The RNLI pulled her out and saved her life. With this traumatic event, she lost her dad, who she was close to. I turned up in her life and she nearly lost me. Putting her through this again with me, was such a cutting emotional ache. An amazingly organised person who is a good mum, I opened an old wound she had.

With Tania, her distance seemed a mixture of multiple inner conflicts. I couldn't help her in any way. This must have freshened the experience of nearly losing me as well, and seeing me as a dissolved part of what I was, I imagined must have been crushing for her. I felt so guilty about this and burdened myself with these chains as punishment for hurting her and others. This lessened my self-worth even more.

Yet these new sensations caused me to see life in a different way. It registered that I could pick up things that could have simply been missed before. I didn't know anybody who had experienced this, so I kept it to myself. I was experiencing this life differently, and this helped to give me the portions of living that were missed. My sensory awareness was in a higher, different place now, which opened up new ways of experiencing and seeing life, whether I liked it or not. The confusion was starting to ease through my understanding of how I could cover the absolute basics. The big drive to accept the uncertain effects of my ailments was pushed away and I was doing my best to get back to my former social standing. I was focused on finding solutions. That might have come from my drive for climbing, for achieving and not wasting energy on the negatives. Maybe it was my personality that gave me this drive. Maybe it was from both? Whatever it was, there was a drive to not succumb to my condition. This injury and its makings weren't winning.

CHAPTER 5

Finding My Way:
The Beginning of Challenges

Man cannot discover new oceans unless he first loses sight of the shore.
– Christopher Columbus

Proudly holding my front up with pain that misses the eye,
Feeling and inhaling the presence of life that was nearly lost,
I now experience new beauties and wonders of living abilities.
Each day has a different song,
Sometimes I sing with majestic harmony.
Sometimes I sing with the wind against my sails,
With my newfound awareness,
I strive to be me come rain, hail or snow.
– Tom Paterson

With all this contemplation of being bound to hospital care, I finally finished my spell, my sentence, at long last, in the Douglas Grant Centre. Finally, with a year and a half of being in medical care, it had come to an end. This tormented imprisonment in one way had finally ended.

I now started to broaden my horizon, spending a portion of my time at Headway in Ayr, who dealt with other people who had experienced head injuries.

I got the train down to Ayr when I visited Headway. It reminded me of the daily travelling to work by a similar train route to Glasgow. This time I was changing trains at Kilwinning bound for Ayr. I was getting quite used to travelling by public transport, as I couldn't drive anymore. My car was written off and the DVLA took my licence off me. The DVLA automatically withdraw driving licences of people with brain injuries like strokes, etc. In losing my licence, I lost the freedom I once knew and loved. There were major health difficulties that I had acquired; losing my licence wasn't as major as these difficulties, so I went with the flow and complied, never mentioning it, as my low confidence affected my assertiveness. I accepted this and looked for positives to justify using public transport. Every item has two sides, good and not so good. It's working out what's better for you at that time to give you the best benefits. Following this, I had to relearn driving for the adjustments I had to make to co-ordinate many tasks at once. It was this freedom that was taken away which hurt my independence. I lost the variety of experiencing different familiarities. I used it as an aim to make the best of my time. This now was hidden from me, yet I could relax, plan and have quality time in my day when using public transport. Under these circumstances, relaxing and planning were vital to me at this stage. This was a better way for me to travel now, as I had acquired a lot of processing confusion from the burden of my body refusing to sing a different song.

Due to memory difficulties from the head injury, planning and relaxing was the crescendo of coping with living. I wrote plans down and made a diary every day for writing practice as well, to help me with this looming burden of forgetfulness that would spread its dark blanket over me. From working before, planning became second nature to me.

This planning technique was taught to me when I was at hospital and from Headway, yet I had always used a diary for organising my job role. Having to rely on a diary was expected. From this, I knew it worked well.

It was great, putting every arrangement in the diary so as not to not clog up my thinking process; this left more mind space for dealing with other events that may be important to me. This showed I was lacking flexibility to adapt to fast changes of thought at this point. By keeping this diary and regularly filling it in, I lessened surprises, to help get myself organised again. Using my diary helped me work out events and not be overwhelmed with the overload that loomed in its presence. My thinking would become faster (with planning).

I just needed techniques, and adaptations to find my way of using them. I wanted to find the most effective ways not soon, but quicker than today. That would suit me.

With having to find my own way using public transport, this in itself posed a grey area in organisation – incredibly slower than what I was used to, although repetitive usage of this helped me considerably. This made events stand out, helping my memory by becoming automatic, and began the speeding up of my logical cognition. It was relearning for me, in terms of memory of the activity as well as names and times to remember.

This is a classic scenario for people experiencing head injury. The basic general experience was similar to riding a bike: you just automatically remembered with your long-term memory. Yet on other occasions, some details of certain memories are missed, giving greyness in contrast to what was so clear. The injuries I experienced made results poor, or not the same as I knew before, yet I thought I knew the task well in my memory. It just didn't happen as it did before. Part of my mind was damaged and that stopped it processing what I required. This resulted in me missing the valuable, needed details of the task, preventing mastery of certain subjects, and forcing me to become a beginner again. This was a blow; to accept such loss from this injury burdened me. This by itself, played on a multitude of emotions; mainly I experienced deep frustration. Other people could only make assumptions as to why I couldn't do it, or even presumed I couldn't be bothered to. This assumption returns to stereotyping a head injury and the inevitable 'pigeon holed' prejudice of what the person presumed from their world that a head injury involves. This damage was so vast; it could affect any part of a person, whether memories or behaviour, so some people construct a pigeon hole for you, of what they presumed.

Although specialists take time to find out what problems you acquired, therapists can condemn this cognitive approach. From my view, it's like repairing a car: find out what doesn't work in comparison with what does work in this situation, then fix it, or as close to that as you can get. Your body parts work together, like a universe in itself. Yes, there is reason for a default in a cognitive process, yet it wasn't known how it was before, if it existed at all. It is difficult to look for a piece of white chalk in a field of snow and without knowing the size of the chalk too. Another aspect is the emotional and life trauma that happens to the person. This may have its own effect on a cognitive process. It can be classed as 'a rock and a hard place'.

This in itself was hard, and it makes life even more complicated with the tangled web it weaves. My determination shone through to go on my own journey, not to be labelled with these assumed differences.

At this stage, I brought my attention to what wasn't correct about my writing: it was slow and it took a painfully long time, never mind my memory took me on to different topics faster than what I could write. By the time I slowly wrote words down, my mind was on a different topic. Due to my short-term memory difficulty at this time, I just continued to finish what I was writing with what was fresh in my mind; this leads to two topics in one sentence, never mind a mixture of past, present, and future: these got muddled up which was so confusing to read at times. What was written was not what I meant. I could say it to myself, but it was so different from what I wrote. The divide in function became obvious, particularly with this. I fortunately had to use my other hand to assist in stabilising my left for physical writing. To me, this was time spent wisely, although it was a visible sign of a disability. This in itself happened to annoy me – being visually recognised for having a disability. It was the other side of the coin. I could not hide it. Having signs of a physical disability helped explaining the injury, yet it was tiresome using this as a primary excuse. I felt obligated to explain to folks if they thought I was making an excuse for a puny effort. It got worse if I didn't have a clear picture in my mind of what I was writing. This was an external extension of how confused my mind was when overloaded with information. This was the beginning of understanding mind control through meditation, which was a major help to me with this and with living in general. I was to gain the knowledge and experience from Buddhist monks to control my thoughts and actions by minimising debris in my mind that confuses my thoughts. Meditation just focuses on minimum content, which works very well with what I was inflicted with, even with not being able to use my left hand for writing.

I kept writing with my left hand because I was indeed determined to not learn to write with my right side. I tried it and it was not me at all. I was a 'lefty' ('corrie fisted' in Scottish). The unusualness of starting something new produces an accumulation of difficult reactions. This just was just not me. I was a 'lefty'.

My bodily components were coherent with being left-handed, or so it has been scientifically recorded. Certain organs of the body are different sizes to those of the right-handed population. I owed it to myself for my own identity. I'm sticking to being 'left-handed'.

I then joined the computer group at Headway to finally learn how to operate computers once a week. That was my first lesson in those things called computers which seemed to explode in popularity through my recovery. This was new learning for me, with no backup in my memory to help me construct similar meaning. I was in at the deep end. Due to my age category, I just missed computer learning at school, which is a big loss in today's society.

I got to know a few other people who were in the group. One of the blokes was from Largs too. This was a relief, that I was not the only one in my area who had a head injury.

I got to know him and we became friends. We had fairly similar symptoms from our injuries, losing our careers and the upturn with our partners and family. We sang a similar song, or even verses of similar tunes.

Our natures were different. He was a chef and had a raging, fiery temper. This was different from me being ambitious and positive.

I knew his wife. She was even in the same class as me at school. This made me realise how small Largs was. They had three kids – two kids to another relationship from the past and one by him.

He moved away from his wife, as their marriage didn't work, and he moved in with another girl. I got to know her and he asked me if I could cut her hair.

It was a basic long hairstyle with graduation around the front. This increased my desire to get back into hairdressing and again be recognised in the community as a good stylist.

With this urge to get back into training with my thirst for what I had before, my health challenges were not going to take this away from me. I was fully determined not to lose this vital part of me in training or hairdressing. It became my main aim in my desperation to fit in again. My aim was to return to the training position, or similar to what I had before. This would be a huge achievement, to get back to that stage in hairdressing, being a training director. I couldn't work in a salon environment anymore, as I was doing haircuts at home with friends and family that took me much longer due to my stance, yet this left hand of mine was not working as before, never mind myself sounding like a foreigner. From an outsider, I looked strained while cutting hair, which I definitely was. This posed great big problems with this dream I had for my life.

Making bread at home had paid off well for hand strengthening and daily exercise had paid off for me cutting hair, yet I still was slow and clumsy with detailed manoeuvres. I had to work on the manoeuvres and angles with cutting. I couldn't reach specific angles, so I had to find my alternative method, compared with the normal versions. I adapted to suit my difficulty in achieving certain complicated moves.

Even though there were adjustments made, this was not economical for working in a salon, with how slow I worked. I couldn't be cost effective enough to cover my costs working in hairdressing anymore. I was drawn not to go back to work as a hair stylist in a salon, but get back into the training of hairdressing again.

I spent day after day going over my training and developing, in my qualifications folder, to refresh the material used.

All the work I had previously done had got me qualifications in training. I also had a mass of practical training papers and folders that were used in my work, as an internal verifier. I looked over this to jog my memory of specific details. I could remember the format. It was ingrained into me with so much use. It was second nature, only being out of working in a salon and with my acquired condition, this produced anxiety hollering over me. I needed to refresh the concept.

The grand amount of satisfaction I got from this, put me on the right path towards the work and creation I had put into this.

I found a quiet space to go over it. This worked wonders for me. The knowledge was in my mind. In reviewing this material, I learned a fact that I use even now. It's essential to processing. Quietness with no interruptions from the outside world is what I desperately relied on for not being easily distracted.

Putting aside my frustrated anxiety and letting my thoughts come through under no influence in a quiet time, brought on the intuition that was becoming normal to me. This training theory and practical knowledge was stored in long-term memory. The only discovered difficulty was making sure all the details of procedures were taken into account.

I kept going over and over the material till the newly sparked adaptations I would use went along with the repetition and inevitably became automatic to me again.

I found out that this process is revolutionary in mind processing for future events. It was like sports, visualising success going into your world to make it a reality. This process to me was vital.

I just needed to check on the details, that it was the same in my memory as in real life, that the details were not distorted in some way from my head injury. Maybe the memories were accurate by themselves. Maybe I had to adapt my disabilities to suit. Maybe what was automatic in memory lacked the details of how to actually do the process again. This is common for everyone to some extent. As the old saying goes, 'if you don't use it, you lose it'. Maybe there was a combination of my attention being taken away while having to deal with drastic life changes, which lessens the priority of the memory of training procedures, and the other ingredient was the actual neural injury. Whatever it could be, I was working on what I thought possibly was a solution. This gave me drive, doing something positive and participating in doing something, rather than do nothing at all. I was making a difference by improving myself.

The same process was used for remembering other important issues. In life, you know how things need to be done and at what times. Sometimes a lack of response results in not successfully completing the task you are aiming for. I knew I needed a particular task done and I couldn't quite put it into practice in normal day-to-day living. Taking time out to create a similar state to the actual event worked, but I couldn't quite put it into practice when busy. My flexibility wasn't there yet. Again, this was very frustrating for me. I kept my cool and went with the flow and didn't let myself get wound up, although it was difficult at times. I could do the task, yet there was something preventing it from happening. I stopped myself before the downward spiral of the problem into a self-defeating paralysis. This was the pain of relearning.

Some things you could not logically explain at this stage. I knew from my instinct what to do, particularly with this kind of learning. Ingrained learning created the solutions. Learning is from repeated success that builds confidence. People just do it and don't think too much about it. It becomes automatic, knowing the exact result will happen with no thought of the process. It happens unconsciously.

This was a new way of thinking about thought processing. Now I was learning to use my mind, experiencing different perceptions. I was aware that my thinking was 'outside the box', thus it was uncomfortable at times. I read that we only use about 8% of our mind's capacity (the tip of the iceberg); this was going to another level of discovery, of possibilities that were waiting for me in terms of how important the mind is. Overall, this made me see things differently and have a different angle to others sometimes. This was transforming. It's just remembering my difference.

Attempts to Get Back into Training

I thought of eventually venturing up to my old work again, weekly, for helping with the training on a voluntary basis. Not with actual 'hands-on' hairdressing training, but the training system that I put into place with the trainers and the students. The trainers were doing a good job. They were on the right track. The trainers and the girl who took my place, were all doing wonderful jobs. It was a relief that they had found a person to follow in my role after the state my car accident caused, leaving them high and dry.

I got in touch with the training company who organised my learning and developing qualifications to refresh my training. A woman saw me from that training company, and took me through additional modules within the training programme I qualified in. With these and the information I had about the system, I thankfully refreshed the training that I developed by going over the modules in detail.

I adapted what I would cover when I went to the Rainbow Room training each week, increasing my imagination with the process. I altered the style to suit me, doing it efficiently and keeping professionalism at the forefront.

Being professional and going with the image I took years to build, I reputedly didn't want to be considered, "Poor Tommy, he tries." I loathed this. I was worth far more than this.

This was a major circumstance which affected the whole of my life and who I was. The last thing I wanted was to appear feeble or pathetic. By no means did I ever long for this perception from people, with their opinions of me and my unseen injury. I had to experience major reshuffling in my life. Working on what I thought I had left of my career, what I could scrape by with after losing time with my boys, climbing with the freedom of the mountains, my physical ability, my speech, walking, balance, functioning ability of my left hand, coordination and communications, having to learn to drive again, never mentioning my difficulty finding accommodation, let alone with my marriage coming to an end.

The very last thing I wanted was to be considered a pathetic human now, with everything else mentioned. All the things I had to work on, they were not right. I presumed my problems must be very evident to others, especially the very obvious ones. The image of being seen as weak haunted me. I hadn't planned to have the accident.

It was my last intention.

I was worth far more than this and no way was this injury going to win. I'm not competitive in nature, though with this, I was bloody going to win in some way. Overthinking limitations of my way forward was the last thing I needed; it seemed a threat to me and wasted my energy. This was not my only way. My attention was on opportunities and what I wanted to achieve.

I got the impression that the owners of Rainbow Room were initially pleased with my return. After seeing me in Edinburgh at the Astley Ainslie hospital, I assumed this confirmed to them that the change they made in the direction of the training was to be permanent, and they had to organise a person to fill my role.

Over time, my presence had served its purpose and it wasn't so easy for me to come back to the role. The last thing I wanted was to be was a threat to the girl who took over. Then it came to haunt me: with injures looming their haunting head, it would be very hard, if impossible for me to come back to this role as a training director. I knew it was a big step for her and didn't want this to be an issue, never mind if I was to return myself. I guess it was denial and hanging on by the skin of my teeth to what was left of me. This didn't include adapting to the work load again. It would take up so much of my energy to barely function.

By seeing her through her actual hairdressing training and her role as a trainer, I saw the effort she put in to get to this role. I had a fear that kept reappearing in its haunting manner: the picked-up tones of, "Poor Tommy, well, he's trying," was always the vilest threat to me then. I am a person, not a stereotype of not doing things right. It was a very difficult situation to be in. I knew the directors and top employees as friends. Friendships and past experiences were all that what was left.

Under arrangement with my old bosses, I then went along to a new training academy. It was located in another building that had just opened up.

All the notes I had taken as a training director, I now saw with new eyes and perceptions. Seeing it from a new angle, from the outside, held such benefits for the company and me. It forced me to diversify into another topic. A topic I was used to, apart from hairdressing training. My aim was to sharpen up my management skills again. I joined a college in Greenock to do an HNC in management, in the evening, two nights a week, although it was management in general, not specifically what I was used to. I aimed to see the management role again and to brush up in a new way could only be gained by work experience in the environment of my old work and at college. This role I had before was specific and the college was presenting the management field very generally to cover all angles. This in itself gave me knowledge of what works in certain circumstances, and what doesn't work in relation to high business style hairdressing management. The Rainbow Room was a leading-edge business and I loved working there. Their delivery was higher than the standards taught, yet it gave me skills in management that would suit other lines of business.

At first, the management system they taught was so vague to me. I couldn't remember some details of the units they were covering. My anxiety rose, trying to sharpen the unknown gaps I had. I experienced confusion fitting the management style the Rainbow Room used to a general basic model, never mind the difficulty I had writing the material on this thing called a computer. I got learner's support on an afternoon, where what we covered felt like basics again, just like speech therapy. I had difficulty relating to this kid stuff that was not relevant to the course material. Yes, it was on writing my essays, but it didn't connect together. They seemed not to relate to me. It was confusing having two pieces of work that seemed to be completely different worlds, yet my way of writing contained expression failed to follow a logical process. If that's what they want, that indeed is what they shall get.

I spent a lot of time in the afternoon in the library covering books of different subjects that I was interested in; they were hard to find. I spent most of my time on motivational management and I got to know the librarian quite well. This made company for the librarian and me.

Another hard task I had, was putting this college learning together with new knowledge of using a computer for exam work. This was difficult in itself, to get used to the new perception of management as a general format. Learning to get by with what I could do on the computer, this helped me identify the mistakes I made while writing. I got confused writing tenses and with having problems remembering what I was saying in my mind, this indeed added confusion to my essays. My written sentences were all over the place.

At times, they were shortened or bits were forgotten, making it very confusing to read and correct. This took a lot of time, never mind correcting the multitude of errors I made. I had a big task to improve this area for academic work. This was survival and I was going to do it.

A lot of my time was taken sorting the errors I found while taking this management course. It was very draining, trying to work out my writing at times.

My injury ensured the need for help from the learning support team from the college. I saw a woman from the team weekly to deal with this.

My grammar was very bad and needed a lot of work to correct it. What I meant would come out broken when written in a Word document. It seemed like I wasn't singing the same song. Even with the computer, it took me on average about four times and more attempts at a small piece of work. The spell check helped, but my composition of sentences was confused by subjects that were intermingled. If there was a lot to think about when writing, my memory drifted and my sentences were mixed, displaying a static approach, leaving a sentence with two conversations, sometimes more. I hung my head in shame knowing what I was doing, yet this kept happening with a lot of information I had to process. No matter what, this was to be addressed. It was confusing as to what sequence was needed when writing.

I could put together, from the sounds of the lecturer and my inner voice, what was right or wrong. With my memory being so weak with regard to past written work at this point, I found it painful to remember mundane items and how to deliver them in an essay. I knew it generally, but I succumbed to blankness trying to write it in detail. I threw an unexpected blank that expectedly happened. This was a big hindrance for me and the darkness always loomed over from a height so I couldn't get control of it, even then. Seeing my work typed on paper, I was given another view of the difference between what was in my head and the words on the paper – they didn't match. I wasn't going to let this get me down. I was going to make the most of myself, even what was not so good about my new life. I would change it. This injury was not bloody winning.

I never completed the HNC, as other things took priority over this, or was this an excuse to avoid confronting it face-on? Cognitively, the time wasn't right for me and I wasn't fully ready to take on board or relearn the skills I needed. To get qualifications in management would have been beneficial, yet producing my work to an academic standard, seemed to lose its function. Where my time would be better spent, I began focusing on what I could do well.

I backed off from doing voluntary work at the salon one day a week to get away from the situation in which I felt I was going against the company's direction for training. I sensed at that time this was not my path to follow, going back to what I knew. This part of my life had ended. I became aware of being alone out there; going somewhere, but not clear where I was and where I was going. This loss, I feared so greatly. My image of myself had died too. I was in a void, where sensations and feelings pronounced certain situations over with the blow of not being able to return to my old career. 'As one door closes, another opens.' Yet I was in an area of no recognition that I had never experienced before. The only recent experience I had with the outside world in terms of how to adapt with my injuries was the day-to-day survival, with no meaning. I lacked expression. What gave me drive was the time I had with my dear boys. My mother was a huge help, not letting me at any chance be overloaded by the presence of my young boys being too active. Myself and the boys painted pictures for a while, under my mother and her art teaching abilities.

With my time at my work, I presumed I could get a placement at college doing HNC management, which I could do with a work placement at my old job. It took a few visits to get set up with one of the company directors in a work placement. I got on really well with her, as we had an understanding.

The thought of not being capable of doing this in these circumstances was frightening, yet frustrating for me. It brought some question to the positive vision of what I wanted against reality. To have dreams and to see the world as an opportunity, but then be faced with the reality of this, went against my aims. I had great ideas, but I was stopped from fulfilling them.

What I worked well as was being a trainer, or other aspects of working with people. I loved the variety and felt at home in this sector.

I found out on the phone by calling Ron at Cheynes training, my old boss with the internal verifying process, that I had also to be practising hairdressing to be a trainer within the hairdressing sector.

This was the final blow to my fingers scratching the edges of a cliff, frantically trying to hold on. I was falling. This cliff propelled me into the unknown.

I had done all I could with my restrictions to get into training at the Rainbow Room. This only showed me more limitations.

They had sort of given me a chance in attempting to get their protégé to go back into hairdressing training with no success. With all the work I had done for the Rainbow Room, this was their way of giving me back what they could. It was also my way of checking my training system was running as smoothly as possible after the years of effort I put in to set this up in unknown territory. The Rainbow Room were organised and they were doing it successfully with my so-called 'training system baby'.

I was definitely lost. This path had come to an end and now, I to find purpose, to fill the big hole in my identity that the loss of training had made, as well as the other parts of my life which had died. Some parts of what my identity was died suddenly, others took a long time to fade. They shrivelled up and fell away, not relying on my support. I had learned my will to fight these limitations kept their existence alive, only to die after this.

When I gave up hanging on to dead aspects, I could grow with new ideas and aims that inspired me with immense energy.

Having eventually decided to end my work placement, I had to also give up my college course. Not seeing the learning I gained from the management course in practice through the Rainbow Room, my ability to reason with the nominal management skills of the course was lost. At this point, my cognition got lost in an array of comparisons of management styles. I was just used to one way of management and I knew it worked well, so why change a pound coin with brass change? It's the same value but I'd rather have a shiny new pound coin than a pocket full of one and two pences.

In the Rainbow Room, they had brilliant styles of modern management to follow. The model at college was to cover the concept of management to give a wide range of services.

In comparison to what I knew, I found it hard to grasp the basics of what was being taught at college. Such anticipated confusion reigned over me. I was under the impression that I had problems with remembering the methods of management I was taught. It was personalised to the Rainbow Room with a huge success in business growth.

The ways I was taught, no matter how fantastic they were, weren't the only forms of management for different requirements.

I would learn from this. If something isn't working in what you want to do, hearing different perspectives opens up different options that are suited to you better. The task is still done, yet the way it is done is more suited to you. There's different versions that can be used. The old saying goes, 'Where there's a will, there's a way.' Only society dictates the generally recognised way something should be done. What's more important – getting the task done, or the preference of fitting in with society? That's the question relating to the importance of the task: is the importance to complete it, or to gain social connections while fitting in?

This was a very powerful lesson. It was an experience in achieving a basis of learning. The more effort you put in, the greater the experience you have to deal with the learning curve.

With what I learned from NLP psychology, there are four stages in learning that can be applied to anything. When you aren't aware that you aren't competent at doing the task, you are unconsciously incompetent. The next stage is when you are aware of what to do, yet you get it wrong: consciously incompetent. The third stage is when you get it right and you're fully aware of this: competently conscious. You know what needs to be done and it takes a lot of effort to achieve it. Lastly, you are unconsciously competent. It happens easily and has become automatic. It just happens naturally. It's like comparing it to driving, when you get to your end destination, and you don't even remember driving most of it. It happens automatically through routine.

I was in the situation where I could remember only certain things that I could talk about and ways that I had done them. I could remember the end result, it was just the details to do this smoothly that were knocked off, sometimes by a lot.

I could remember the big picture, I just lost sight of how to achieve this in detail sometimes. This was frustrating.

I always had cut my family's hair and thankfully it was not in front of a mirror where I would be drawn to how I adapted my cutting and my posture to cut hair. It got the job done.

This gave me the chance to break down my cutting style, chunking it down to details to suit myself and how I would hold hair at different times, especially cutting blunt-edged styles. What was important to the cutting style and what did people look for in a haircut? It turned around what was meant in society when getting your hair cut. What things to explain, what things to just expect and so on. It turned it right around on its head, looking consciously again at details that were always presumed to be the way. This began my opening up of other people's worlds. With hair, it was how folk managed, washed, styled and looked after their hairstyles. This was more of a one-to-one counselling approach, discovering problem details that were usually missed. It was getting into their world and working with them to find a solution. Using one-to-ones I found out the benefits of getting their hair cut the way they wanted. This again, was the start of me being aware of what people wanted and what they were trying to say in another way. In their view of their world, with the help of my sensory acuity, this was picked up so much. I learned how to tune my senses to what could be missed by others. Some parts of this sensory awareness I was aware of, but there was so much I wasn't sure of. I'm not saying I could see folks' fate and other such psychic tendencies. I could pick up a lot from someone from the way they dealt with situations or other people using my senses. It became eye opening for me. I couldn't believe I missed so much before then. I had become more attuned to this.

What I had acquired from my 'wee car bump' was skills that I was just beginning to use, although scary at times, picking up so much detail from others that it made them feel uncomfortable. I began learning when to speak about this and when to keep quiet. I would spend years picking up intuitive signs from people. It was maybe their personality traits, emotions that were deep, the way to react to their beliefs and values and so on. This was clearly a new market for me in giving personal care while cutting.

Delivering Positivity Classes

In my times of going to Headway, after dropping the idea a few times, I finally talked to Jane about letting me do classes with the other Headway members on Tuesdays. She thought that was a good idea and replied with a statement that stayed with me, about my personality and presence.

She said she had never have met someone with such beaming positivity at Headway and she had been working there eight years. We decided with this in mind, to call them 'positivity' classes.

Getting organised for them was a mammoth task for me, although I loved every minute of it. I had studied lots of playable CDs of great speakers and self-help topics that interested me. I listened to tapes and read books. I also read some of my books on leading and training with NLP. I uncovered an old favourite author of mine, Anthony Robbins – *Awaken the Giant Within* and one called *Unlimited Power*. This helped me frame the style of training I would do and not be bogged down with the humdrum of people caught in a medical predicament. It took me beyond that. It made me think outside the box.

I was inspired and highly respected Tony's style in the way he was working. He was my role model for giving training talks at my work. We had such different lifestyles, though his energy drive was where I was coming from, in its own way.

My main focus was on training that NLP could help me deliver. I thoroughly enjoyed the NLP style for training, even way back when I was doing training as my job.

These books and tapes landed me additional knowledge from different angles, to get results for the Headway members and staff. This style I aimed to deliver was a modern-day exposure to active psychology in terms of how it could help, in my view, create breathtaking results.

I began mapping out what I was going to cover in classes and topics to use. I planned out the training sessions and made up on the computer, with new skills I had discovered, what I would give as handouts.

I had the idea of borrowing a VHS video camera from my aunt to rehearse what I was covering and my delivery. I went over and over and over them, performing, watching, adjusting and covering all angles relating to the NLP techniques.

My speech was not good at that time, yet my body language emphasised what I was saying. This was stronger, and gave more meaning to what I was saying. I found a way of slowing down what I said to make it sound meaningful and thought provoking. I just practised and practised and practised with these tools that improved my delivery.

My vision for the talk was seen in my mind's eye and told of the enthusiastic passion for what I do, and that came across. This added to the meaning of my theme for the talks.

My aim was to give meaning with more than words alone. There is by far more communication in the tone of voice and body language than the actual words, which would assist in portraying my meaningful theme. This was a very important lesson. I experienced it during all I went through with my injury, in delivering understanding to build motivation, and 'walking the talk'.

I eventually titled the themes of my classes: 'What you think is what you become!'

The talks covered three topics: Body Language; Increase Your Energy Levels; Beliefs and Perceptions.

The classes took 45 minutes each. The time was to be short, so as not to have the topic of a single subject going on for a long time, which would test my memory. It was just the right size for me.

Because of my slurred speech, the concentration required to invent the most suitable subjects for them, and the sheer effort of practicing my delivery, put it all together. In my mind, my first class on this subject was looking so good. It forced me to look at speech and communication in a different way. There was so much that was missed in the delivery of sentences, it was the beginning of a major transformation in communication for me. Again, learning of missed details opened up different doors. What people observe is psychologically driven, not from what is being said, but how it is said – pauses, tempo, volume, especially speed and pace – and this revolutionised communication for me. It was like having a new toy I couldn't wait to play with. It was only the burden of the cross I bore that held me back. It's like getting a new second-hand car with all its glory, but it has problems starting at times: it may not work the way you want it to, when you want it to. This was the cross I bore.

This was the key part of everything I had done that's still with me to this day as I push myself. I had a 'want'. In its way, it produced an addictive buzz, going to the edge and not being afraid of proving to myself that I could do it. I only saw successful, positive outcomes.

Pushing myself was without doubt for me. This was to prove I could communicate in my own way with better results, after losing my previous path on which I communicated before and was of great importance to me then. I wanted to do it better than before, making it my way. I gave myself aims of what to go for to make things better than before, or add new things. I wasn't going to waste my time wallowing over the past and what wasn't right. Improve me and make an advantage of this for me. Make the most of it..

I ventured down on the bus at 9 o'clock in the morning to Ayr. I focused on my recall of what I was to cover with my class. I got buzzed up, ready to help and motivate people. My aim was to give them cognitive understanding of how they are special, in different ways to suit them, changing their living and how they view themselves from now on.

The course content went down well. When they got used to me talking to the group instead of being in it, they picked up on my positive conviction that brought attention to what I was saying. This sold it to them.

At the end of the sessions, I still held that role. I had one-to-ones with the group members who needed some personal help. Nobody told me or suggested this was a great way of giving specific help, I just assumed it would be needed at this time. Even just taking time to listen to them intently, was worth its weight in gold. Someone they could actually open up to.

When the class was over, what I wanted to achieve was met – seeing their faces glow with new expressions. This was the purpose I had looked for. Was this the reason for me being kept alive? I summed up all the learning I had gained from all of this. Coming from training, this was normal for me. Another boost to my self-esteem in a huge way and my confidence soared. This whole concept was off of my own back. All my very hard, determined work was starting to pay off. This theme of motivating others was what I aimed at for the 'new me' and I felt very comfortable with it. It just felt right.

Next I made adaptations to suit other occasions, and that took time. Having experienced these life changes and a major life turnaround by losing just about everything, I was putting it to good use by making it my strength. People would know they could relate to me, as I 'walked the talk'. People would perceive this from my delivery alone; this was so powerful to me. All that had happened to me was an advantage that would help other people. Coming from such extreme losses, I was enthusiastically jumping to put them to use.

After such a thrill of taking a class after my change, I then went up on the bus for an hour and a half to college in Greenock to do management till 9 at night. I then went to my aunt's for a lift from my mum and I got back home about 10. A 13-hour day for me then. Long days were what I was used to from my teens and they were coming back now. My glowing energy was being focused.

My week at that time was becoming full, although it took a lot of concentration.

Monday was doing homework and preparation; Tuesday – Headway and college; Wednesday – I went to my old work for helping with training in Glasgow; Thursday – college; Friday – homework and Tai Chi; Saturday – preparation; and Sunday – time with my boys. Even though I missed my boys so much, my healing was called for. The more I recovered, the more time with them I'd have. Every day was crammed with daily exercises of improvement that set my day up, as well as still making bread. This was putting structure back into my life and I now could measure the improvements.

Tai Chi

I heard from people that a Tai Chi class was going to be in Largs. That conjured up good memories of doing the Tai Chi form before in 1998. I was in a class in West Kilbride and learned the form, as I used to when I opened the shop in Glasgow. It always set me up for the day.

In Largs, I went to the first class session with a walking stick to show that my legs had physical difficulties. Alvin, one of the seniors there, took me under his wing, having experienced childhood polio that affected his legs, his right more than his left. This was the start of becoming good friends with Alvin, Liz (his wife), and Irene was to be a colleague of mine later at stress management.

Training to do the form back in 1998 was three years ago, and the sequence of moves went blank to me after my wee car bump. I remembered very vaguely the form, I just couldn't remember the specifics movements; some I would have to adapt, to put it all together again.

At this stage, going over sections slowly at first gave me the details I needed, again with the adjustments to the moves I had to make. Sometimes, it was a strained adaption.

This was hard. Even more so, my limitations with my pelvis and legs made it even harder, going so slow.

Still, I was going to bloody do it. This spurted my willpower to fit in and complete the form. It was perfect timing for me. I got to know new people in the class. I got to the first cross hands. Usually, when this was reached, people went on to complete the form. I picked up that others in the class had a good appreciation of what I was achieving. Yes, this matched my determination to learn the form again.

Even with the memory problems I experienced, the repetition of the movements became automatic and I didn't have to consciously remember them, they just came to me automatically. This was an important learning process I had with memory: repetition. Also in discovering other forms of martial arts, second-nature movements are essential in cutting down time for defensive responses. The memory was in the subconscious and gracefully came automatically to me. Everything wasn't lost or messed up at all.

Alvin helped me to find my own way of doing certain moves. Physical expression was important to me, not being able to communicate with words well; in this case I just relied on the needed moves. I made the movements flow smooth and calm, even with the limitations my foot did give.

As time went on, I eventually completed the form. The completion was such a big achievement, physically and with the memory skills it helped develop, I had finally had completed it. I remembered by repetition. Completely remembering the form was such a relief, adding to what I had overcome that others accepted in day-to-day living. It was just like passing your driving test. Then you had to learn how to drive well from experience.

I discovered that there were other Tai Chi classes by a man who taught our class leaders the form. They went to his classes and were still there. I went to these classes in Greenock, where it was taken by a man called Bob in a church hall that had a long, big room. Bob was a third dan in aikido and now ran Tai Chi in this area. Tai Chi, with its martial arts aspect, was his theme. I had full belief I could continue with Tai Chi in this way.

I found out the grand master who set Tai Chi Chuan up was Chen Man-ch'ing: a master of calligraphy and Chinese medicine. In his early life, he had a brick wall fall on him when he was young and was in a coma for weeks. Suddenly I could relate to this aspect of how he broke through. Everyone is different and can sail through some things, yet some bear a cross to carry from similar experiences.

There was someone who had gone through a similar accident and came out with colours, and I had found a role model. This was sweetness to my eyes, and opening them wide I found out more about him. I had envy for his skills in constructing the short form as well as his other master skills following Tao.

In Bob's classes, I picked up more by repeating learning the form, and also by joining other classes and doing the form in different circumstances. I'd seen it in other aspects. This strengthens anything you want by heading towards mastery. Being a senior in Tai Chi now, I place myself in a good position, with all the other seniors, so folk can see the form being done from all angles to keep them right.

His teaching had a fantastic, different edge for me. He based it on the martial aspects that were influenced by aikido.

In teaching each and every movement of the form, he told elaborate tales of Tai Chi, martial arts, the Tao ways, and some of the famous people involved with the form over time. In his class, we were told that we were seven times removed from Chen Man-ch'ing in learning the form. He emphasised this fact on a regular basis. The talks he gave, helped with the way of Tai Chi and Tao, in life and all of the classes, making things a lot easier and improving life day by day. This was the holistic approach; it made complete sense and it made me wonder profusely how people didn't follow this way of seeing life as a whole. All things affect each other, good or bad. Energy, and the whole world having different energy levels, how to achieve calmness and inner power from within.

Boundless enthusiasm came through these words of wisdom and set me up to follow this way of life. Tai Chi was meant to be for me, in terms of helping my movement, the Tao way of living, keeping focus, and disengaging from stress to a relaxed state. This was life changing.

Our class was taught by drumming in the martial art aspects of being, with movements and what to do, with time talking of martial arts and the Tao way, which related to and blended so well with my twists and turns of life.

We did 'push hands', putting the form we learned into combat reality, yet relying on sensing the other. This was to discover what we would experience when someone was in front of us; how to keep cool and not show or react to emotions and be grounded with the moves learned. It would result in the automatic motion of putting the moves into action if someone should attack. This was 'going with the flow'. Go with them and put them off balance. It was drilled into us continually. Certain movements looked so easy and so effective, knocking the other off so much.

I then got involved with weapons like the staff, the Japanese sword and the Chinese sword. These all loosened my mind to the humdrum of day-to-day living, and ways to express, to act, and think in situations. It became a relaxed process of adapting speed, strength, flow and action. There was one time I teamed up with another person to use wooden staffs. I got the hang of focused control to such an extent that my first strike against his staff shattered it. Bob was pleased, yet I was shocked by it and felt bad I had broken the guy's stick. By this stage, I was going to three Tai Chi classes a week.

The secret was to cut out all thoughts, just to think of achieving the technique excellently. Clear your mind of anything else. This person in front of you is going to kill you. You only get one chance or you lose your life.

To be relaxed and focused, going with the flow of the other, then to turn it to your advantage, sensing they're off balance, gives you control with selected movements. This style was based on the ancient history of self-discipline. It gives the life skills you need. The philosophy covered what was needed for controlling yourself through life. A lot of history proves how intelligent humans are, like the construction of the pyramids, or Stonehenge: the accuracy of constructing these structures is phenomenal. Human intelligence in past times is not given the correct representation.

Overall, Tai Chi was vital for me in managing, processing, and having a purpose. It helped give focus and purpose to daily living. It interrupted non-productive thinking by doing the form, something more productive, and putting things into proportion. It helped give me focus and this alone is my sole purpose. It was my one and only focus when needed. This was a gift, training my mind to be more in control of myself, which I valued so much.

What's more was being told by Bob that if your opponent is big, that's an advantage, because you can get him off balance easier and he comes tumbling down. This revolutionised my confidence. I never had the feeling that someone could overpower me physically and mentally. Everyone breathes, pisses, shits and sleeps like everyone else. Nobody can be in power over you. It must be psychological in standing. They have created this overpowering image, so I could generate 'I'm not taking any shit and no prisoners'. I focused solely on being convincing and true and this always backed them away. Psychological aspects are more valuable in terms of being able to physically be on top. This drained a big fear of mine, of what could be projected socially.

Furthermore, putting the form to use in real life self-defence, I could see how it useful it might be. While learning the moves in real situations for use, Bob would come round observing and he would occasionally stop me and I would describe to him how the movement happens and what I found hard, saying that by next time I would do it right. He always said to me, "You are dead. Always do it with conviction and under the circumstances, you don't get a second chance. You do your best to survive." This has never left me and applies to any aspect of life, to be able to walk away: to perform with conviction and not rely on a perfect theory. The chance of it being a perfect application is very slim. It's having will and conviction that gets you through.

First Munro Again

At least once a week, mainly Sundays, I went walking up the hills at the back of Largs. This time was devoted to sort thoughts and situations out in my head and also, I measured the routes I would walk. The hills, being of uneven ground made this a challenge to my balance at times. I counted the amount of times I went up and down to measure the same height, if I was doing a Munro (a mountain over 915 metres/3,000 feet). It was an average of five times I went up and down and yes, it was the same distance in height, but it was known ground I ventured on. Doing a Munro again would involve a dramatically longer distance. This was the closest I got and I didn't want to hinder anybody waiting for me to do a Munro with another person, as I would be too slow compared to them. In my mind, it would be similar to an adult waiting for their young kid. I didn't want that. After all, I was on a recovery journey that folk could not see; it was very personal, therefore I'd do it myself. By now, I was getting used to achieving things myself.

My sister was venturing up north to take one of her girls outside Fort William for a day. It was for her ballet advanced learning class at a location up there. I'd seen this as an opportunity and asked for a lift up, and to be picked up on her way home.

I had marked a Munro near to the very first one I climbed. The hill I aimed for was called An Caisteal just before the village of Crianlarich.

Going into this area myself was a big step. I was filled with such determination that my disabilities were not going to win. My sister knew that, so instead of saying no, I would have to find some other way of doing it, at least this way was more controlled.

She made sure my mobile phone worked and I followed the path. Slow walking, but I was on the road to some part of my life I thought I'd never experience again. I was actually doing it. The route was ingrained in my mind, but just in case I found certain parts too difficult, I could find an alternative.

The first section was grass-covered steepness that required me to infuse my efforts with monotonous counting to gain distance. This took a long time. I got to the peak of that section to open up to a graduated steepening flow to another peak. It was easier: my legs worked much better than they did before practicing up the Largs hills to build up strength and stamina.

This put me on track to go faster up this starting section than I had expected. I got some fantastic views of the mountains nearby. I stopped occasionally and imagined what path I took to climb them a while ago, before my accident. From these views, I observed what looked too steep for me at this moment, and what parts looked feasible and meant there were other mountains that could now be accessible. My energy needed motivation, with little exercise in comparison, as well as wondering whether I could do certain sections because of my injuries. This alone took up so much energy, looking for the alternatives as well as doing the normal route. This was my emotional rucksack, this was a burden me at times, but I wasn't going to let it win. I had Mars Bars to keep me going and sandwiches when, or if I reached the expected peak.

The steepness eased off and it was coming up to a possibly tricky part I could faintly remember. It was a steep rock formation with easy holds, but a long step over a large gap at the peak between two rock faces was required. This was too steep for me to go down and around. With the steepness of angle, there was a high chance of me falling. I was back to nature, a place I thought I'd never see again. It's just that I thought, *I don't want to get injured up here.* I had to step across. I had got this far doing what I thought I would never experience again, so I found the best space to cross this large, deep gap. I prepared myself to calmly achieve it, made the committed move over to the other rock face with a lunge, and I was successful. The buzz was flowing in me at full steam now. I followed the faint path up and the last rounded steepness of the final peak.

I had made it. I had done a Munro again.

It felt like such a monumental time for me and the views were breathtaking, especially when it wasn't that long ago I thought this kind of experience was to be no more for me. I was finally in complete freedom from my imprisonment. If you are a hill climber, you know what I mean, going to these places so far into the wilderness, although in saying that, sometimes they are busy. This one was as peaceful as I expected it to be. There is a difference, being in such wilderness that hasn't being plagued by the human race. I was in love with this experience of nature.

I celebrated this momentous time by performing part of the new horizons I had taken on board. In this quiet area, I did the Tai Chi form. It was my way of gratitude, following Cheng Man-ch'ing's form. I modelled the way he changed things and I had achieved what was presumed I couldn't do anymore. I had my sandwich with lots of water and felt so contented, although I was just halfway; I still had the way back to go. The journey back down the mountain was waiting.

I followed the path down to the rock crossing again. I composed myself and went for the lunge again. By this time, the gap felt so wide and steep. My abilities were drained, yet I could do it as I had done before. I went for it again, imagining my foot placement going beyond the gap to make sure I securely crossed.

I had done it again.

Venturing down the steep part, my legs began to protest from such continual strain from being stuck in repetitive conditions for a long time. As time went by, I was on the last big grass steepness; I thought I would go down it quick, but I was going down slower. It was soon going to be the time Margaret, my sister, would be there with her daughter, so I decided to give her a call. There was no reception. I thought of her waiting for me at the lay-by and getting worried. She could possibly see me coming down this part of the mountain, as this part you can see from the road. This worry added to my tiredness and I just ploughed on.

Eventually I arrived back at the car with relief and they told me about the ballet day. It wasn't long before I fell asleep, being so tired after achieving this landmark for myself. Such feelings of gratitude for my sister for helping me get there, and the others who helped me to do this. The time was right for me to achieve this. It was one of the main components for me to experience what is called spiritual growing. This kept me young, and energised.

School Talks for Headway

Headway was doing a talk for a school education programme about head injuries with medical and ambulance staff in Ayrshire.

I joined the team that were delivering their piece in the educational part, and discussed with Jane what we would be covering in my piece to the students. She discussed what the class sizes were to be, how many classes we were to talk to, and what the medical and ambulance staff would cover.

We were there all day at the school, covering five classes. There were four of us that would talk to the classes about how head injury affected our lives.

My aim was to go over what I was going to say lots of times so it was well rehearsed.. What techniques I would use, what my message was, and how to dramatize my talk. The time and the content of what I was to cover was quite rightly paid attention to. I practised and practised, until I felt confident. My speech would be great, with the delivery that I had in store for the pupils and the other folk presenting. I saw the result clearly in my mind's eye.

On the day, first was a talk by a medical staff member about what they normally have to deal with in casualty, then the ambulance crew, all with slides, and then our talk. One by one we from Headway would say our piece.

My talk appealed to all of their senses and was different from the pace and style they had anticipate.

They listened to me. People actually listened to me. I delivered my speech with confidence and this worked well. Teenage kids were listening to me. This was brilliant. I am important and they had an interest in what I was saying. My words were at times confusing, but by having confidence, it took away their attention from my speech quality to what I was saying. It was an act. Life is an act and is full of different performances, it's knowing when and where to act to get the best performance.

I started off hyping up my successes and the fun of climbing, showing the adventure and daring that a teenage mind could relate to. I also made it seem exciting and risky. I had a beautiful wife and a brilliant career: everything was going excitingly. I climbed more and more. One time on returning from a climb up north, my car skidded and crashed into a tree.

I dramatized the crash to accent this life-changing point. "WHAM!" I almost shouted and stamping my feet and banged my hands together in one single sharp blow. This contrast accented event that happened quickly and so dramatically changed my life.

They took in that just one single event could completely change one's life, just like that. I then informed them in a different, factual voice what happened – broken bones, coma, not being able to walk, my talking was very poor and my left hand was barely functioning, my time in many hospitals and the daily struggle I have. I lost my job, couldn't drive again and my wife left me. This gave such a contrast to the risks of climbing. I made it fun and exciting for the pupils to hear about my life. A big build-up, then WHAM, the shocking sudden contrast, then a factual account of what happened after that event got them thinking. All because of being caught up in the adrenalin rush of climbing: not being aware, I lost everything.

I did a good job for Headway and the pupils that day. I was proud of what I achieved through my drama skills and facts. I hope this gave them a new perception away from society and developing through late teenage life that maybe pulled them to behave in a different way and avoid bad consequences.

CHAPTER 6

Beginning to Find Myself:
Built with Determination

A journey of a thousand miles starts with a single footstep.
– Lao Tzu

London Awards

Jane at Headway said she had the great pleasure of telling me that I was to go down to London to pick up an award at their annual meeting: 'Finalist achiever of the year' in the United Kingdom. Jane informed the main office of Headway about me: my positivity, drive and determination. This was an award of accomplishment after a head injury. I was being rewarded for the effort I had put in to get back on form again. It was for being given an opportunity to live again. A feeling of pride came over me. This was gold dust when I felt all this hard effort was being lost doing menial day-to-day tasks again.

Jane must have written a magnificent letter of notification for me to their awarding body. It was all that I had done, plus the weekly distance I travelled from Ayr to Greenock by bus, taking groups, then going to college to a course I joined myself.

There were three other winners in different categories from the Ayr Headway. I can only reckon it was just by chance and by specific circumstances these people were all there at once. Jane and her team must have done a very good job in doing the application forms for the centre. Her recommendations got us all through.

Maybe it was solely on Jane's letters. Maybe it was just by chance there were certain standards of people in a certain area and Jane justified rewarding them. It probably could have been a combination of both. The other award winners were from around the area of Ayrshire that Robbie Burns, the famous Scottish poet, lived and wrote his most popular poems and songs, as in 'Auld Lang Syne', the internationally known song sung by all after the bells at New Year.

After the buzz of flying again from Prestwick airport, which was soon to play an important part in my life's future, I didn't think I would fly again, or have the opportunity to, and there I was, in a plane again. I loved flying. This was exciting.

Meeting all the people from Headway at Prestwick airport, we all travelled down in the plane to Stansted. It was great being back in London at the Hilton hotel. Only going through the door did I remember this place. The Hilton had brought memories flooding back. This was the same hotel I stayed at for the national hairdressing awards a few years ago. Tremendous energy of joyous times was with me. I was filled with contented happiness of then and now, what was to happen, and my self-worth was present and alive.

At meeting with the entire group beforehand, I found the ticket from *The Hairdressing Awards* of the exact same hotel in the pocket of my suit that hadn't been worn since then. It brought back the glam and the electric energy I experienced that day.

In the big boardroom, there were lots of large, round tables for the possible winners, and our team from the Ayr Headway sat together.

Each category of the awards was presented by a celebrity. Some of the celebrities you would know easily. They were just about all males, except for one gorgeous female. I found out it was Miss Universe of Britain: Katrina Hendon. She was a stunning, glowing presence that stood out so much.

I couldn't believe my luck when I found out the only female was presenting my category. That was immense luck. Who needs to win lottery tickets? Winning the finalist award in Britain, being flown down to London, having that beauty Katrina give me my award – this was my lottery winning. This didn't seem real – a self-defensive way of protecting me from what appeared to be 'pie in the sky'. I was expecting to wake up at any moment from my perfect dream to the dulcet drones of the alarm clock buzzing away in the background. I glowed with vibrant energy and my eyes sparkled with excited joy.

The categories that were presented were going through very slowly. My category was coming up soon. The excited buzz flowed through me and quickened my pace. I handed my camera to Bob, another person from Headway in Ayr.

"Can you take lots of pictures of her giving me the award?" I said with a glowing cheesy grin and eyes that shone bright.

Laughingly, he agreed. Then my name was called out. That feeling of ecstatic excitement was as full as it could go.

I got a kiss from Katrina and then a professional photographer took our photo. So quick and it was over. Can you imagine how immensely gratifying this was to me? What an experience. The only female celebrity, so stunning she was, and I got the honour of her giving me my award with a kiss.

I got back home (with such a big cheesy grin like a toothpaste advert) in a triumphant daze and fitted into my weekly routine again. It looked like I had been given some drugs that put me in a daze. Still, on the defensive side, this felt like a very, very good dream that gave the fullest pleasure of fulfilment. It now seemed plausible. Things eventually were taking off after the loss of the life I had before.

A New Home

Tania decided she wanted to go her own way, unknown to me at this point. She had studies to do, as well as organising the kids and the house. I felt pushed away to the side, which in a way was good for me to recover under my own steam and not let people impose on my difficulties with their version of fixing it. All this got too much for my wife after experiencing a deflated and broken version of the old me; she wanted her own place. Maybe unknown to me, the relationship wasn't as good as I thought and with this major upturn, this was too much for her. This was painfully out of my control.

With my wife buying a house for her and the boys, the house we were in was to be sold, so I had to look for a small place with the finances from the sale of the house. It was arranged the majority of the funds would go to the boys and her. I couldn't look after the boys myself at the stage I was at, and the ages they were. This was crushingly upsetting for me.

Having to help sell the house that I was now in alone brought me back to the solitude of experiencing life that didn't connect, and I didn't have anyone to share my experiences with, to enjoy life together anymore, as it once was. I used to get lost in physical activities that took my attention away from this devastation. Twice a week I'd make bread to keep me focused on exercise for my left hand. Making bread created such a pleasant, fresh, caressing scent.

The family house was too big for me. At least I had the company of my two ginger cats that we had for a good few years. Their independent living brought on my affection and respect for them even more. They were friendly, but never imposing their own territory. They were living in the now.

I loved cats, particularly ginger ones – ginger toms, bringing the total to three ginger Toms in this house. With my ginger hair, we teamed up. How they just got on and adapted to coolly suit always impressed me. This gave me enjoyment in relation to what I was experiencing myself.

I can remember of our first house, one cat made me laugh so much. I was in the front room and in the hall was the back door fitted with a cat flap. I heard the most unusual disturbed noise from the cap flap. One cat was trying with all his might to drag a bloody herring seagull through the cat flap with its wings banging the back door, not letting it in. It wasn't successful to my delight after shooing my cat away. If the seagull had come in… I don't know anybody that had a seagull in their house. It could have been the beginning of many funny tales, or wing in this case.

Back to looking for a new place to live, I saw a few flats that just weren't right, but good to see, and eventually one flat filled all that I was looking for, yet it was just over my budget. A great location and facing south to get the warmth light from the sun all day in the main room. It felt just right for me. I went by my instinct. I put in an offer and got it. Slowly I would build up again from being so low down after that episode in my life.

Moving to my new flat just after the matrimonial house was sold, I got some help from my mum to get the 'one-up' flat in which the main room was south facing and got daylight and heat all day. One floor up and it had a railing with the stairs. I went out of my way and was slower going up the stairs, not holding on to the railing to prove I didn't need it, and I did not need it, making my confidence grow. A good saying for this is 'slow and sure'.

I dearly missed my boys and distracted myself with lots of activities and projects to work on to cease that destructive train of thought that was out of my control.

I eventually got my boys every Sunday. They had comfort and enjoyment of the father-son relationship. We grew stronger and stronger through one day a week.

I would look after them for the whole day and was offered the help of others, mainly my mum, every Sunday. This help from my mum and good friends, was a saving grace for me. To get help like this was a blessing and helped with the priorities. Being a father as best I could, was ultimately best for my sons in my view. We all benefit from a father figure.

I had the opportunity to discover who my friends were when I needed help or support; they automatically came like the 'law of attraction' – it brings a connection and draws you and others to a needed point in their life journeys.

I saw Dee and her cousin Grace with her girls now and then, spending time doing activities with all of our kids. It was fun and different to get help doing new things.

Dee was in my class through the years of growing up. Grace being cousin to Dee, I had the pleasure of knowing them both for years. Their support was needed at this time and it's only through events like this, you really know what true friendship is.

My mother, who was now retired from the local academy, was an art teacher. She let us do painting and drawing pictures, myself and her grandkids, every Sunday visiting her. This increased their imagination and lightened up my creativity. It melted me with happiness to find my creativity again. It was then I realised how creativity was primary in my life and for a while, it was lost. I wasn't able to take the boys any other time through the week, as it would be too much for me at that stage to deal with the ages they were. That tore my heart. How great they were, having time with me. I loved this so much. Their single personalities shone so bright. So much love I got back from my boys that was pure and true, which strengthened my motive to be there for them.

After doing this activity every week, I wanted to give them something else we all could get pleasure from. It became an event to take them swimming on Sundays. At that point, Adam was four and Euan six.

I usually went down first with John for an hour, giving him full attention. Then my mum brought Euan to get changed. I just stayed in the pool for each session with them for their personal attention. By having them separately in the pool, I could spend specific time with them, improving our bond, and I could improve their swimming. It jokingly went through my mind that this was like doing different children shifts.

This worked so well, hand in hand with the skills I had learned through NLP coaching.

I made it so entertaining fun for them, providing enjoyment with them learning to swim a breadth across; going to the shallow end of the pool and bouncing further down up to the middle of the pool; holding their breath under water to bounce off the floor of the pool consistently; going up to the deep end and jumping in; diving in and touching the bottom. From breast stroke to front crawl, I put in the effort of swimming one length, to eventually achieve lots of lengths over time, never mind the advantage of exercise.

Taking them weekly to the pool was enlightening for my progress. There were ways I couldn't help them in normal life, like when they were at their mum's house. This was a way I could, by giving them one-to-one time and improve their swimming. Being a father to them, this was sharing in something that was a core to my life —

keeping fit. The hours devoted to swimming gave me great exercise. I got super clean, with the chlorine making me even paler, being a Scottish person. The whiteness made my freckles stand out against my short red hair, giving me even more of the look of a typical Scottish person.

I worked on what I was good at and worked for me in terms of trusting myself and getting results. I wanted to have the feeling of physical accomplishment again. This time, it was different. I was trusting myself, going with the sense of my own intuition in what felt right, rather than someone else's rules and ways. This influenced my trust in myself and acknowledging what I was good at now compared to what I was good at in my old life.

Doing this every weekend was hard, physical work for me then, but worth it by far. My week was filling up well, although I got the impression that my placement to oversee the training of my old work, which helped me with my college course, wasn't going anywhere. You get a gut feeling that things are going well, and it suits them as well as me. I had to make a grim decision. Feeling uncomfortable up there, I had to give up that ghost and stop going to the training salon. This decision had a knock-on effect. I was under the impression that you needed work experience to go to with the college course, and giving up going to my old work, I had to give up my college course. For some reason I thought that was the way. It logically made sense to me and I needed to see the theory in reality (hands-on). After having to give up my management college placement, I needed to find another focus of interest that would give me motivation.

I finally found a work experience placement at the Heart Foundation shop in my town's main street through a girl my cousin was seeing who was working there. Talking with Headway, they referred me to a company called Momentum whose role is to get people with injuries back to working.

I told Ann from Momentum, who I talked to at first, that I didn't really need her to organise me a placement, as I had work experience in a charity shop. I had found it myself. There was a group meeting every Thursday with other head injured people. It was eye opening for me to see the conation they had constructed after their injures and the way their life was now. Momentum's aim was to rehabilitate them back into normal day-to-day living. Having knowledge of the effects they were experiencing, I saw this as limiting themselves. How these negative thoughts affected their body and themselves was an important discovery which could be made by actually witnessing it, rather than reading from a book.

I knew where they were coming from due to my personal experience and the knowledge I have of psychological theory which left me with unique skills for knowing how to help them. This beckoned empathy from a managerial position, looking out for their potential.

Weeks of the meetings went by and then I told Ann about the positivity classes I had done for Headway, and that I could do group classes for her. We discussed the topics I would cover about communications, beliefs and energy.

My drive for 'hands-on' psychology loomed and became more driven on my way back from the day-release hospital appointments. I was motivated to find out more about the mind and its workings. I have always had a fascination with psychology and all my attention was forced to make sense of this now. I was to see if my previously gained knowledge from training would help me now. Digging out the old material I had on this connected to training and motivation, I was on to a new direction, finding out how people learn more efficiently. This showed me, with the help of my strong will, that I had the qualities and techniques of learning. This was the ticket for me.

With the help of NLP books and CDs, this sent me in the right direction again. Now, I had clarity over the painful discovery that I was on a different directional path in life. I could not go on the path I had any longer. This one was a scary new path. I was unsure of its direction. What I did know was that I felt this was who I was, and felt very comfortable with motivating people. No matter where it led me, this was my path.

Spending time doing work experience with my old hairdressing job, I met an old client of mine. Talking to this old client, she mentioned a woman she knew through counselling who had an NLP class. She phoned the woman whose name was Mina and then I talked to her. The group was on Tuesdays in Glasgow. I was told the address. The Tom Alan Centre. I planned out how to get there by scanning the street map of Glasgow. I was ready for this.

The NLP Group

Going to the group, it was quite busy. I felt very conscious of my difference. My walking and my speech were prominent. Mina was so friendly, and with the other members in the group, I felt very comfortable. To join with people that have a similar focus was of importance to all of us.

The group was taken by Mina and had two other trainers, Jeff and Rintu. I got to know them more and they shared their skills and knowledge with me. Mina was in her 60s but didn't even look in that vicinity of age at all. She had a youthful, energetic glow about her, full of fascination for subjects and a vast interest.

We went over techniques and psychology in the night sessions. Going home on the train, I applied them to my everyday life, if the techniques were relevant. It was without a doubt solving the problems I was experiencing in adjusting to my new self, and solved a lot of psychological adjustment I had to make to fit in with society with all its trimmings. This was brilliant for me. Going through the material weekly, the patterns were beginning to link. With my poor memory, this regular activity with meaning gave me ways to remember things and get the most out of my mind.

It made me realise I had qualities; this was the start of a journey of self-discovery and helping others. There were so many fantastic hands-on skills to learn that helped me rehabilitate myself, fitting in with the world from a new point of view.

I was seen differently in life and people of the group responded differently to me. I just stuck to the fact that I am bloody worth it, clear in my mind, no matter what their initial opinion was of me. I was not basing myself based on what I presumed to be going on in the other person's head. I wasn't going to let that assumption ruin my day. This was a great learning experience from NLP, and more. This was the transformation that changed my course, giving me control over my life and meaning, which would not be affected by social assumptions. It brought out me as a person. What skills I always had were identified and used to my benefit now – that made me unique and special. I am different and proud of it. I could confidently stand out for them, selling myself in a different way than before. How you present your image, is what people pick up on. Be shy and they will think you shy. Be confident and they will think you confident. Be intelligent and they will think you intelligent. Anything you put your mind to that is sold with conviction, helps make up their view of you.

Each week, I learned more fantastic tools, and during my work experience at the local charity shop, I took my notes with me and revised when it was quiet so I could put them into play. I put the learnings to use in different settings to see when they worked best.

For just about two years I went to the group and found out of they were having a practitioner's course. It sounded exactly what I was looking for. This got me very excited. I eventually found things that were true about me, and then this – I had found my way. Now it took time to gain the knowledge and experience of the true destination for my inner self. Hairdressing played a main role in my life and back then, it suited my lifestyle. My life had changed and now it suited another way.

After going to the NLP group weekly for two years, I saw Mina, Rintu, and Jeff about whether I could take a week's intensive practitioner's course. I was stuck in what I presumed my limitations were from the brain injury, and what society presumed I was limited to. They said it would be fine for me. This put me at ease as the momentous darkness that loomed that I was far from perfect, with a very poor memory, and I couldn't cope with this. A sense of failing was newly put into play because of my belittling injury. This made me not raise any hopes of being able to do it, never mind of passing. With them telling me I could do a few days and see how I got on, and if needed I could always go to other practitioner courses at no extra cost, this was a big relief for me. I claimed the benefit of experiencing positivity from another person's point of view.

With all the exercises and tests I was given, they were based on memory of a subject that wasn't stressful to memorise. You just took it in. Maybe it was the way it was delivered that helped and made it easily understood, instead of trying to work out what the other person was trying to explain, never mind the content they were supposed to be explaining. Just let it absorb in a particular way and review it in the same way to gain the information needed. I would discover later that this was one of the keys to memory retention. To have a want for the knowledge of the mind and also a desire to get to know the different areas of psychology increased my passion to know it.

The course was seven days long and in two weeks, two days to refresh the course.

I laid out all my clothes, breakfast, bag and writing material. Getting up much earlier than normal, going for the train to Glasgow, I had already done my usual morning exercises that needed to be done. The perseverance would make progress in my view.

The first day the course began, I got the train up from Largs and it was the same train I used to go to work in Glasgow for years, getting the train the whole journey right from the beginning of the line. It was good to remember that time and the fun travelling this way, with the anticipation I had then, of actually working in a high street salon in Glasgow.

I couldn't sleep on the train that day. I was full of anticipation. I arrived at the centre where we had our regular meetings on Tuesday evening, only it was set out differently with seats in a semi-circle. The nervousness of starting a new class was there, yet there was something different about this. It was a strange amount of excitement I was experiencing. I couldn't believe I had got to this stage. One half of me was so excited that I was on the road to what I wanted. The other half of me was waiting to be discovered by the course – I shouldn't really be here, or I failed. After such a long time of being constantly belittled because I had a head injury: compared to other people, our ability is lessened, some to a great degree. Because I was in that category, I shouldn't expect anything different.

I had so much confidence that I would recover to some degree, if not better, I wouldn't be limited by the assumption that I couldn't achieve what I wanted. Nobody could determine this for me. Only I could determine this. Maybe it was not the same way it was delivered to suit the general public, but I would achieve it a different way that suited me, with my disabilities, that made it work.

With all this fantastic material, I found out my learning style and it just didn't follow the common average expected by schooling and society anymore. A lot of folk were like this, having their own way of learning. There were lots of different angles, yet the most common one was how you mostly take information in using your senses; how we interact using sight (visual), hearing (auditory) and kinaesthetic (feeling). These were the main ones, yet taste and smell had their relevance, depending on the state the person is in.

Depending on the situation, my main modalities were visual and kinaesthetic. I learned about communication with myself and others, and how this is an important factor. I could pick up whether I was on similar modalities with another person, and knew how to change what I said to suit the situation.

The main learning process was communication, in terms of how the mind communicated with the body and vice versa. What was also important was how to communicate with others. For efficiency, we were to model what we wanted to improve from others. It relied on the mainly on the subconscious. Modelling was one of the keys of NLP. There was so much that one could find out from someone from their beliefs and values as a person. I learned to pick this up and see what stage in their development they were at, to influence their motivation. I then understood where they were coming from and mimicked them to achieve what I wished in their behaviour. Matching the amount of detail they used as they spoke also brought on rapport. It matched their model of their world and gave the illusion of being on the same level of thinking.

With language, there were two categories to work with in terms of what level a person chunked up at. The two levels were meta-modelling to counteract details in language, and the Milton Model which covered vagueness with underlying presupposition. This was a form of hypnosis. Milton Erickson was the most famous hypnotist of this era. Milton, the American, was a psychiatrist and took hypnosis away from the formal approach and showed how it could be applied to conversation. Healing and learning comes from the subconscious and hypnosis worked with this.

Milton produced some amazing results with issues that had never been solved before. It was in an angle that there was a void in health for. Primary health had factual solutions for the working body. This opened up secondary mental health.

Milton had polio and was in a wheelchair. His sensory awareness was famous in addition to this new version of hypnosis. His fame generated from being aware of people's reaction to inner conflict. It was noted from the sight of their blood vessels changing flow as their pulse rate changed. He noticed their reaction (the mind-body connection – the body responds to the mind) and altered his delivery to suit, taking into account how they reacted. Erickson wrote some very interesting books.

It was working on the person's subconscious that got results. Instead of battling against the block found in their conscious mind to give them direction, it was suited fully to their subconscious. This bypasses the blockage by focusing on what is better for them. It's awe inspiring.

Milton is no doubt a prominent person in my life, due to the way he achieved so much in his life with polio.

With my voice, I had to talk slower than normal and go over every single word. This was ideal for Ericksonian Hypnosis. It helped break up the normal pattern of speech and then I could talk slower with confidence. What and how words were said posed such difference, and by using vague words the conscious was occupied in working out what it meant. Then presuppositions were given to back up the person's aim to overcome their conscious blockage.

Against the odds of my disability I had with my speech, yes, daily practice worked and words sounded better – this was so suitable for me. Even when the person was relaxed, my pronunciation of words confused their conscious mind. My speech wasn't a disadvantage anymore. It was pronounced as a condition of dysarthria where I had acquired difficulties in pronouncing certain tones in words. This was confused as a foreign accent, which fell into a certain script that I used regularly to deal with this in another way.

Cheng Man-ch'ing and Milton Erickson were my role models for making a mark in society after an injury or illness. They gained further knowledge to a high degree and I wanted so much to follow suit. Finally, I wasn't alone. Others had travelled the same path. This produced a strong belief that I was on the right path. All my suffering had its reason in preparing me for my future travels. Hypnosis fitted like a glove. I used self-hypnosis CDs for relaxation and knew they worked. This added more to my delivery, as I knew what sections worked from experience and delivered them with conviction. I would never have ventured into hypnosis until this time, after my life changed so dramatically.

Driving Test Again

Per the DVLC, I was not allowed to drive again after my accident, due to having a head injury. I was to sit another driving test to prove that I could cope in traffic.

Getting in touch with the DVLC, I told them about my accident and asked what would happen now. They mentioned about a test at the Astley Ainslie in Edinburgh. I had to go there again, only this time, I was just visiting.

Jane from Headway told me whom to get in touch with about my driving assessment. I had driven daily since I had passed my test the first time at seventeen. For me, it was second nature to just drive.

I got a time for a test. I was excited that this was coming to a supposed ending, eventually taking a major step back into normal day-to-day living.

My mum offered to give me a lift through to Edinburgh on the morning of the appointment. When I finished the test, I had to go back by bus, then train, and that gave me the welcomed experience of using public transport from Edinburgh. To be with people from different walks of life, was refreshing for me having been imprisoned for so long.

In the grounds of the Astley Ainslie, the actual section was a place I had never been to before on my slow walks or being pushed in my wheelchair around grounds I remembered so well. What I was experiencing then came flooding back. A fabulous service, yet I was at my worst and was haunted by my imprisonment.

It was on the left side of the main building by itself. It was so good to be there just as a visitor this time for my driving test.

I had a seat and waited for the woman to see me. It brought back the old sensations I had with my first test. I was just seventeen, my legs could barely touch the floor and the others in the room looked so much older than me. This time, I was under the challenge of functioning differently.

She introduced herself to me. We had a brief talk and headed out to the car with manual gears. At that point, my co-ordination was a difficulty for me. I knew how to drive, only I had problems working the clutch, the gears and the accelerator in co-ordination. We were supposed to go out in the Edinburgh city centre busy streets. That would be hard for anyone who didn't know the details of the roads around Edinburgh. I was going to bloody do it. This would have been a big step for me, getting my licence back.

We just went around the hospital grounds. I wasn't ready yet. She mentioned about automatic gears. This sounded good and made complete sense. My attention would only be on driving. She gave me the number of places nearer to me to arrange another test and getting lessons with automatic gears would be my next stage before sitting the test again.

After phoning and phoning, I eventually found a driving school that does automatic car driving lessons. The Paisley Group had someone who could do this for me. He was the only one in this area at this time. It was a relief getting this stage organised. I couldn't get my licence back straight away, I would be doing this way.

Our first meeting was at Gourock, which was halfway between Paisley and Largs and Greenock, where my aunt lives. I have fond memories of the area from growing up, visiting her and my grandparents at every school break. My dad, being at sea was home rarely, which led me to spend a lot of time up there.

Driving about in an automatic car was fun. I found areas I had never quite been to before, discovering details of Gourock, Greenock and Port Glasgow town all joined together, which is large and long an area compared to Largs.

It didn't take me long to get the hang of driving again and not bothering with the gears, although when I stopped the car, I automatically went to push the gears into first. Occasionally, I would go to make gear changes automatically, as part of the process before that was built into me.

My instructor was good. I was interested to learn things I had trouble remembering or dealing with due to my physical injuries. I was so focused on segments I could improve. I found out what was needed and I used to practise as much as I could physically or to visualise myself achieving the manoeuvre.

This was a successful method of practice for me. The breakdown into small chunks, planning time to do it regularly, visualising success and rewards for myself. I did this automatically, as if I sorted it out by myself to get it done and feel good about myself, giving me balance in my life.

During the week, as with the other activities I had, I used to run along to the pencil in Largs and back again, going over what I had learned and putting it into play continually, so it would become an automatic reaction. Twice a week in the evenings, I would visualise myself successfully completing sections I wanted.

I got the go-ahead from my trainer to see about the test. I phoned and arranged a time and place at the Paisley hospital. I asked them what they would be looking for. They just said my driving in general.

I told my instructor about this very general statement. He just set out as if I was sitting the full test, covering all the driving code theory questions, and went over every manoeuvre.

I had to be picked up at Paisley railway station and drive in a busy city area covering where the test may be taken and the best places to go over procedures. Paisley is much faster and busier than Largs by far. By repeatedly going over the areas needed for my manoeuvres, it just sank in. Not details of street names, but the vivid memories of the areas I drove in. It is called procedural memory. This came more easily to me. This is how I work with anything. I just like to do things hands-on, not paralysed by analysis, just doing it. Experience, rather than an academic accomplishment, give me greater rewards, attached to my feelings of being right or wrong.

After practising the actual techniques manually, visualising myself succeeding, and getting my cousin Robert to take me to a car park to practice my manoeuvres, the hard bit was going over the driving code theory I had to remember. Yuck. That took major effort to do. Continual repetition eventually worked, leaving me feeling confident with what I knew for a pass.

The day before, my mum and I went to my aunt's to meet up with my sister and her family there as well. We had dinner and a good laugh with my brother-in-law Raymond.

On the way back home down the coastal way, outside Gourock,

there was a stop and traffic stood still. We waited and waited. A person came running up asking if there was anyone who knew first aid. It was a car crash. The emergency cars came by and eventually, we moved slowly to pass the car. How fragile cars could be. I knew that from past experience.

I kept up a focused front and ignored the emotions that could have brewed up. I wasn't going to let this ruin something I spent months practising and what it meant. I was going to do my best.

The day came. I came up as usual to Paisley by train to meet up with my driving instructor for a quick lesson before my test. We went over techniques again and driving in a busy area.

We ended up at the hospital where the mobile driving centre was. There were two men there. One was to go out with us. We left the hospital and covered the area I knew so well by now.

I was driving confidently. Because I was heading towards a test, I had to lose all the habits I gained for quicker, relaxed driving, like putting my left hand across the passenger chair to balance while reversing, or crossing my hands turning the wheel and so on. Things you never really think of until you are put in a test situation.

I was given a chance to change my old driving habits.

He just said where to turn and watched my manoeuvres at the hospital. I was to show the techniques I had been practicing so hard and visualising in my mind.

When I was told a specific one, I was prepared. I was ready for it.

The first manoeuvre in a way, was humorous. There is a low speed limit of fifteen miles an hour and I had to do my emergency stop. He watched my technique and that was easy. What was hard was the three-point turn in the car park area. It was very compact. Thankfully, I did it successfully. The next was parking by reversing into the space. Not easy in these grounds with someone looking over your shoulder as well. Not easy.

Back at the mobile centre, I had a talk with the other guy who I got the impression was of a medical background.

Relaxed, the traffic code questions were answered okay. I displayed nervousness for a test, which contrasted the instructor's relaxed way. The comparison made me ease off from being in such an attentive mode for the theory questions. I was trying too hard for perfection, to cover everything just in case. If you go to such lengths and be lax about some things, it's more often those things will get asked. 'Belts and braces' is an old saying that makes sense.

I eventually passed. My instructor drove me to the station, as usual with driving tests. I was hyper with achievement. My mind was racing at 100 miles an hour. I remember the time at Astley Ainslie, being in a wheelchair and not knowing what I would be able to do from then on. Even the basics like walking, talking, would I ever work in the career I was in, drive and so on? I had now got my licence back.

This brightly glowed through me with the confidence it created.

I thanked my instructor and if I can recommend business his way, I will. I had such a cheesy grin going back on the train. Who would I tell first? I was so chuffed with myself. Now the limitations I had, were fading faster and faster. I could get whatever I aimed for. The effort and methods I used, was a good way for me. For the first time in my life ever, taking control of the situation, knowing the outcome and putting into play what's needed for this to happen, I could achieve whatever I wanted. The limitations that were set before, were now to my fullest advantage.

I imagined all the way home what was possible after completing my road test again. Now what had been an incredibly limiting experience, to be crippled with disabilities, was not so. I had earned a prize people would take years of experience to gain – even just a part of the life skills I had experienced. This gave me an awareness of the skills I now had. It's like the yin and yang symbol. If one side lessens, it is more on the other side, to compensate the whole self. Things were taken away from me and replaced with others so special.

I was given a second chance at life. Part two. Everyone builds up limitations from their childhood; now, because I had to relearn the basics, I wasn't going to fall into old ways that aren't useful anymore. This time, I could change my set ways of do some things, only better this time.

I had experienced the hardship of losing the basics and my set ways in life; this loosened off the frame of my life, to show me anything I want is possible. It's not what happens to you, it's what you make of it that's important.

An old saying that stuck with me from NLP, from the legendary hypnotist Milton Erickson: 'People create their own problems and have the solution within.' I proved this today. What a complete, enriching feeling.

My next aim was my speaking. From NLP, I used valuable techniques and said out loud my goals from a sheet I made. I practised daily and taped my voice as if speaking to a crowd, to see if I could deliver in a different way to counteract the problems I had with speaking. I was continually improving, and still am. I didn't give myself a chance to change my moods by awaking early every morning at the same time, giving a structure to my day and working on how I wanted to sound, as best as I could. I drove myself with a vision of how I wanted to be. Nothing was stopping me from giving myself the best life I could. This was my second chance.

With this. every morning, I did weights with a pull-up bar to strengthen up my left grip, with my posture and Tai Chi for balance, stability, and calmness in my mind. I did this routine every morning before my day started. Maintaining a martial art form, I set myself up for any emotional attack from daily living. All three routines took over an hour.

I was determined to improve, even with being by myself. I had to improve. There was no one else to rely on. That's one of the good things about being a couple, the option to rely on each other at times. The creative power of working together.

These exercises became a way of living, done daily to set me up for the day.

I was going to the NLP group in Glasgow every week and their ways seemed to be where I was coming from. The way of their minds was in sync. It worked so well. Something was on the same side as me, going the same way. The techniques I was learning were making my improvements slicker. The people in the group were so pleasant to me. There was no mention or feeling about my speech difficulty or my limp. This impressed me and I would never forget the sensation of this, not feeling different. The 'I'm a person' sensation.

I heard there was an NLP in health one weekend. This was great fun. Some of the techniques I had learned, I now saw them put into practice. It helped create ease in my mind about myself and addressed things that could have held me back.

The NLP master practitioner course was coming up. I told my mum of the progress I was making in life now and she said she would pay for the course for me. This was almost surreal. I had found NLP and this was so similar to where I was coming from. With NLP, one of the main descriptions they use is 'the pursuit of excellence'. That suits me, being a perfectionist and going out my way to do things well, no matter how long it takes, more so nowadays.

I learned to listen to myself, to learn what I want to do. Get into what you are doing with a passion, 100%, and the learning becomes easier. The psychology of how the mind works: what makes up communication, the deletions, distortions and generalisations used in by people when they are communicating. It showed me ways of communicating through different types of language, making it detailed, or ambient. To decide which to use is called chunking up or down to suit the person and the outcome. There are a combination of different main role models. Virginia Satir, the relationship counsellor who created Gestalt, and Erickson, the legendary hypnotist. It is classified as cognitive and behavioural psychology: the best and most useful segments of other professions.

The trainers from the group, Mina, Rintu and Jeff, all had their strong points and worked well together as a team. This alone taught me how important teamwork is and the energy this creates while teaching, and the response this generates in the class.

The others on the compact seven-day course were a mixture of different people from different walks of life. There were a few people that worked well together. There was one girl, Maryanne: we seemed to hit it off. The scenario with groups is that some folk just cluster together and complement each other; we are on the same wavelength and co-ordinate our thoughts, as two heads are better than one, especially when we are on the same train of thought.

It was similar to learning counselling. Coincidently, Mina was a counsellor as well. I had a lot of respect for her. I liked her method of working. She quickly got into my world and I thought this was inspirational. I wanted to share this with people who needed that.

Rintu was fantastic with language. This was my favourite subject within NLP and he was filled with so much talent in the use of cognitive delivery. He is my role model within NLP.

This time I was putting the trauma into a sort of reality, although still unsure of the permanent after-effects of my wee car bump. I was taking control over the confusion instead of waiting to see what would happen naturally. I didn't know what would happen, but started to look at what I could do. I was to bring out what skills I had and discover how much they were affected somehow. After all, this wasn't going to win.

CHAPTER 7

A Holistic Discovery:
Built with Determination

If you want to build a ship, before you give them tools, teach them to yearn for the vast and endless sea.

– Antione de Saint-Exupéry.

At home I was still doing haircuts for friends to keep me involved in being creative. One of my relation's friends, their daughter was seeing about a course at college in Greenock. It was quite different to what she was doing before, and that got me interested. She was going for holistic therapies. When I thought about it, that suits working with people, working with energy like Tai Chi, that would suit my desire to help people.

Inspired, I got the application form and filled it in. In my meetings with Ann from Momentum to discuss my interview, she said if I wanted, she could come to my college meeting. This offer was of a good nature, yet my ego was in protest of this. I had gotten so far under my own steam. By being seen at the very beginning of the course, I wanted to show I was my own man, displaying my independence and drive. It was appropriate and in their view required for some person from Momentum to be at the interview with me, but that wasn't for me. It could be detrimental to me if I got someone to highlight my disability, starting me off at the lowest point. I wanted to blend in and find my way in life. I said thanks but I would do the interview myself, knowing what the college would cover in the interview for the course from my educational work history.

I was nervous before I went. In a way, it was good that Emma was going for the same course as me. I met up with her there. It helped us both in circulation with others.

In the interview I was introduced to different people from different towns fairly similar to my age, yet all girls. At the interview, I was on form. With my past history of being involved in training still fresh, I knew what she was covering. With the visible effects of my injuries, entering another section of society I could be perceived as average to dim, which was so different to what I have experienced. Cleverly answering the questions with enthusiasm, I got in. The start date came in quickly.

My first day at the class for the whole year, I was early as usual. There were mostly girls with only six males on the course, which relaxed me a bit. There were to be two classes, we were told by the tutor – class A and B. I was in class B. Four guys were in the A class and there was two of us in the B class. The other guy, I knew him from school at Largs but I had never seen since and would never imagine him doing this course. He lasted about a week. I was the only guy in the year now, although there was no change for the other guys in class A. I enjoyed being the only male in the class. I was used to being in the minority from the hairdressing industry. I much preferred this idea. I was in a good mixture of classmates, a varied collection of people.

As time went on, the class established and there were cliques developing within our collection of people from different walks of life. Our Holistic Diploma course was for just one year and bustlingly compact, covering nine subjects, and I was to sit another two extra units: advanced body massage and Indian head massage. The head massage turned out to be my absolute favourite massage.

There was a small group gathering support to each other.

I had one very good classmate that I got to know and we worked well together, although we rarely paired up when learning massages. The more we gained experience from other people, the better.

There were three people who had done the previous Level 2 complimentary therapies courses. One of the girls was automatically given the class representative role by the class and the tutors. Due to the intensity of the course with such a heavy workload, she fell short of that role and created more of a class upheaval.

Because of my past role in management, I was voted into this role by my other classmates. I felt very at home having this role and it made me fit in more with the class and the teachers. This was the link between them both. I would do the job if someone helped me with the paperwork having to be done faster than I could do. I got someone to help me. Dorothy was a character. This gave her a role in the class and helped build a team.

We covered practical therapy lessons to learn the needed movements and theory. We covered anatomy, which was an astounding amount of work. A test every week as well as having to do four models at home, of the massages we were working on: facial, aromatherapy, body massage, reflexology, advanced body massage, Indian head massage, physical assessment and first aid. Also there were practical tests in all the practical classes.

There was one girl in the class, Catherine. She was attractive to me. Her long dark hair, her slim body and her timid personality just glowed. A generally quiet girl whose caring nature came through. I enjoyed talking to her. She had a beautiful soft voice that verged on the quiet side. This interest kept me going.

Writing in class was difficult for me. I found it hard to keep up with the fast pace it was conducted in. This was a reminder that I still bore my cross from that life-changing accident. Writing slowly, I had to remember what was being said and the constant facts being told to catch up with my writing, which proved difficult.

Another difficulty was remembering what was important for tests we got regularly: a minimum of a few a week. This was really hard with my memory being so grey on details and facts, though it was improving.

The effort of writing quicker and memorising brought tension and tightness inside of me. This was scary. My short-term memory difficulties opened up some challenges for me. Could this be too much for me? Would I give up? This was not getting the better of me for one minute. For what I had been through already, I would find a way to get the better of this, I would bloody make sure. I went with a way of shutting out what was not needed and brought forward ways of keeping focus. This is what makes memory work the best, being state dependent. (You remember the same state you were in – happy, excited and so on.)

Knowing Tai Chi, this gave me a way of keeping overload at bay, to calm down and prevent cantering myself either emotionally or physically. It brought out the life-changing fact that I learned through Tai Chi – we work holistically with the whole of ourselves. All our learned skills combine when dealing with other events. I had the ability to feel the energy within and to alter it by adjusting movements with control, just like that.

At lunchtime, I gave myself time to do the Tai Chi short form in the corridor up on the top floor, waiting for our next class. This balanced me, taking away the stresses of the morning, plus sorting out all the information of the day and putting it into place in my mind for my memory. A feeling of control, working this way was true to me and did not respond to the hassles of the course and life with its ways. Each time I performed the form, for each and every movement, I was hearing my Tai Chi tutor's voice telling me to watch the movements, make them correct. Imagine there are enemies around you. Feel the energy flowing through you. Don't resist energy blockages, go with the flow and be aware of Tao. Relax. Follow the movements that happen and focus on the way. Think of nothing else: movements alone. It is the most fantastic experience of feeling the energy of the whole area, not just that which comes from me. It is the energy of life that is all about us and can be missed: the spirit of magic. I would have never believed myself in times past, what can be felt in the energy levels within a person. Going with the flow, I now have the ability to sense this. What a gift I was given, or acquired as some folk would say.

It got to Christmas and it felt like halfway in the course. It was so much work compressed into a short length of time. We were guaranteed at least one test per week and always had a weekly test in anatomy and assessments with the massages as well. That was guaranteed, without question. Revising for other classes, there was always an aromatherapy project to work on and hand in, which in itself was a lot of work with revision, research, internet work and project development.

What was good fun was the health and safety at work class for cuts, broken bones, electrical shock, or drowning.

The worry of making it or not was easing – completing the course was the focus. The people that were going to leave the course had left by now, knowing it wasn't for them, or their lifestyle did not work for the course.

It was like Tai Chi to me; getting to a certain point was just a matter of getting my head down with complete focus and putting everything into it. Time spent dreaming and wondering about a new career was becoming a reality.

I really enjoyed aromatherapy with the theory and the practical giving it reality. In fact, I really enjoyed that course. There was no subject I found difficult, it was just giving them what they were looking for. That took away the emotions and focused my attention on the process of achieving what was required, the performance criteria and the range for evidence.

In advanced body massage, which mainly was shiatsu, the theory was absolutely brilliant and I was fascinated with this knowledge. It was heavy on psychological aspects, making the client think in a different way. I did the massage with a type of hypnotic movement, making a big deal of the pace and my given attention. This devotion was required to achieve change in a client with troubled priorities. The main priority that created an emotional response switched their focus to something else, another emotional response away from their problem.

Out of the class, I had acquired a friend. Tanya lived in Skelmorlie and had two kids and a husband. It is quite a thing how folk realise friendship through certain learning styles and also similar experiences in life. We both were into finding out as much of the detail of the material as possible and didn't understand why other pupils didn't want to gain a complete understanding. Our focus was similar, and funnily enough is required with higher forms of education. Tina went on to do an HND in complimentary therapies, whereas I went on to diplomas in counselling and an honours degree in psychology.

This was a big help for both of us, giving each other guidance and reassurance that we were on the right track. The class of females had its difficulties with folk clubbing together, and we gave each other support when we experienced isolation.

My most favourite massage technique of all was the Indian head massage. I was drawn to this from hairdressing where I taught students shiatsu head massage. Originally from India, known as champissage, the Indian head massage was used in the west by therapists, barbers and hairdressers. The founder was blind and felt his way through it, mainly on the face. I took that to heart and relied on feel rather than sight. He relied on feel, to take it to another dimension. Going by kinesthetics and pace, meant you tapped into the client's world to give them personalised relaxation. This was the beginning of finding a specialty of my own.

Building up our portfolios was hard work and similar to folders I checked as a trainer. Different context, yet the format of the folders was similar, like the way evidence was stored.

The excitement was growing tremendously. I was actually going to complete this and be qualified.

Meeting with the guidance tutor, Anna, I discovered I had won another award that I was not expecting. Yes, being the class representative was fun for me, despite the extra work. I just wanted a smooth flow of working for everyone.

Anna told me I would be awarded 'student of the year' for all my efforts. It was so good to be recognised for what I had put into the course. What I aimed for, not forgetting the incredible amount of hard work and effort I put in for the academic side, I got there. What I aim for, if it feels right for me, I will achieve it. This was a monumental life lesson that would serve me. As well as eventually picking up the qualifications for the year of immense work, I was awarded the student of the year. I was achieving and forging a direction now, somewhat harder than I had ever experienced before. I gave it all of me and it overtook my life for this very intense year.

Stress Management

In the hall at the college, we received our awards. We were next to the stress management people. That's exactly I wanted to do next. It seemed next for me. It felt so right. Stress management was my calling.

Through Sandra, my aromatherapy tutor, I got the number of Rose who I called to visit the stress management centre the college used as a placement for this particular course.

We went out to a community hall in Greenock, way up the back, to deliver group stress management. I loved it. It was exactly what I was looking for. The holistic therapies were a catalyst to get into this way of caring for people.

I was to go to a meeting where I was accepted into the stress management course, to my relief, eventually finding my way.

Tina went onto to do the HND in complementary therapies and there were some old faces I knew that would be in my class. One of them would be Catherine. That confirmed my decision.

Starting back at college this time doing stress management, we spent the first sessions filling in forms. This year was a different kind of business compared with last year doing holistic therapies. There were less classes and more 'hands-on work' at outreach placements. This promoted a lower volume of work in favour of the actual intensity of the work.

We were also to do clinical practices – putting therapies into a clinical setting. This gave me more experience that was powerful for me and has always stayed with me. I also took advanced aromatherapy, which was brilliant and I thoroughly enjoyed it.

The tutor Ann had fantastic knowledge of this field, though with everything else I wanted to specialise in stress management. The workload these three courses gave was too much for me, all in. The class contained some HND girls from their second year. I thoroughly enjoyed every subject, but now it was time to make a decision. After quite an agonising debate that lasted a few weeks, I left advanced aromatherapy, one of my additional subjects, which was a very hard decision for me.

I felt in a way left out, because rest of the class were doing three subjects and I was only doing two. I felt a difference, not being able to cope with this, and did my best to sell the concept of why I wasn't doing all the subjects.

I said my focus was on stress management (which it was) and the concept of NLP married beautifully with this. This was my thing. I was focusing on client solutions and ways to achieve this.

It seemed to work and nothing was really said about the fact that I could not handle the work load. I would find a way to progress through this somehow and accomplish them all.

After talks with the stress management tutor, we arranged for me to join her reiki class in the new year. It was all about energy and not so big on the homework field. This, I liked. Everyday energy became very important with this subject, an area that seemed not to be covered much. Maybe energy was a niche for me.

Reiki has a reputation for being heavy on spiritualism and some folk go down the road of angels. This wasn't for me. From the suggestive questions and the way your hand hovers over or just touches certain energy points, I worked it out that reiki was the same as hypnosis as a way of pre-framing a client to improve themselves with lots of presuppositions for self-healing.

This was truly of the Milton Erickson statement: 'All the answers are within.'

It was fun in this class on a Tuesday evening. I always went to my aunt's for my dinner and had a good chat, enjoying each other's company, which set me up for the class.

The class had about eight pupils and we got clients just about all the time. Again, I was the only male in the class. I enjoyed the attention this gives, making me pay more attention, because folk noticed me more, so I had to take a more professional approach.

Clinical practices involved me going to nursing homes once a week to do therapies for patients. The first nursing home was an old building well transformed to the highest standards. The staff was friendly to work with and the old folk loved the attention from me. This was more on a clinical level with procedures and being observant of medication.

In the class, we were shown the power of touch and the calming effects this has.

The other nursing home I worked in was modern and just like a hotel, run mainly by nuns. There was such a peaceful environment in this home.

In both homes I saw patients in their bed, their bedroom, or a specific room for therapies.

In the placement I had for delivering stress management to the general public, the team leader was fantastic at her job. There were some full-time therapists that worked there, five of them, and some volunteers also. The majority of the staff was placements for the college. Everyone got an outreach centre to work from. My placement was with Carers Inverclyde that was down the road from our centre. I felt at home there. Knowing from myself what is involved for caring for someone whose health is not good, I could easily relate to this. I didn't show any judgement ever, just listened to them intently. Having difficulties with speaking, I listened often so suited this well.

Working in a group in the same building for working with clients, suited me to the ground.

I did a relaxation talk to the aromatherapy class, on how it is done correctly, so they would understand the feelings they were to pass to others. This was, in a way, to show my previous class what I could do. With all my NLP knowledge and my newly quiet voice, it was part of hypnosis and it seemed to work perfectly for me. It put my voice differences to their best use and suited this so well.

In the college, the class week had a compact structure: massaging was my strength. Using my hands in the area of sensing, is what I have always showed skill in, from school to hairdressing and massage. I could instinctively change my delivery to suit the person's needs. I got this intuition from my accident – without any words spoken, I seemed to know what was needed. I seemed to identify exactly where the pain was through their energy. I identified energy blocks. My sensory awareness seemed high now.

With an accomplished relief, I finished my course of stress management and clinical practices. The stress management was in order to actually go to the next step of getting an income again. To achieve this, I had to find out about going self-employed. I eventually found the way through lots of mistakes that took up valuable time. I was eager to get up and running. With help from the Job Centre which sorted out my income tax, I then got in touch with Business Gateway in Irvine. Being technically classed as living in north Ayrshire, Irvine was to be the centre I was geographically based at. A phone conversation with them led me to at least go to classes to do a business plan, accounts for VAT, marketing and time management. This led to a fascination of how they would deliver these categories. What style would they use and what would be its main aim? My interest increased.

Each week, I was with the same faces in the business class, which I got to know, only for a short time, although we socially got on with each other to make it more simplistic to experience unknown knowledge. It wasn't really the class content, but the excitement of starting up a business. We received the lessons from a trainer of Business Gateway. I found these interesting in terms of working out his delivery of the classes and what was important, was his material.

I kind of knew where he got all of his marketing and time management knowledge from, or at least a very similar version I had gotten to know from past years, except for accounts and doing a business plan. These I found mundane. I'm not very good with figures. Arithmetic I can survive, yet maths I struggled with. Doing accounts got me in an initial fluster. I have never been drawn to this side until now from necessity. I persevered, knowing how good an outcome it would be, being able to do my own books at a basic level, and when I'm told or have the impression that I can't do something, I will go hell and leather to do it. I was going to do it some way. I hate being told I can't do anything. With the events that happened to me which categorically changed my life around, my perseverance was with me all the time, 24/7, and it wouldn't switch off. It was more than just becoming a habit, there was a deeper meaning of accomplishing something grand. I didn't know what yet; previous ideas of doing some fantastic extreme climbs were replaced by some other scale that in its own way was grander than that.

The people in the class were covering totally different subjects. It must be a great part of their jobs in Business Gateway, seeing some of the inventive ideas that folk come up with. There were some different ideas in our group that would take off; within every group, there must be a general section for things like car cleaning, massage therapies, hairdressing and so on.

Learning about business plans, we had to put together our own plan to see if we would get some funding. My age went against me. It was all right if you are about sixteen into the twenties, but for me, the way it is set out, I would just get a couple of hundred pounds, being an old guy, yet I have no grey hairs. Only my red locks preserved a youthful look. I wonder if there is business funding for redheads: maybe, maybe not.

It took time, fleshing out my business plan and writing it out on my computer. It was like college, getting what information was needed dealt with in the right places. This burned a lot of concentration, with the incentive of completing it being that I would get a grant to get started with my own business.

Organising a business account at my local building society was straight forward and this added to my collection of credit cards I had collected. It seems nowadays that most organisations give you a credit card sized card, even the council library.

I got the go-ahead, and I eventually got the funding of just a couple of hundred pounds. This now it seemed the right direction for me – being my own boss. I didn't take any wage money from my business account, it was there to build my business up. Then, I was to take a wage once it is running itself. I used it to pay for travel, the car, training, equipment needed and books.

My aim was building the business up to eventually pay good wages that I only imagined was possible. I opened up every opportunity for myself, wondering what was possible.

I was working through being self-employed at two centres, with occasional work found here and there, yet mostly I volunteered, gaining work experience from the stress management placement and Carers Inverclyde. It was looking promising at this stage. That aspect was soon to come to an end, due to lack of government funding, which closed some stress management centres down.

The times at the centres gave me valuable experience in working with certain illness, disabilities, and mental health: mainly depression, anxiety, schizophrenia, neurosis, and victims of anti-social behaviour with its broad range of clients and problems.

I would find a way, a niche for me, to get my company up and running and successful. I was determined.

In a bout of inspiration, I was drawn to provide therapy and coaching to expatriates in France, giving them wellbeing and health improvements. That didn't take off as well as I thought, though there were amazing trips, thanks to cheap airline tickets, to different parts of the world filled with mountainous scenes I could never, ever get sick of. France was one of what may be my ultimate destinations.

I was also continuing to assist with NLP training. No future in progressing with that one at that stage, although I gained more skill with the techniques, seeing them from another angle. I even repeated listening to NLP training tapes in the car, which helped give me mastery in subjects I had already listened to. It was the next best thing to going to a 'train the trainer' course. I could not afford it at that point.

I was drawn to mastering the NLP topics. It gave me a direction to follow.

My next step was down the road of designing and delivering motivational training sessions. I did two and learned I need to involve another; being alone and my own boss, this seemed to be my calling. I had good ways of getting feedback from who I was delivering the courses to, and I needed that edge to take me on further to where I wanted to go.

Because I didn't claim any wages from my business and got this checked out yearly by the VAT, at that point, I was covering my costs and using the excess for training and materials needed, so pressure was on to make sure my bookwork was up to scratch.

I was then applying for jobs as a back-up and this became my so-called hobby. This in itself got my direction confused, as applying for certain jobs, researching the position, I had decided that these posts were what I could offer. This confused me, with the importance of being self-employed. In doing this, you become absorbed into being a part, and my main dreams were dulled at times.

Having cut costs for so many years, I was eager for a regular income, instead of being on the poverty line. Once you have had to cut corners to financially survive, it never leaves you. I guess Scotland having a reputation of cutting the corners to not waste anything, brought this into understanding. I felt flat and lost in my direction. That got me so frustrated and anxious that I had to go away from this pain, and this gave me the needed motivation that would spark off my determination. This was one of the many valuable life lessons I learned, of flexibly changing my focus to suit different situations and not be burdened by a closed road on my journey.

Also, it taught me that until the lesson is learned to create that needed change, the pattern of behaviour will keep coming back in different forms. I found out that I needed to keep changing the question I asked myself, till I got a solution. It came to me that this was getting rid of what was stopping me from doing something. Something was blocking my way. No matter what it is, this blockage is present in most people, even everyone. This was a lesson I could pass on to others. Having gone through hell, I bloody won the right to pass this on to help others by changing your thoughts, producing different results. If you know you can, then you are right. You open up possibilities that may have not have existed in the first place, rather than just accepting that you can't do something.

Overall with my personality, I have a strong character and would find it difficult working under a boss. I think 'outside the box'. That would be no problem if it was a boss who I respected and not a boss who knew less than me, had poor personal control and let their ego take control, gaining power from their position.

This is a time when having gained much knowledge is a negative; they do not give people the benefit of the doubt when there is so much invested in employment into their company. This held me back and was considered a weakness, if picked up wrong.

I was reading a book about leadership and showing confidence so others believe in you and follow. A commitment in congruence with what you have: lead by example (walk the talk); think of the big picture, showing its value and worth, and have pride in what you believe.

This is me. Maybe I am more destined to be a leader. This just feels right and it suits the whole of me. I guess this added to me helping others. Knowledge of the attraction theory kept raising its head. Thinking something feels right attracts you to other things, broadening opportunities. This is true, and many things have turned out with this in mind.

Through not consciously thinking and having this naturally come from the whole of you, it sends off energy to do with this subject and all things connected, are drawn to you. They find positive results from you because it comes from the whole of you and is attracted by this.

To be honest, I was a bit disappointed when I found out more about the attraction theory. I thought it was something to do with successful dating. Later I found out the prime directive of this theory in terms of the effects it has: how it can change your life around with the full and true beliefs you have, making them work by themselves with minimum effort.

Working with stress management at Step Well, I used a personal profile of the clients' traits. This was a big NLP and psychological element of working with the client and understanding how they think and act. 'To get into their moccasins' is a great expression.

With my sensitivity, I could pick up traits fairly easily, and with the great help of the book *Words That Change Minds* by Shelle Rose Charvet. This was more straight forward than the NLP version, and I could pick things up easily. This book astounds me, describing what the categories are and a system for looking for them. In the same way and style of absorbing the books daily, I read *Bouquets of Bitterroots* by Betty Lou Leaver and many Erickson hypnosis books. Small chunks were filtered into my life easily.

Having a structure was good, for my memory was still in a delicate way at times, yet getting stronger and stronger. A phrase I enjoyed was that memory is state dependent, meaning that matching the state you were in at the time, is the way to remember the contents.

For a few years at college, when studying, I listened to relaxing music and used rosemary essential oil for sharpening my memory. Every time I went into exams, I took a tissue covered in it to be in the same state. I always sailed through exams and even doing something positive was helped by this.

Eventually, spending the investing time in working out personal traits, it became instinct for me and I understood how people's thinking works and was able to get into their world. This gave an experiential, educated view of their world: results that suited them so well.

Understanding the process of modelling, I could now see how to improve almost anything. In understanding their thinking broken down, their strategies and procedures and their motivations fitted in an ideal way. Discovering the aim, their thinking and their strategies, was put into use and suited to stress management. This seemed part of my niche.

My personal traits were understood now and I always looked for opportunities. I organised training for the new stress management students that were there on placement with Step Well.

I had a talk with the team leader about group training I could offer with the technical experience of training I had. She went away with the idea and came back and suggested training for them, the public and other health professionals for National Stress Week. That was a wonderful opportunity to input NLP with stress management. This would get me known in another way, about what I do and the different angles in which I could deliver my chosen profession.

I planned out the sessions using what was vital for me with my challenging memory, a mind map of what I was covering. All the information for this was found in one single sheet. A word for each topic, it was like a tree trunk running to many branches that were all connected. This mind map technique, I used constantly and still do. It's a very visual way of working that suits me.

I went over the topics of identification, why it comes about and fast and easy techniques to put into action. Using the basis of identifying the aim, taking control and identifying strategies for achieving it. Then the benefits this would create, to better their life in being flexible, always trying, refreshing their aims and then just do it by putting all of this into play. I made handouts and talked again to Rose for feedback on what my aim was and the delivery of it. This gave me more confidence that I was on the right road. I was getting excited to use my training with what I wanted to do: be a public speaker in stress management and NLP.

I didn't really have to justify my speaking would be okay for this, as I had techniques of adjusting the pace to create different levels of thought. To speed up for motivation and raising enthusiasm, and slowing down to generate more thought process. What I learned about body language and tone, was to serve its purpose.

This gave me motivation, and there was still courses I wanted to do, as well as wondering whether I would find employment or my business would take off. Whatever came first, I would take the advantage of filling my day as much as I could. That would never leave me.

At James Watt, advanced aromatherapy seemed the course for me at this time, compared to all the other courses that were on offer at this stage. It would give me more knowledge of a therapy I was very fond of.

The class, again, was the HND complementary therapies, all girls. We covered a lot on the chemical properties which brought oils to a more workable level.

It was a spirited class to be in and I seemed to fit in, despite being the only boy again.

In this class was my friend Tina from holistics, which made it easier for me to settle in with the HND second year group.

We covered different ways to deliver the essential oils, like inhalations, compressions; some I found very useful and others just created confusion with me in terms of their actual uses.

We had different clients with varying needs that showed me how I could use a combination of my skills to suit them.

There was one client who had a number of medical problems and seemed frustrated. My sensitivity picked this up and I gave her my full attention, which is what she needed. I used a blend of oils that would relax her and ease her medical complaints. In this case, Indian head massage would work, making her feel comforted.

I spent time repeatedly visualising using it for an event I had to do in Millport, which gave me mastery with this. I used my feeling touch, more commonly known as sensing, to decide the movements, the pace, the tempo and the pressure for a complete relaxing flow. I also broke up the expectancies of movements that clients assumed were happening. This in itself produced relaxation and they could get lost in the 'now' time. I used my senses to go over the intuitive moves that suited the client well. It gave them a journey inside of themselves: relaxation at its fullest. For them, complete escapement.

This used physical activity to soothe the mind. To visualise achieving what you aimed for, taking time to do this repeatedly in a relaxed state. In a way, I had gained strength by doing this for anything in the future – to visualise myself achieving what I wanted, worked well.

I seemed to learn this myself, only to find out that this technique was to be used in coaching, aiming to achieve what was previously presumed unachievable. This was invaluable.

From that client to a bloke who was a sports student, giving me the other side of the coin. With him, I talked about running and other sporting events that he was involved in. This brought us into a unity of energy with this subject. Choosing the oils to suit muscle injuries, I remedially massaged his legs, which was a great combination to me. He was pleased with his visits and asked me some advice on muscle recovery for the future.

There was lots of preparation work and folders to make, with the experience gained from Ann, the tutor, who had the most amazing knowledge of aromatherapy I have ever known.

Having some time in the previous class and a bit more experience, I got through it with no major challenges. Now I wanted to join a counselling course. Funnily enough, there was one at the college and even better, in the evenings. I thought that I should be asked to go to the James Watt Christmas night out, as I could be seen as a tutor, as I spent more time there than some tutors.

A Motivational Thing

Getting organised at Headway and Momentum delivering my positivity classes, had set me up for doing what I do in the public eye.

I did group classes for mentally handicapped kids in Port Glasgow in relaxation and sensory gain. Understanding where they were coming from with the frustration they felt from their impairments, I generated relaxation and they picked up on my nature of wanting to help in a calming way.

With the need to always challenge myself to keep my mind active, I came up with the idea of providing a motivation class in Largs for a few sessions. My target was general people. This was a new angle for me and another step towards my big dream of reaching fame from this.

By now, I had a hobby of applying for jobs; as well as doing my stress management weekly at four centres, applying for a full-time position was something to keep me focused on another aspect of myself. It wasn't really about whether the job seemed right for you, it was how you filled in the application forms and followed the format that is required for job interviews, including the interview techniques. This was the way now. It was completely new for me and it had to be learned. I did not want anything getting the better of me. There was a reason why I did not die and I am here for a reason – to help others break what's preventing them from improving. I just needed to find my way. Trying many ways was my way of finding it. Experience tells me whether it is right or wrong, not just assumption.

I had the idea to deliver my sessions to the local public.

I researched halls: the size, cost, location and accessibility. The hall on the front owned by the council, looked the best.

The marketing I would use was an advert in the local paper and flyers around hairdressing salons where I knew someone who worked there. This way, I could promote the nights I was on.

I practised and practised the routine and contents I would cover, explaining how to relax, let stress go, with better learning and aims. For them I selected all the materials I was going to use, handouts to give and promotion material of Mind Body Connections and other services I offer.

The first eventually night came and I got the keys for the hall. I then organised a float of money for change and guessed how much to have. I set up all the chairs, organising the layout of the room with tables for the material I would give away. The selected music to promote learning was my ultimate favourite. I loved this music and used it myself when studying or planning what I wanted to achieve. It brought on such creative vibes to assist in gaining breakthrough solutions.

I asked my cousin and his wife if they could help me. They were the first to arrive and we waited and waited, yet no big rush or busloads of people.

Only one showed up and that was a friend of mine who showed interest in self-help and learning to improve.

I started anyway and made it a one-to-one training session. It was such a disappointing turnout, but going to such effort in organising, and going over the material I would use, had its advantage. If I hadn't experienced any of this, I would not have learned what I needed to go in this direction.

This wasn't a successful exercise. If it was successful the first time, it would have been lucky. With me going by experience, I learned from this fully and it would move me forward in terms of doing motivational classes. Most of life's successful results rarely happen the first time around.

It was just another case of 'biting the bullet' to learn and move on to better things. Life is too short (as I found out the hard way). Not to waste time and energy hanging on to something that didn't work, I learned and improved on it. Emotions are emotions and they are a product of a way of thinking. I thought it through to the end result and digested the lessons. Emotions are created from how you see the end result and how it affects your self-esteem. Dismissing the feelings and thinking only of the results, produced motivation and good feelings that gave me drive to achieve. This was a blow, but pushing it aside, learning from it and moving on to better things had its advantages.

Newspaper Headlines

Time drifted on and with being stuck, like the saying of 'a rock and a hard place', I struggled to get employment. I couldn't get a job to get work experience, yet I couldn't get experience because I wasn't working. Not having a partner for a long time contributed to this weariness too. Both represented this relentless struggle uphill with the wind in my face. It took much strength of will to not let this get the better of me.

In a new unexpected light, I had my tale printed in the local paper in a full front-page spread about my ordeal. I was in the next week, with me and Miss Universe at the Headway awards in London, getting my award.

Then a bit later, Rintu, the trainer from the NLP group, mentioned there was someone he knew who ran the *Greenock Telegraph*. He gave me his phone number, saying he wanted to write a story about me and NLP.

His name was Tom too and we met at a coffee house and talked. I told him about me and my tale. He said that would be an excellent book and he would have a senior reporter meet me to do a story on me. He also said that I would get my photo done. The photos for the Largs and Millport news, was one of my own portrait and one from Headway at the awards in London. It would be brilliant getting my photos done by a professional photographer.

I met with the journalist for a coffee in Greenock before I started work that day, on a Wednesday. She had done some research on NLP before which made things a bit easier. With NLP, it's about how we think and to change our thoughts, thus affecting the result we aim for. She had looked up different aspects of it, because if you go on the internet looking for NLP, you get lots of different angles like selling, management, sports, hypnosis, and its vast range as well — persuasion language, romance and so on. I gave her the vision of determination, caring; a strong personality and always looking for improvement.

It was arranged for me to go to the head office to meet the photographer and get my picture taken.

On my way up to another stress centre called Healthy Living Initiative in Clydebank, I popped in. I had my whites on and made sure my hair did not need cutting, making it look smart.

At the beginning, I got the impression she was busy and wanted to get them done as soon as possible. She went through the usual form of getting folk ready to take their picture. The same lines she uses all the time.

This was my chance to put into play what I assumed makes a good photo of me, delivering what I am like as a person. I found out what she was looking for and closed my eyes, telling her to wait a minute.

I thought of nothing, then the excitement and passion I give in delivering what I imagined to a very large audience. I was motivating them, giving huge amounts of inspiration. True beauty comes from within and my thoughts were only of the purity of it.

She asked me to point my finger as if going over a point of inspiration.

"That's perfect. Have you done this before?"

"No, and I am having fun," I replied.

My idea of how to create a good photo worked. The power of the mind raised its head again.

The same day it was printed on the paper, I bought a few copies and told people I was in the paper.

It was a brilliant coverage of the story on the centre pages with a big photo of me pointing a finger as if saying something inspirational. The look in my eyes showed passion in my delivery. It was a great story of me and what I do now: There was a big section on Rintu and his NLP coaching company. They worked well together.

I got some work out of it coaching folk in Greenock who needed some direction in their life.

So my paper coverage was getting good. Overall, I got a front-page story, page-three coverage and a fabulous centre-page spread. This made my sons think it was normal for their dad to be locally known by most folk. This part also helped us become stronger, in my view, having had a focus of mine met. To show the boys that you can achieve anything that you aim for, within reason. The papers, motivation and positivity classes, and spending time with them, would take us to another level of bonding, showing the boys that by opening up, you make things possible for yourself. What can stop people is not believing in themselves and going for it, gaining an understanding of themselves from within.

Using my hands through hairdressing, I had followed this by getting involved with therapies. This seemed like the most suitable thing. Through acquiring knowledge and understanding of health, I could relate to others about how their health was. After all, I walked the talk. Yes, there are so many health issues, whether due to environmental factors, or social factors, but I had so many similar themes experienced, so I would have an understanding and could to help them. I was starting to learn about the skill I had acquired in sensory perception. I could pick up that which others may miss. This experienced attitude gave me an edge.

CHAPTER 8

Pulling My Own Strings:
Taking Control

Two roads in the woods diverged – I took the road less travelled, and that has made all the difference.

– Robert Frost

NLP Master Practitioners

In the weekly meetings of the NLP group, I had got to the stage of knowing what technique was being covered, even in different conditions. There was talk of another master practitioner course that was coming up, and I was drawn to this greatly. This would specialise my skills towards where I wanted to go, so I went looking to see if I could afford this important course.

I sorted through my all my bank accounts. Even through building society accounts in the 90s that were going to be public and get a good pay-out. Unfortunately that didn't really happen. Oh well. I had accumulated enough funds and now I just needed a bit extra to cover the cost of the course. After all, this was very important to my rehabilitation. Telling my mum, she said that she would help me.

One day I phoned Mina about going on the next master practitioner's course. She said there was a place left in the one coming in the beginning of 2005 and I could have it. I was ecstatic to be taken on. This would be a brilliant experience for me, learning in more detail about what I had a passion for.

I spoke to Rintu about doing the course and asked if there were any CDs like the practitioner's course. Unfortunately, there wasn't. I asked if there were any tapes I could borrow and record them. Thankfully he said yes, he had a master practitioner's set and he knew about my training delivery background. He let me borrow a 'train the trainers' set. He knew I was financially in difficulty and he knew I would do it at some point. Also with the way I learn best, I could observe the topics covered and get comfortable with them.

To get to the course, I got the train into Glasgow from Largs. This gave me a chance to listen and study what was covered on the course the day before, and gave me time to prepare myself, work on affirmations and distract my attention with a little shut-eye, practicing relaxing hypnosis that I have used with the stress management college class.

Getting near to Glasgow, the train would busy up with folk standing and I would try out what I had learned about catching someone's attention using energy. Because I was sensitised to this, I got results regularly. I made folk turn and look at me.

Being aware of energy in this sense astounded me. With my Tai Chi learning and understanding, energy levels fascinated me. This idea was taken from ancient times, yet it is almost forgotten nowadays. I rediscovered energy with the massive amounts of relearned content I had to get through, yet I relearned the more up-to-date version with new perspectives. Focused energy and being aware of other's energy to work with them, is the way I wanted to go. With NLP and Tai Chi, energy systems were very important to me.

Against all the logic of what social attention is, this proves to me there is more to what is assumed.

With this understanding, it is controlled unconsciously, hidden from your attention. Again, the power of the mind changes all. What is assumed is not always the case in terms of illness. Illness effects are presumed; patterns are presumed that only have one conclusion.

Believing in yourself gives you confidence to alter folks' presumptions and those presumed results. One thing that worked was following the presuppositions of NLP to reframe my thinking and not be caught up in their presumption of in this case health, or anything for that matter. You can take control of the direction of thinking with language. This helped me greatly with my accident effects and other aspects. This was one of these core development lessons I had. Maybe it was a fundamental one. To take control of a situation by reframing it using language to get a better result, was an important lesson I would always remember.

Going to the actual NLP course, a full day of intense working was finished off with a relaxing hypnosis – a way to check you understood the session's learning that I still use to this day. This gave a great ending to the work, needed to put it into practical, usable terms.

The subjects I enjoyed most from this course were 'reframing' and hypnosis that involved language. This hypnosis was the start of the most major discoveries for me: health, metaphors, how learning happens, and of course language. It made me see the delivery of language differently to what was assumed before on the surface. It was all about the deeper meaning.

For Rintu, who was one of the trainers, language was his forte. He amazed me with the knowledge and control of language he had. Such control and manipulation over the English language astounded me.

The very words used – changing the tense, the situation, accenting different words – produced different results and a detail that was called chunking. (Chunking up for abstract and a larger meaning that suits more things, or chunking down to more detail that gives specifics, both produced different meanings.)

Conversations are either one way or another and we practised chunking up and down. This created unity in what was being said – to be more in their shoes and then reframe it for their benefit.

This was evident by chunking up things like hypnosis and chunking down to details for meta-modelling, and gave different levels of language control.

I was fascinated by this and he was a mentor for me. Needless to say, he was very good at hypnosis as well.

Mina and Jeff had their specialities too. Jeff with meta-modelling and Mina with her counselling approach. Counselling appealed to me greatly also.

With all this learning, we were to put it together and perform a breakthrough with someone in the class or an outside person.

Overall, I had two people to work on and I was a client for someone else.

We followed the book and from rehearsals on the train, I delivered it more smoothly.

Relaxed confidence and determination helped with my delivery. This is crucial in gaining rapport with the client, knowing you know what you are talking about.

I was exhausted doing them, although it was a great learning experience. This boosted my confidence to an all-time high. Being a model, I learned more by having it done to me.

For me, the counselling approach was successful and it suited me well to get them to understand through different language, and get them back on track. This gave me my balance back.

Improving my learning in this field, I started reading cognitive and behavioural therapy information to do with thinking and stress. This was the start of reading many books in different subjects, relating to the mind and therapies. I read a few pages a day to let the daily intake integrate at higher level, plus saying it out loud to be recorded, made me use this experience in two ways: actual learning and a catalyst to improve my speech with something I had a passion for. With a small amount of time spent going over what I wanted to learn about daily, this showed me, amazingly, how the subconscious works better being in a trance. It is a very good way to learn, to not miss details of the process.

Trance is found to be of use all the time. It involves inward relaxation to see things from another point of view. This is used in sports all the time, as well as other professions where they require a certain level of performance, like the police and medical staff. They experience unconscious scripts, conditioning them for their job roles. They have to get into a certain mode of thinking, to get results suited to their profession.

I began to go over the processes in detail to learn them well and to get a full understanding of them.

It is a shame that NLP isn't a recognised profession yet, due to the different standards of training. NLP Scotland was first-class training and I could get help if needed. It was good to know the help was available.

I took this learning and put it into use in helping out at their NLP training courses. I went to various courses covering different related topics. This helped greatly my learning and on many occasions I helped with training trainers NLP.

With Rintu, on his courses, I got the chance to teach his practitioners about energy. I really enjoyed this and it got me back into actual training again, where the whole class listened to me.

Further Counselling Skills – CBT

Now I had discovered new parts of the world that were unknown to me. This introduced a new era of discovery for me. Talking to colleagues who worked at Step Well through stress management, counselling seemed the best direction for me with my NLP psychology skills. There was an evening course at college taken by a teacher I had for the counselling aspects of holistic therapies from a few years earlier. I enjoyed her teaching. This worked out for me in filling my time with the introduction of some new concepts, instead of moaning that things aren't the way I wanted. I was taking action. If I didn't get anything out of this, that's okay, it got me recognised skills and a qualification that was accepted. It was two evenings a week for a year, although after half a year the class numbers were too low and we had to wait a year before doing the other half of the course. This allowed time for integration and we got together every couple of weeks for an evening at the tutor's brother's flat. She saw clients there and he has lived away from this area for years.

At the beginning of each class, the teacher asked everyone about their week. For some, it was a major offload for them. It gave them experience from a client's point of view and it allowed the teacher to evaluate their state, so she could adapt the evening's learning. With me and all my challenges in life I kept it process-based, rather than feeling-based. This produced functional results. Each method has its advantages and disadvantages. With this course, not taking onboard other folks' problems kept me clear and focused on passing. It was good, being in the environment of similar-minded people, as far as wanting a counselling award. I had too many life changes, both physical and emotional; the class at their stage did not know how to deal with the likes of me, and so I kept it short and sweet.

The content of the work was good and along the lines of certain NLP concepts. I enjoyed the studying. I was still challenged with my writing and messing up sentences. I seemed to get confused with tenses and if I had lots of content to cover, my mind would race ahead of my slow process of jotting down the contents. This added confusion while reading it. If it was something confusing and unfamiliar to me, this was normal. I loved the course content, so this lessened the problem greatly. I just needed a quiet time to let my creativity go. I did well and the break in the course let me integrate the work, and this took away some pressure.

One good quality of the group system was working with triads. This was three people; one was the client, another the practitioner, and the third an outside point of view. This technique was familiar to me from NLP and was very useful in gaining other perspectives. This was a 'found out' core skill for therapy, counselling, coaching and any other concept dealing with people. I enjoyed this, as it gave me more experience in working with another angle of assisting people.

It was nearly the end of the course and we were to receive an award at the town hall from James Watt College. The course was equivalent to an HNC so we were included. We had to hire gowns, we got our picture taken and were presented with a certification.

The event was much more formal than getting the holistic therapies award at college and it also involved a broad range of courses available at James Watt College.

The big hall at the council buildings was laid out well, although there were stairs made so all of that college year's passed students could get onto the stage. I just hoped I wouldn't trip going up these steep stairs with no hand rail to get my award. I haven't relied on hand rails for years, but with the pressure and fast turnover of people; I didn't want to fall after waiting a long time for my name to be called out. Eventually my name was called and I went to get my award. I didn't fall. It felt great getting an award at this level.

I got the photos taken in my robes and holding my award. I took one for my own flat to keep me reminded of achieving this, one for my mum and one for my aunt, so they were both proud of one of their family holding an award. It looked like I got an award for delivering newspapers – the one I was carrying.

This gave me more practical skills and a recognised qualification that took me forward.

There was another award ceremony evening I was in, for my class mates of the HND complementary therapy course. I was in a few of their classes. It was in the Inverclyde sports building in Largs, which was handier for me. It was concerning the complimentary group I was with for advanced aromatherapy. They all had ball gowns on, and I had a suit on.

The evening was fun and full of excitement. After 10.30 when it finished, a few of us were saying, "Where can we go now?" Being a Friday night, one girl suggested going to the local night club, which would full of people at 18 years of age. We agreed and got a taxi down. The girls in their ball gowns looked like they were going on a night out. I looked like a parent that was looking for their daughter, all suited up, or I looked like a CID police officer. When I went to the toilet, the area cleared so fast when I came in. It was busy with young guys and they thought it was a raid, so they rushed out, not wanting to get caught. It was amusing. I followed the walk in with an authoritative demeanour.

It didn't seem like an ending with the course work at college. In a way, it just felt like a weekend gathering that was fun. There was more to come.

A Foreigner on a Night Out

A real friend is one who walks in when the rest of the world walks out.
– Ronald Reagan

Pleased with my progress, I told my climbing mate Kenny who lived near Stirling where he worked.

We then had arranged a night out in Stirling. In the winter's night, it was cold and dark. I was to drive up to his on the Saturday night to have a night in Stirling; I would then take up his couch and drive home the next day fed and watered. That sounded like a good weekend to me.

In driving there, a problem started. I couldn't quite remember how to get to his house in the dark. From all the years of going up north early in the morning hill climbing, there was some new road works that completely knocked me off, and then I discovered glasses for the twilight night driving. On that day, the weather was smothering rain which lowered the visibility as well – I was struggling to read the road signs. I took the wrong turn-off and found many ways around Stirling. It was just like learning to pass my driving again, only this time in Stirling.

This was the beginning of going up there for nights out and still losing my way again and again. I found new routes in Paisley with my driving lessons and now it was Stirling's turn. It was broadening my horizons, seeing and experiencing different places.

Eventually with added help of Kenny on the phone, I arrived at his flat. My vision of signs in twilight and dark was too limited, therefore I passed the junctions I needed to go to. I would need to get my eyes checked.

Because he worked for a home improvement shop before, he had made some changes to his flat that were absolutely astounding – the main living room, a total transformation to his kitchen, and he reformed the bathroom. I was so impressed and wish I had these skills to create such a difference.

We had a few beers and then got the train to Stirling to all the good pubs and clubs in the town centre. We met some of his police colleagues who were a good laugh.

In our second pub, which looked busy, it started.

We got talking to a few girls and then what happened next, gave me a template to use when talking about how I sounded.

She asked me where I was from. Hearing I was from Largs, she asked me where I stayed before that. Where, abroad, I was from?

I was looking into Iceland for the ice fields and great coastline for kayaking, I said Reykjavik in Iceland. She said my accent was lovely, with a sparkle in her eye. This surprised me greatly.

Whaow! When asked, I could say I'm foreign. Instead of making it a problem, I would turn it into my advantage. I felt so relieved; this massive life problem I had acquired could be turned to my advantage. Instead of looking for perfection in improving my speaking, I would go with the flow. Speaking confidently puts the doubt in the other persons way of thinking – it 'puts the ball back in their court'.

This is my answer now and it's far from perfect. I changed the rules I created surrounding my speech development, which dramatically improved my speaking. The confidence was back. I had spent what seemed like a slogging lifetime trying to be understood and I broke through this. The keys were confidence and a strategic script to put this in play. A perfect example of what's called pre-framing: making the frame up at the beginning to condition their thinking to accept differences in how I say things. A foreigner gets certain pronunciations wrong. That fits in perfectly. It's giving an okay version for them to ponder over. It brought a realisation that changing how people think, changes the reactions to my so-called speech problem.

A quote from Erickson, one of the greatest hypnotists of the twentieth century: 'The problem to any solution is found from within.' This was a quote I never forgot and have full belief in.

What had been a major problem, I had turned around to make it work for me.

I used this all the time and folk imagined where my accent was from; I ended up all over Europe and more. With what they had experienced of foreign languages, they thought they heard those styles listening to me. People thought I was Spanish, French, Italian, Belgian, German, Norwegian, and Swedish because of the tonal expression I used with certain words; I also went over every word, covering every letter, relearning how to speak again. It had become my way of not sounding regional and that created interest. The most common were Belgium and Norway.

I followed a routine: when I was asked where I was from I said, "I live far away from here." They would ask where. I would say Largs. And if they asked, "Where did you stay before that?" I always asked them, "Where do you think I'm from?" They would decide which accent they could relate to the most and say that place. Depending on the person's reaction, I may smile a confirming smile, not saying a word, or then say I was from Iceland. This routine worked so well and it became funny hearing the different answers from other people.

Another side of this turning to my advantage: there was a time I was providing stress management education at a school in Port Glasgow with other therapists for Step Well. We were to work there all day with classes in social education and we all had different sections to talk about stress to the classes. The ones I had were nutrition benefits and thinking differently.

We had different classes for the day. The first class was no problem at all and just worked a routine for our sections. By class two, it started. When it was my turn, I got up and talked. There was a boy who said consistently, "Where are you from?" I kept to my form and he still went on. He kept interrupting me. One of the times he said, "Where are you fae?" ('From' in Scottish). I said Iceland automatically. I cringed while saying this and it actually shut him up. What a relief to work in my format without distraction. Never again will I ever say this in schools again. That's the boundary.

I felt bad about saying this to the other therapists at lunch time down in the hall with all the other pupils. The other two therapists were facing the pupils. I was sitting at the other end of the table with my back to the pupils.

They said, "Look, they are pointing at Tommy."

Never again, I said to myself.

Then, back at our class in the afternoon, some pupils were in and there was a girl whose inattentive staring followed me across the class. I felt very aware of this, repeating to myself, *Never again.*

Before my turn to begin, she looked bursting to talk to me and tried her best to catch my eyes for attention. She then said, "Where are you from?" The way she said it with such intent and interest, I felt cornered into following up what I said earlier. If I said differently, it would have lost the credit we had with the pupils in what we were there for. I was cornered.

I said unwillingly, "Iceland."

She glanced away then said, "My aunt lives there."

I thought, *Oh shit,* to myself and replied very quickly with true automation, "Oh, that's good. Where does she stay?"

The girl looked instantly puzzled and shocked. She replied, "Oh… I… don't know."

I said, "Oh well… You should go one time," and turned round and began my piece of stress management for the class.

That was so close. What a relief I dealt with it in that way which kept my creditability about being truly foreign alive. That was too close, and now I would only bring it up if my only option. Still today, folk question my accent and the majority of this was at stress therapy, dealing with folk at a personal level. Mostly I was working in Greenock and after time I followed a sure format that cleared this up.

If someone asked me where I was from, I said that I live far away from here. This gave instant curiosity and then I said Largs for a humorous approach. This brought humour into dealing with stress and sometimes it carried on.

I had taken this lesson from that situation; this gave me a new approach to deal with different situations. With the gift I got from NLP with hypnosis, my quieter voice and pace gave itself perfectly to this and became a speciality of mine. With my nature and the way I spoke, it seemed perfect from my view, for this. Stress management seemed to be suited to me like a hand is to a leather glove. It felt right for me.

Masters Swimming Group

As part of improving my physical health by going to the gym, I would go swimming a few times a week. At the pool, I asked the pool lifeguards about how many lengths make a certain distance and they told me to see Sharon, the swim coach who takes the North Ayrshire swim squad. It was a length of swimming you had to do for triathlons. Talking to her, she suggested I should go to the masters swimming group on Monday evening that she takes as well. I thought they would be way ahead of me but a big part of me wanted to go to this. She knew about what happened to me and that I was limited in strokes at this stage, which helped. I went along to the group one Monday evening. There were four lanes for different levels of swimming ability. The last lane was mostly people who were in the North Ayrshire swim group. It was kids at school who train constantly. The ones who left school who still wanted to swim train, this was perfect for them. There were some swimmers that could swim very fast and they joined this lane too. The majority of people were found in the second lane when I saw them for the first time. The third lane was intermediate and the fourth was the slowest level. I started in this lane. Talking to folk there about my condition, it was great to be understood about how I am slow at certain moves. I used the explanation of my head injury having similar effects to a stroke, which a lot of folk understood. Maybe a member of their family or someone they knew had a stroke so they could relate to this with me.

My leg movement was not good. At times we did drills of certain moves like just the arms or legs with different strokes, but my leg movements were too weak. With running, my legs were muscle-bound. The up-and-down that running movements promoted was okay, it was just drawing my legs inwards as in breast stroke that I found I had major problems with. Technically I had weak abductor (inner leg) muscles because my broken hip joint reset differently. I assisted with stronger arm strokes to compensate. It wasn't right, but I had an excuse. At this stage, this was the same with the other swimming styles. I used my arms mostly which increased my upper body strength a lot. I was acquiring that triangle body shape of good swimmers, which I was pleased about.

We had to do different moves each week and when these leg movements had to be stronger, I struggled. I did as much as I could then watched the highest level of swimming in the group do this part. You can pick up so much by watching, and swimming is ideal for this. This idea was taken from Bandura, a renowned psychologist; one way of learning is from observing. I used time while I couldn't finish the set watching how others did it.

Being in a group has its benefits. You have things keeping your mind occupied, like catching up with the feet of the person in front of you. This also worked when you felt someone touch your toes and that made you speed up. You focused if your coach was watching you do a certain stroke and when in her range, you accented doing the moves as powerfully as you could. There were more, but this increased your ability, with more lengths of a particular stroke at speed. Swimming in a group helped performance and speed greatly and swimming alone gave you a chance to practise the strokes to master the movements, which was good in itself, yet this lacked the motivation of your performance with the group.

I would swim on the Monday night and practice twice a week. It is one of the best fitness activities you can get, as there is no strain on certain joints, or pressure on a certain leg that gives you hassle. You build up muscle and flexibility to its best. Before, I was going to the gym regularly and by doing my daily exercises, I was built up and quite muscly-looking. In comparison to swimming, you can look good, but that's all the muscle performance can do, except for some strong movements, they just look good. It's a visual thing. With swimming, you exercise the whole body – cardiovascular, stamina and muscle strength, never mind the psychological benefits you gain by pushing yourself. My build looked less impressive, but with more effective use. Eventually my look became athletic. Over a good few years my leg wasn't going tight; in practising leg kicks for front crawl, I hit the fastest movements I had for a decade. Running was quick, but this kind of swimming was at full speed. It was amazing achieving this. This led to a big discovery that swimming is the best form of exercise for me in building my strength, stamina, discipline, and is invaluable for improving my body functions. It is far more effective for stretching and athletic swimming offers more flexibility. Flexibility is a calling that occurs from age thirty onwards and becomes in great demand in your later years. Keeping flexible is keeps you young too and stops that physical decline. It is very, very valuable to your health.

With swimming, it is very important to know what can decrease your movements and what you can increase in your stroke to improve your potential. It is best to keep your food intake away from manufactured food and back to basics. You use a balanced diet, mainly with carbohydrates to replenish used energy. It's all to do with acids and alkalines. Alkalines are easily digested and stop the blood from clumping together with cells that can reduce energy. They keep your energy level even as well as the food groups like carbohydrates, proteins and fats. At varied levels connected with basic foods, this works wonders in giving you so much energy. Lastly, it is worth finding out more to help give you the energy you need. I compare it to old-style petrol being two-, three- and four-star petrol. If the engine is a four-star fuel engine and you give it two-star petrol, it affects its performance. It's the same using the best food; you get tools for better performance. A key to this is drinking water and keeping away from other drinks like coffee and fizzy drinks, as this affects your performance. There are so many benefits just from drinking water. It's good for your skin, digestion, joints, thinking clearer and more. So many benefits, that it's worth regulating this.

The swimming group gave me a level of fitness I thought I would never see again. I had finally found a way to keep fit.

Swimming gave me more conviction while listening to my body. I got to know what things I felt right working on and giving it that extra resistance to improve, and when to take it easy. This applied to my physical input as well as other things from doing writing on the computer, to spiritual aspects of increasing my self-development.

It also showed me things I could use for my classes on the Fridays. It seemed a good combination to actually use the swimming exercises to improve swimming techniques. After all, this was another 'walk the talk' situation. It was always best for me to experience what I was talking about. That way, I knew what people were experiencing and they knew what I was experiencing.

The masters swimming and two practices a week, not just swimming, taught me an important lesson in learning. A basic way that swimming is taught at this level is through complete repetition until it becomes automatic and you don't think of the movements, they just happen. Tons of lengths and eventually you fine tune your technique to improve through trial and error. This is true with just about all things in life, yet if you have a plan or an aim so you particularly work on improving a specific technique, this shortens dramatically your time practicing. Yes, this way proves more efficient in learning, yet how you are at the time, meaning which state you are in, affects the quality of your swim. This is where lots of repetition comes into play, making it automatic and building strength, flexibility and stamina, yet some kind of planning in your training is called for. You have something to focus on. Improvement comes from conscious discovery. That's how you learn. There are times when unaware, repetition produces mastery and it just happens. You don't know how. Maybe the focus was on improving stamina, not completing the technique well. Your attention may be on other things, yet this holistic approach improves many aspects, not what you focus on. It really depends; if you've got the time to spare, repetition is suggested. If there is a time constraint, some clever thinking and planning is called for.

With the masters swimming, this was the best form of fitness I could get, never mind also improving my posture and stance. I used to go to the gym five days a week. This gave me the build that was what I was looking for. I looked healthy and fit, and not artificially structured that looked good but served no purpose rather than just for aesthetics. With improving my swimming, I improved my ability to walk more than a little – I just flowed. I had a strong top build, because my legs didn't seem to function as far as propelling me through the water, although they are well built and muscular. They seemed to favour assisting with balance when I stretched out to get a maximum pull. It also improved the strength of my left side. There is no difference now, but it kept things in even participation during strokes. In keeping an even pull, this maximises your swimming and your balance in life. I had eventually found what could substitute my climbing, as there were a lot of aspects to think about, not just swimming. It was a matter of keeping maximum streamlining and the correct technique for propulsion through the water. This was the technical side. After mastering this side, there was the flow in the water. To feel the water and the movement so you flow through with as near to perfection in movements as you can get. You feel the flow of the water and you are part of it. This was close to getting lost in free climbing with flowing movements on the rock. This was the same as mindfulness to some degree.

I then started going to the early Thursday swimming for the masters with the North Ayrshire swim squad. To start swimming at six in the morning, I was up at ten minutes to five to do exercises to help flexibility. I just did the stretch exercises, as I was going to get my arms exercised by swimming. This was the only occasion I didn't do my set of exercises first thing in the morning like I have always done and it set me up for the day. It wasn't going to win by me seizing up or not having the right frame of mind and discipline achieved through daily exercise.

The only thing was on Thursday mornings, the other swimmers were mostly from the highest group, so the pace was very fast. Yes, it improved my speed and stamina, but also brought on what I thought was lost through my 'wee car bump' – my asthma shone its light again. It just made me aware of social influence that got me uptight, and I tried not to get uptight swimming and breathing. Relaxation and a change of focus was the call of the day with this too. It looked like relaxation was the call for everything to get results.

Teaching Swimming

After joining the masters swimming for a while, I still took my sons to their club as normal, to see them come on in their swimming. I also took them on Sundays and I swam a few times a week as well. At that time I was doing more lengths, with the intent of completing a mile, which I did. I also did it without touching the sides. I was getting proficient in the water, except my right leg played up and became sore with spasms at times. The standing bouncing I did eased off these leg cramps and spasms. I would do breast stroke, then one length occasionally on my back doing the breast stroke legs.

I thought about training for doing a triathlon where swimming, running and cycling were used. I was running on the treadmill at the gym and was pushing my speed and stamina up. I took my dad's old bike and I went cycling once a week. I found out the triathlon distances and matched their sequence to going to certain destinations. I put it together a few times but with very slow transitions, meaning getting changed in the pool changing rooms. Under my haunting health constraints, the long transitions were okay in my view. I swam first, then cycled, then ran. When finished, my legs lacked control for detailed moves because I was fatigued, although I always slept well after.

When taking the boys to their swimming lessons, I asked the person who ran it, Ann, if I could help with teaching them. She said yes. I felt anxious because of the disabilities I had, but I was getting a reputation with my physical involvement in exercises and I delivered with confidence with the hope of being in a teaching role again, even volunteering.

It was perfect timing, as there was a course to aid a trainer the next week and I went. This was not a problem, as with my years of being a trainer, I had so much I could offer them. I had spent a lot of time researching exercises and health, so I was interested in the delivery of coaching the kids. The health and safety related to the pool was new to me at this level and was interesting with its common sense.

After a few sessions, I went to help them with the classes. The lead swimming instructor asked if I wanted to go with Euan's older class, although I opted for Adam's class. It was a bit earlier, but I went for him first beforehand to take him to his class and that suited us fine. She mentioned that the cost of my training would be free if I gave them voluntary help weekly for a year. If not, it would cost me. This was not a problem, as I aimed to do that anyway.

I was helping with the top group in this section. The guy overseeing the group, I knew, and it was fun. In helping, I added my tutor experience and NLP psychological techniques to help bring out the kids in their performance. It was challenging for my speech in a noisy environment. I slowed my voice down and learned to project my instructions. This worked well. Also, when coaching, you simplify your instructions to avoid complications. This suited me as well, although it was hard work filled with, yet again, practice to become clear.

Brian, who oversaw the group, wanted to see how I dealt with situations. This was a privilege for me with what I had been through, thinking I had lost just about all of me to become a second-class person, to experiencing that interest from someone again, learning themselves from what I showed in teaching.

It was so refreshing to get this back again. There were skills I had before that allowed me to move on to better things. It put light on my achievements before, and how much of this was created from previously gained knowledge.

Months went by and I was enjoying it so much. This style of training involved different strategies in delivering to gain control of the group. I made them feel as if I was having a one-to-one with them, yet controlling the group at different paces and levels, I found enjoyable. I was like a kid with a new toy. This was brilliant; back to teaching, another aspect of coaching, and more athletic knowledge to help my own skill as well.

I had an urge to better my training in this, as I had so much interest in it, as well as for personal reasons of taking a class to a better degree and improving my swimming. The course was at the Waterfront in Greenock and I was the only person that wasn't Waterfront staff. It was good in a way to see how other organisations delivered their training, although I did at times, feel a bit like an outsider in learning a course, whereas they were putting their learnings to direct use.

The knowledge was fantastic. It covered the stroke movements, the class formats with different ages, health and safety, the psychological aspect of training (which appealed to me greatly) and anatomy (that also appealed to me greatly and I gained a better understanding). These were the points that stood out for me.

There was about eight people and three of them were dyslexic, which helped me in not having that alone thing again. There were three guys and five females, which was an interesting mix. Two of them were full-time life guards as well, who worked for Renfrewshire Council pools. There was one guy who used to work at an old pool called the Hector McNeil, where my dad worked servicing the engines of the pool after he had to come back from sea. This was due to self-inflicted health problems he got related to excessive drinking. I didn't know how he was there. This in itself left me feeling unsure of what wasn't said when he spoke. The drink had affected him there as well. He just continued with this self-destruction of his health, never mind the inconsistency in his moods. Alcohol is so destructive to the person and their family. Years after he had died, this still haunted me and I thought I had let it go. This made me more determined to give my best to this course and prove that he was not a family trait.

A lot of the training you had to deliver used what I knew of NLP, such as what sensory information the kids would be using, either seeing, hearing or feeling. In applying your instructions to suit seeing, hearing, feeling, the kid would relate better to their guidelines, meaning someone was on the same planet and understands them. The delivery of information showed them the 'whole', explaining parts that led to putting it all together. I loved finding out how to use the techniques I knew with something else, like swimming. I thoroughly enjoyed it.

In writing about manoeuvres and body position for the test, I used an anatomy description to describe face up, face down (prostrate, etc.), the leg and arm movements and so on. It was a bit difficult at first using the terminologies in a different setting, but for me, it gave me a better understanding with relation to something I knew.

We had time in a 'classroom' and delivering training to kids in the pool, which was fun. These classes were less time and more compact than what I was used to. What didn't help, was having to bring class planning sheets and write evaluation sheets. This in itself took time, as from previous experience in delivering training, the evaluation sheets had to hold proof of the teaching learned.

With my enthusiasm for seeing things differently, this appealed to certain kids. Taking classes like this, I could see what needed to be improved in a kid's performance and find the most time efficient way to make them feel individual. What I would then show them, improved their swimming. I also used a lot of my psychological coaching, as I could observe barriers the kid had created and knew how to break through that limitation they made for themselves.

It was on weekends and we had finally got to the point of sitting the exam. I was classed as dyslexic too, as that would be easier to explain than the complexities of head injury effects.

Ann, the leader of my swimming group who knew the head of the Waterfront well, was to come up and help by being a scribe. She asked me if I wanted a scribe. For me, this would only complicate what I was going to write and would add to doing the exam, so I declined.

I was to be given a quiet space to work, although there were a lot of us in the quiet room. There were us three blokes and one girl. They all had scribes and I wasn't going to take the risk of that kind of help.

After a few hours, the exam was over. Those weeks of training and study proved beneficial. There was no point, I struggled to find an answer. I had to wait a few weeks till I got my results back.

I got them, only I had to answer a few questions, as my descriptions were hard to read. Due to the fact that I was classed as dyslexic, I was given the opportunity to rephrase them. I did and passed a few weeks later.

The sense of accomplishment was inspiring. It wasn't something that was very taxing to do, but I loved the content and felt at home with it. This used all my skills to their advantage. I love this and my trueness came out. It's what I had a passion for: I was using all my skills together. It was coming from the whole of me. I truly loved being a swimming coach and trainer. There were so many life skills I could add to help folk click while improving their swimming. It seemed to match up all my skills and passion into one subject. Whatever happens, this will hopefully always be present in my life.

I was employed by North Ayrshire Council to be a swim teacher for kids a few hours a week and I took a leading role in the amateur swimming club on Thursdays, which suggested that this was my way and unconsciously I generated my passion for swimming.

Pyrenees

I got talking to a girl who enjoyed the hills too. We talked about the Scottish hills and also running. It was so good to share this with someone who didn't know me before, or what I could do. This was about now time, not the past, and I wasn't trying to fit in with my old identity. This was my new one. I didn't have to prove myself and we just savoured the joy outdoor life gives.

After hill walks, Wendy asked me out of the blue if I wanted to go to the Pyrenees for mountain walking and camping. This opened up so many possibilities of what we could do and in different locations. Going away with someone on holiday to a place I wanted to go to, was unbelievable. We would be living in a tent for a month. This brought a brimming excited smile to me. I thought that was a distant memory for me, camping and mountains. My outdoor gear was to be used again for an adventure.

Flights were arranged down to London, then to Pau. I was flying down to Stansted airport, only this time I was to go further afield. We had to pick up our luggage and transfer it to the French flight.

We arrived in Pau in the early evening and took a bus to Oloron-Sainte-Marie. We stayed overnight at a cheap hotel. It was lucky that Wendy's French was good to make it easier, because she negotiated a taxi to drive us a distance to the camp site near Cascan. The camp site had views of the surrounding mountains that left me drooling and hurried to see how I could get to their memorising beauty.

Cascan, this old town was steeped in old buildings with narrow winding streets, with a chapel off the middle of the town. It was absolutely picturesque and stuck in time with its beauty, along with the relaxation won with its laid back pace of life.

My money, for me, was just limited to just scraping by. To buy the basic food was what it came to and with France's fresh, natural food it was a blessing in a way. Back to the very basics, camping, mainly just drinking water and back to solely enjoying the elements: the beauty of the countryside and being at close quarters with another for a month. That could promote some taxing times with anyone. You just need your own space to wind down at times. Such a co-dependency of sensations and actions made it an adventure I would always joyfully look back on, bringing warmth and excitement to me.

We camped at four different areas covering the mid to left portion of the Pyrenees. It was brilliant and free, just living with just the basics. It was back to nature for me. There were times when we stayed at a hotel in between valleys. There was one time when we got a train to Lourdes. It felt unusual with a spring mattress, sleeping in a room again. Lourdes is an amazing place. I am not religious, but the unity of positive energy will always stay with me. It was enlightening. We had the experience of seeing different parts of the Pyrenees through different camp sites, valleys, some remote and some places were busy ski resorts in the winter.

The most memorable was when we visited Gavarnie, famous for winter climbing in La Grande Cascade, the famous huge gap in the mountain range between France and Spain and mountains of sheer beauty that weaved their presence to humble you in the impending view of nature.

On a journey to the gap between France and Spain, we walked up the long astounding valley. Turning right at the end of the valley at the beginning of the impressive rock faces, we began a long scramble to rock climb for over 1,000 metres in extremely exposed vistas. It was a low grade, and due to the length of the climb and the challenges I now had after my accident, this was the first climb I had completed outside since that part of my life came to a halt. Complete focus, and slowly and safely I then proceeded with extra care.

Having to adapt my movements due to my left hand not gripping perfectly at that point, my right leg protesting with pelvic troubles, and a balance challenge from changing what I was looking at, some scenes made me lose my bearings. This was 101% effort for me.

There were certain times when traversing on exposed sections, I relied desperately on my not-so-good balance and could slip down hundreds of metres, straight off the cliff. I moved position by position, creating a trance state for the flow of movements. I went into the world of the rock formations and the movements were flowing with ease. If it wasn't, that was a sign you were doing it wrong and impending danger lurks ahead. But I was singing the same tune as the mountain. My movements were smoothly flowing. I was in the moment and indulged in the process. I relied totally on relaxed, sole focus. All fear disappeared as I got into the flow of my movements.

We were past the most vertical terrain, which eased off to complete it. I gave Wendy a big victorious, emotional hug with a tearful eye, saying, "That was a major accomplishment for me. I missed this so much. Thank you for waiting for me and having patience."

We ended up at the *Cabane des Soldats* lodge high up in the mountains in the middle of nowhere, up in the steep slopes and crags. As a big reward we bought a bottle of Coke and a Mars Bar each. It stands without reason that the prices for these products were expensive, and it was well worth it for the pat on the back for us, especially me.

We decided not to go back the same way we came, if possible, and we headed down a faraway gully.

There was no one in this area. Heading down the gully hours later, we headed across the mountain slopes to eventually come back to our beginning. We occasionally saw some mountain sheep about in the distance.

We trundled on. By this point it was becoming a trudge. We came across one sheep that was sitting down. It sat up and gingerly moved, then sat down again. Passing it, we noticed its legs were half mauled off and the wounds were filled with flies and scabs. The wounds looked so old and it was in a tragic situation. The sheep couldn't eat; it was on its last legs. It was so weak. You could see the absolute pain in its eyes. After discussion about help from the farmer, we knew this wouldn't have happened. We were in the back of nowhere. This animal was on its last legs, so to speak, and it wouldn't get any help. This was a major incident to Wendy and she wanted me to smother it, to put it at ease. I said no, I couldn't do that, but I would hold the sheep. She brought out her old fleece. That last spurt of action had drained the sheep. It couldn't get up. The sheep was smothered and died quickly. It was the best thing to do and we couldn't leave the injured sheep and say it wasn't our responsibility. We couldn't let it suffer with what looked to be so much pain. The pus, wounds, and the tons of flies feeding on it, were too much, we had to take action. After one of the biggest points in my life, on the same day we had come across this. No words were spoken on the way back. It took till ten for us to get back to the campsite. It was a very emotional day. It was an exhausting day. Then I had to have energy to make our dinner and have a shower to end it.

Later at night we experienced thunder and lightning so close in the valley. It strengthened nature's dominance over humans. I counted in between the lightening and then thunder to see how far away the lightening was. Five-second gap between the lightning and thunder, then four, three, two, then one. It was very close. I shuffled away from the tent poles. It was very off putting, yet excitingly magical.

The loudness with such clarity and brightening lightning in a campsite far up the valley, still leaves vivid memories of that time for me.

I now had a love for France and its way of living.

Our flight home went okay. It was good to be on a plane again with comfortable seats, although I must have smelled of the outdoors a bit. Yes, lots of fresh air to hide smells, but the clothes demanded to be washed after their hills experience.

Back home we seemed to not get in touch with each other. Trying to get in touch with her, she ignored me. My mind went wild with possible excuses.

It may have been too much for her, dealing with me in such close proximity. I conjured up how annoying it may have been for her to listen to the way I spoke. Maybe she was coming to terms with her own life. Overall, I didn't know. It was one of the most amazing holidays I have ever had and I achieved a life conquest of climbing again in the mountains. This was another monumental step for me in walking away from my injury. I wouldn't let it win, making major differences in spite of the injury.

Grenoble

Passing my time on the internet, I was getting closer again, talking to random people, which I missed from hairdressing, with people opening up to you. In this way by using the internet, I had a new way of getting around the situation of letting them know about my accident, and they could find out about me instead of me already having a label. They got to know the real me as a person and I wouldn't be instantly judged with assumptions that happened so often.

Talking to these people, they were told my tale. It depended on their interpretation compared to what they knew in their world. This was too much for some; having had so much life experience compared to them, they had difficulty putting it together with their constructive understanding of life as they knew it. They didn't take in, or were not ready to experience the vast change around as I saw and experienced the world anew and differently. It was so different and special, although the loneliness stuck its head up at times to haunt me. Another reason they fell out of touch with me, was that maybe we were simply not similar people and lacked compatibility.

By telling my tale of reality, I got to know some people who had experienced trauma that upset their life journey. Events that could be difficult for them to explain to others, I understood – 'walking the talk'. We had a connection and no matter what it was, from broken relationships, unhappy childhoods, stillborn babies, even getting married again and again looking for something, it didn't matter a single bit. This was an opportunity to air our thoughts that we didn't get the chance to in day-to-day life. It was a form of counselling, each having our own agendas in privately talking. We appeared to overcome barriers and move on. This can be difficult for some people, to figure out what barriers they experienced. They just cannot or will not compute it, out of non-acceptance or denial. It is their way of coping with it.

I thoroughly enjoyed talking to others. This was my passion: communicating with others gave me further learning in terms of what I now knew about people. I had a skill in it and could pick up so much more now with my sensory awareness.

Dealing with other people's problems gave me more experience helping people in my career – that was going to be my thing. To use my experience to help others was ideal, finally giving me a purpose. They picked up on the unspoken non-judgemental understanding I gave stacked with practical common-sense advice. This gave me so much energy and purpose. I was given an edge, a special edge. I could pick up far more than the average person. In my communication, this gave me an unconscious tool to use. I didn't know what it was logically, I just intuitively picked up from the person. It came from feeling or sensing.

Then I got talking to Lisa, a lovely woman from Grenoble in France who was a French English teacher. What luck, the perfect place for me with mountains all covered in snow in winter and inspiring crags of sheer vertical rock in specific locations. The awe-inspiring beauty of the place blew me away. Looking at maps, the sight of craggy, steep mountains and remoteness exploded my inner excitement and made my heart race. The location inspired me, but as always, it was the person I was talking to that held the most importance to me.

We talked every night on MSN or by phone for hours. Time escaped when our contact joined. I got the impression that I lit her fire and she told me she had feelings about me without even meeting. I was enthralled with such joyous explosive excitement that flowed from my heart in hearing this.

Time went by and we got on with our constant talking. With all this time, we really got to know each other through quite a lot of intimate, personal details. It felt right for both of us.

We arranged for me to give her and her lovely girls a visit.

After separation from her husband, she had the girls all the time, except at weekends where he had them at his place.

We decided that we would meet and if anything else happened between us, it would be seen as a bonus. This was being safe and sensible and very logically done, not giving disappointment an opportunity.

This was my third flight after my 'wee car bump' – the first time going to London to get an award, and the second to the Pyrenees experience. This time I was going abroad to another part of France, to Grenoble. This had me on a buzz filled with the excitement of meeting a French local in her country. This country I had begun to love back in the Pyrenees.

The plane landed in Grenoble airport and I was to meet her outside where she would drive me to the industrial town or small city.

I waited for a while, going only on what photos I had seen of her. After about five minutes, a beautiful, slender, tall woman came over. It was her. I hugged her and we kissed passionately. She looked a lot taller than I expected with a most beautiful figure. This was a pleasant shock and learning adaptively, I wondered how this would be for her. The difference of my accent was okay, although hearing me on the phone was different than in real life. I was more focused on my leg, as her apartment was a few floors up. I put all my effort into giving her the impression that I was not a hindrance to look as natural as possible.

The drive to Grenoble was breathtaking. Her girls were at her ex-husband's and we made our way back to her apartment. The idea of just being good friends lasted a very short time. We both had the same instant feeling after meeting each other.

The view from her apartment took my breath away. From the window from the front room and from the bedrooms there were majestic mountain scenes. To create a crescendo to this, going out to her outside balcony you got 270 degrees of mountain vista and could see the houses of Grenoble, the real Grenoble that is away from visiting sights. This gave me a feeling of belonging. Santa could never have given me this.

Her two girls were delightful. A bit younger than my boys and an age I could relate to. We could communicate by expression with me now being more aware that communication is not just verbal language.

I met a lot of her friends that weekend, going out for a meal or up at their houses, and this was absolutely brilliant for making me feel special. All the effort she made showed. In a way, it depended on what her friends' impressions of me were on seeing me for the first time. I couldn't help but think it was a time for her to check with her friends if I was okay.

The long weekend went very well. She was better than I ever imagined to be with. Her friends were great company and the city was breathtaking.

I was asked by one of Lisa's friends if I could do some coaching or therapy with her. She had repeated ovarian cancer and needed some outside one-to-one to help her have holistic strength. She was English and over a few visits, I got to know her very well. She and her French husband had adopted a young girl and this brought so much happiness to them. I was very pleased for them for finding what looking after a child would give them.

She needed strength in certain areas to get her through this. I boosted up what she had and wasn't aware of. That is very common. I gave her new strategies to cope from a fresh new perspective. This and Indian head massage boosted her energy and confidence greatly.

She wanted me to meet one of her and Lisa's friends in the city at a tea shop. The girl was Canadian and settling in Grenoble with her French partner and young child.

Meeting in a tea shop was ideal. She liked where I was coming from and opened up to me and I counselled her.

She burst into tears and Natalie, the woman I coached, said, "That's me and her you have brought to tears. Are you always like this?" in a joking way, showing her sense of humour. I thought, That's good, I'll need to write up this skill of making folk cry for my CV for future jobs. This was a good sign for me that she was back in control again.

I travelled there as often as I could. It was just like a dream for me. A country I began to love, a beautiful woman I fell for and she fell for me, and the countryside that was a landscape I had dreamed of, not knowing how majestic it really was.

The costs of flights varied. In the winter, it was direct and cheap. In the summer, it was down to London, then Grenoble. That was expensive.

Lisa asked me if I wanted money from her to travel there.

Being there and being very careful with my money, as well as thinking I would be taking advantage of her, I stupidly refused and over time got myself into financial trouble because of my male egotistical stubbornness.

I used to get the bus from the airport to Grenoble and find my way to her apartment.

There were trams running near the bus station. This was my first time actually seeing trams working next to the railway which looked like underground carriages. I used to always walk and I loved the atmosphere of this city. Next to the bus station was the train station that linked other cities together. At the very centre of the city was a small mountain that you could walk up by stairs. It was always busy.

It was about half an hour's walk and it was brilliant meeting Lisa coming back from her work.

There was one time I was there for a week and picking the girls up at another city, Claire, the youngest, had chicken pox. Lisa was worried about me catching it. I told her I had them when I was young and I wouldn't catch them. Having to be absent from her work, I said I would look after her. This was a good move. Claire and I got on so well together.

On the day, we watched Tom and Jerry cartoons I brought for them. She taught me days, months, seasons and weather from a wall display she had. This was a great way to get her attention onto something else.

I had a vocabulary book of words if I was to say anything specific.

This was a rip-roaring success. I had Lisa's number if there were any difficulties. We had an absolutely brilliant time. She got a lot out of going over the French words with me and I encouraged this to happen. Claire got a buzz out of showing me what she knew and then we played some board games.

Claire was a character, full of energy, and it was fun to look after her.

When I was there, Lisa and I used to go for runs and many times I went myself when she was working. It was a good way to find my way about. I went a few times, running to different parts of the city.

We went to other places nearby like other towns, lakes and up in the mountains.

On a good sunny day, we had the girls as well and we went to a nearby lake called Grand lac de Laffrey. It was so relaxing with the warmth from the sun and what Sunday gives. I can always remember what her Claire said to her mum. "I am pleased you get so much love from Tom." No words spoken to them, and they picked up on this love I had for Lisa and her girls.

For me, with all the unrest I had with my accident changing my life, this seemed like the reason. A new country with mountainous scenery, being given the chance to see if I could set up therapies with the expatriates, a beautiful woman that actually was an English teacher, two lovely girls and an apartment with vista only my dreams were made of.

One time we went for a ski at a resort that had a good reputation. The last time I skied was in Alaska and I showed good potential. I loved walking in the mountain snow and doing technical tasks. It was pure fun. This still carried on in my head, yet I experienced the wee car bump which sang a different song. My legs didn't work well and my balance was a problem.

I just went to the nursery slopes and constantly fell over. Poor Lisa was all eager to ski and she had to cover me as if I was learning again. I was so embarrassed with a feeling of frustration of letting her down. What impression did that give her? I wondered to myself. I asked her if she wanted to go up the ski lift herself and come down the big hill. She said in a nice way that to spend time with me is important.

That cheered me up, yet letting her down overshadowed me.

On the phone, we planned on us doing the Grenoble ten-kilometre run that she had done the year before. It was not the distance, but the being in a run and not running myself, that was the appeal to me.

The run was in Grenoble and two times round a particular road circuit with sunny weather, was a very momentous point in my life. I had walked again without any aids or sticks, now I had completed a run in France. I was in an accomplished place.

I have no doubt that my ego assisted in this. In aiming very high and always against the odds, was my ethos seeing an accomplished example.

Not long after this, Lisa came over to Largs to see Scotland and I had a family get-together planned, to show her my side with my two boys, as the proud dad that I am.

On her return, I was under the impression that she thought this was too much, yet she seemed serious about showing me her family. Our relationship wasn't going to her plan, or maybe it wasn't what she expected. At that point, it fizzled out between us. I was in such confusion. Our paths didn't follow on from there. Everything seemed just right but maybe the reality of me wasn't what she had in mind for her big picture. I could give her love, but maybe I was too much for her to worry about in myself, being a foreigner having to live in France who was poor at speaking French. It would have been too much for her on top of her own life worries. She was an au pair in Ireland for a while and felt the isolation that would have become my constant shadow. One time, leaving to go back home, she came down to the bus and gave me an unusual long, passionate kiss. This was strange and it gave me an uncomfortable feeling. Talking to her at home, not directly, but giving me cold replies, I picked up something wasn't right. We were planning a holiday up north and she told me to cancel it. This relationship had come to an end. Early on, she claimed love for me and I think she backed herself into a corner before getting to know me, yet our talks could class this as that. I think it was with me not having work there and not speaking French. The glove didn't fit.

With this loss, I was devastated and became very low. My dream had been shattered. I had such a looming darkness upon me. Then I picked myself up and said, "Maybe that direction was not for you. There will be a better time ahead. Believe that there's something waiting for you."

I had the drive again, in a different way, going for another path. That way only brought sadness and such hurt. I wasn't going to have pain like this anymore. I'd find a way of putting myself back in the right direction. I have been through a bloody hell of a lot and wasn't killed. There must be a good, important reason I am still here, and I'll bloody find it.

CHAPTER 9

Pushing the Barriers:

Making It Work for Me

Fall down several times, get up eight.

– Japanese proverb

Talks in Edinburgh

One day, I got a text from Ann who was in charge of Momentum in Irvine, where she said a girl from the head office in Glasgow wanted to talk with me about writing my story in the Momentum magazine for the UK. I openly agreed to see her and meet her down at the Irvine office in Ayrshire Central hospital. A time and day was arranged and I drove there after working one Monday morning.

I wasn't too sure what to expect from her and was surprised when a caring, attentive young woman entered the room. Getting to know her, her personality was so refreshing to be with, and she was completely non-judgemental, I could tell her about myself fully, knowing I could trust her.

She was telling me about the magazine and other folk who had articles in it. This was to give hope and direction to others who read the magazine, which appealed to me greatly.

I told her about my life before:

A successful position; wife and family; great house and of course, climbing.

The accident and its effects: couldn't walk, my speech poor and my left side suffering similar effects to a stroke.

How I wasn't going to be beaten by this. They took my bed away for trying to walk, eventually leading to me getting to walk and asking about running.

I was doing public talks, groups and more. The press coverage I had gained in newspapers, my stress therapy and doing an official run in Grenoble, soon to do the Glasgow half marathon.

Normally I get a look of disbelief compared with their opinion of what would happen if that was them, but she had an enthralling look of inspiration towards what I had done, deciding what my good points were and going for it.

I had to ask her in another way to see if this was a real reaction from her.

I asked her if she hears tales like this often through her job.

She said it was a great sensation to hear from other people all in different angles of society, how they coped, created a different path and showed courage.

It was an amazing story of me she wrote and found it very inspiring. I didn't know if I would turn out to a have that kind of strength years ago.

She seemed very intrigued by my story and asked if she could put it in the Momentum magazine, in an article covering me. Time went on and I got a copy of the magazine delivered to my door. It was full-page coverage with another page given to a photo of me that was taken by Laura later in that day.

The article was giving motivation for others, in a role model format that could give inspiration to others.

It was humbling, explaining in writing in a specific magazine to others that I've experienced what they are experiencing, rather than the very grey explanations the health professionals gave, to cover themselves.

With injuries of the head, the effects are different per person as to the extent of recovery. It depends on their actual injuries, their previous health and their will to recover. With me, I gave them direction, shown them an aim, giving them a will to do it.

I phoned Lauren and thanked her, hoping it would help her in producing a good article. She created a win-win for us.

I phoned Ann from Momentum in Irvine to see if she had seen it yet. Yes, she had seen it, and there was a trip to the Austrian Alps that I could see myself doing one day. The Alps was very appealing, yet it had taken a long time to get slight recognition in any form with the line of work I was in. Sadly I had to turn down the trip.

Months later, Lauren called Ann to arrange a meeting with me again, as she had a proposal for me. This intrigued me, wondering where she was coming from. We arranged a meeting at the Momentum offices at Ayrshire central in Irvine.

She had a great drive for her work. In meeting her, she was on the side delivering a formal approach, which gave me the impression it must be quite a big deal.

She started by talking about a company similar to Momentum in Edinburgh, looking after people with forms of disability, normally brought on in their life.

Momentum was doing talks at venues by Ian Winston, the British Director at this time, and someone who could give inspiration and was helped by Momentum. It was to be delivered in a hotel in Edinburgh to over 200 people of different disabilities of all ages, their helpers and staff.

"Would you be part of the Momentum speech with Ian, the company director?"

I couldn't believe I was being asked to be involved with the company director of Momentum.

First, taking positivity classes, then motivation life coaching classes led to doing talks with Momentum's company director. I felt so electrically alive. This was a big stepping stone for me in being recognised for help.

I thought about how to make it different and I recalled a poem of worldly reflective thought that would match the flow of energy given with this.

I got this poem from my grandad and I used this in helping my memory and speech. The poem was 'If' by Rudyard Kipling. I learned this and gave an emotional delivery to my speech therapist on a return visit. This aim was to improve my flow of words and I wanted to create passion through my delivery.

I gave the poem a flow and built up a crescendo for the ending to a peak of sincere emotions. The pace of a technically flowing delivery with times of emotional meaning, gave me the edge I was looking for.

In delivering it to my speech therapist that I had involved in my delivery, she was agape during my delivery of the poem that glazed her eyes and at the end of the fourth verse, she was near to a tear. It hit the exact emotional chord I was looking for in the way I could deliver poetry or talks. Emotions are so important and have immense impact. This poem had achieved my aim.

I was so pleased with my delivery of 'If' with the creation of so many feelings. I aimed to get this reaction from Lauren – that would have the most effective impact.

I suggested using Rudyard Kipling's 'If' with my speech for Momentum. Laura was happy for me to use this. I sent her what I would be saying as well as the poem. After she gave me a brief on what Ian would say, I sent her adaptations in my theme of positivity that I was going to use. This would work with Ian's talk.

I practiced as much as I could with the poem, my delivery and what I was covering. I visualised successfully performing the talk and poem and that created the good feelings with a compendium of emotions.

Talking to Laura, we were to meet on an early train to Glasgow, then take the train into Edinburgh. My train time was the first train out of Largs. Lauren would join me halfway at the Kilwinning station. She was to meet me on the first carriage. Before I went, I got a call from Madeleine, with her intent on giving me the feeling of not being alone. That helped, and it was a bonus, but the day was a big day for me and I focused on giving a monumental delivery.

I was relief after meeting Lauren at the station because I didn't know where the hotel was and she said Momentum would pay for my travel.

Our chat got us caught on other issues, as she had a lot to prepare for her boss and had a pile of handouts from Momentum explaining what they do. This gave me a feeling of pride, representing Momentum in Edinburgh.

Reaching Edinburgh, the MacDonald Hotel was on the Royal Mile that leads to Edinburgh Castle. It was just a walk from the station to the Royal Mile. This MacDonald Hotel was close to the Scottish parliament. When we went in, I got to know the main people from 'Places for People'. I then checked out the presentation room and the tables, perceiving the reality of the amount of people that would be there. It was quite tightly spaced and I had the impression that the hall would be huge.

Behind me was a large screen where the words to 'If' would be displayed.

That gave me a buzz and I couldn't wait to talk, though anxiety rose.

We were second on. Ian talked first and impressed me with his work history and having a child with a disability. What he and his wife experienced was a story by itself.

Then it was me. I was just focusing on the presentation and had a good introduction, mentioning the power of positivity.

The people and 'Places for People', never mind Momentum, didn't know what I could deliver.

My talk began, showing energy from myself and humour was used to tell a sombre story of what happened with my injuries. Adding fun into my parts of my recovery, with the different approach I had, built an alert atmosphere. I showed them techniques they could use with situations to give them control and self-worth back in usable, common-sense ways.

Then, I gave a good introduction to the poem, explaining how this poem was helpful to keep you on track and in balance in life. How much difference 'If' can make.

I started 'If' quietly, slower and clear, and used my hands to add more visual description. With every verse, I increased the emotions and intensity. They were now very attentive, drawn in with the emotions that gave meanings to words and phrases. This then led to a crescendo that represented the power of taking control of what happens in your life, to make it give you strength.

I got an astounding clap and folk stood up. For all the time practising, this was worth it. It was my ultimate reward. I helped show folk direction. Four people came up to me, clients and carers and staff, to shake my hand, and told me how good that was. It was a surprise for everyone. They never expected my delivery would have this kind of impact.

I got a supreme response from 'Places for People' staff and they kept in touch with me.

It done a good deal for Momentum and finally I was being noticed for the impact in changes and motivation I could have.

My self-worth had reached what I had pictured in my mind.

Glasgow Half Marathon

By this point, I was running five times a week and stretched the distance I could run. I got a book called *The Non-runner's Marathon Trainer* by David Whitsett, A. Cole and T. Kole, giving me the knowledge and motivation I needed. I was running alone, just like most things I had done by myself. I didn't want to hassle people with my slow progress, and my prospect of being a hassle to others always haunted me. I got leg muscle problems relating to my sacroiliac injury, thus tightened up muscles sometimes made them rigid, mainly my calf and my leg wouldn't straighten. I had my physiotherapy foam roller and that helped a bit. Also, a cold shower to ease the swelling was called for. I could handle coldness because of this.

I kept going, and books like this one freshened up my direction and will to achieve. *The Non-runner's Marathon Trainer* drew my attention when the previews mentioned they got a person with a disability who couldn't walk at first to run a marathon. This appealed to me and I had to get this book. It looked like we were roughly singing the same song. This book showed weekly training exercises and what was important to me, was the psychology that is primarily needed. Psychology was similar to athletics, yet made less complicated by following a theme. This made me plan out where I would run to and what time suits best each week. It showed me exercises to improve my speed and stamina. I had to make sure I stretched before I ran and after, to help loosen off the complex tightness in my right leg. Sometimes, it was tighter than others, especially when I got worked up through the day, as we all do at times. This gave me an internal sign that something had worked me up and this made my leg tight. I found out because of the damage I had on the right side, my nerve sheath was less flexible. There was pain around my right pelvis when I ran, although I visualised healing liquid entering the top of my head, flowing down to and around the area with soothing healing. Over time, this worked and the pain faded away. There was a lack of movement in my hip joint and this resulted in overcompensation by the left leg, to adjust movement. Knowing about this, I made sure my movement was even while running and this gave me something else to do to pass time instead of focusing on whether that day you can or can't run so well. A big secret was changing my focus. I used affirmations like 'I can do it', saying it repeatedly, until my energy was focused on achieving. I also used meditations of what I learned was 'the inner smile'.

When running, I went over every part of me and smiled inwardly from tip to toe. Then I went over all my organs. I learned where they were and their function from holistic therapies, then smiled at them individually. It was a conscious trance and I ran a lot of distance going over the whole body smiling. This improves your energy greatly, working as one with no parts of you in dispute.

I learned this from NLP. Occupying your time with different thoughts is a winner and a perfect distraction to stop yourself being over protective, which in turn stops you from achieving things you want. It's best coming from the whole of you. There is an old saying that when you are running you can solve the world's problems. It's one of the best exercises to sort your head out. It's active meditation, so you feel physically and mentally healthier.

Lastly, the joint between my leg and ankle gets tight and this affected movement. It adds to the tightness of my right leg at times. It even got sore down to my big toe. I initially thought it was sciatica, but my spine was okay, and that normally catches the sciatic nerve. I thought it may have been another muscle located horizontally deep within your pelvis, which can catch the sciatic nerve, but it wasn't that one. Not moving my legs in particular ways, my abductor muscles which brought my legs in, were weak. Running didn't affect this, only swimming leg kicks.

From this book, I learned that cold showers, particularly on my legs, helped so much. It cuts down inflammation.

I had motivation regularly, which was brilliant for keeping me from wallowing in self-pity and I felt I was achieving something. Being involved with fitness is a love I have always had. I could be fitter in a different way, with all the other benefits this gives, like the better functioning of my body. Your digestion works well and your nutritional intake becomes important. This gave me even more energy, apart from the will of wanting improvement and sorting out my head. This also kept me young.

I needed something to aim for and someone I knew asked if I wanted to do the Glasgow half marathon in aid of his brother's cancer. I happily agreed. This gave me more conviction to run this event. His brother, who had throat cancer, owned a pub in Largs. There were three of us running, one was his brother and the other was his son. This situation promoted a mixture of emotions for me. One side, this gave me motivation to do well, as a lot of folk know me through the pub after helping Tony raise funds for throat cancer. With this, I had to gain sponsors with a sheet and this produced an expectancy of me completing it and not having to explain why I wasn't successful. I was motivated by running for a good cause. My grandpa passed away with throat cancer, so there was a family reason for me. The pressure of so many people rooting for me inspired me, although this added pressure of not failing them. Yes, it was stupid to feel pressure from this – it was a healthy motivation to achieve it.

I followed a running routine daily. I was left with a tight leg that eased off after running, yet it affected my running capability. At worst, it was tight with sore calf knots. At its best, I was flowing so well it gave me the impression of my leg getting better. My determination for doing it gave me the initial drive that got me through. No way was this injury winning. I would bloody show it. The idea of failing was never thought of. I refused to give in to it.

Pleasantly, it became an obsession to make time each day to run, and a long run on Saturday for distance. I ran five days out of seven with two days recovery with a precise focus. This gave me a sense of balance to improve. I was clocking up the mileage and was ready.

One of the guys from the pub was going to give us a lift to Glasgow, so that was one problem not to worry about. We got there and got ready in George Square in Glasgow. I was fairly up front to start with. A lot of stretching followed. I had been over the course so often in my mind, I had no nerves. I only wanted to complete it. The race started off up a hill and I got into a good pace. I was used to hills rather than long straights. I got into a rhythm and we went into the south of Glasgow to parks. These changed my thoughts and what was inspirational was people watching egging you on. It produced energy from nowhere. This was new to me as a solo runner. It was so good and motivated me to carry on.

With all the practice of long runs, I knew when I would need to think about other things to keep me going. The joy of a trance state which I was used to was so beneficial.

I picked up refreshments when running, then chucked them away after I had gained a mouthful. At first, I laughed to myself at the Portaloo toilets, but used one later. I understood that they were called for.

I reached the last section and got a burst of energy. It was so close now. I started to speed up and finally seeing the finishing line, I sprinted and crossed over the line. YES. Years I had been building up to this, from not being able to walk, to walking, to slowly running a short distance, to achieving this. My injury didn't win. I won my personal battle.

I met up with the others. Yes, my time was slower, but I did it. The timing wasn't important to me at all, it was completing it. I felt triumphant. On the way back in the car, my leg was cramped up in the back and then it started to protest. Normally with runs at home, I went for a cold shower to ease my leg muscles, so that's exactly what I did when I got home. I then phoned my family with such brazen pride. They had witnessed the state I was in before; achieving this was a major breakthrough and more importantly, I won my personal battle.

Solitaire Sea Swim

To follow this, there was a swimming event that caught my attention. It was a swim from the Isle of Cumbrae to Largs via the Clyde. Swimming in the sea water was another task in itself – the coldness for a start, and more would be floating in sea water. There was the variance of waves and wind, never mind jellyfish, which seemed to come out more in the summer spell. The weather and shoals of jellyfish, if they were to be present or not, is out within your control. Relying on how the elements are on the day, never mind if it was sunny or raining, big waves or windy, it was a gamble.

I found out more about it. It was called the Solitaire Fund for people needing an escape to property in Largs from the cities. It was formed by parents who lost their daughter and were interested to help families.

The information was on the website and I went into their shop to talk about this, in my foreign accent. Again, it required a sponsor sheet to fill in and so I had this pressure all over again.

The distance was a mile and a half, which wasn't that far, but the difference in the weather could make it completely different. There was a rehearsal sea swim at the marina a week before and I went to it. Beforehand, I bought a wet suit to help with the cold and more importantly, to avoid jellyfish stings. On crossing on the ferry, at times I saw a cluster of them and if you swam into them, it wasn't inviting at all.

The temperature of the sea is at its best in late summer – it gains a few degrees to an average of 14 from the summer warmth.

I was suited up with a cap on for heat and to be seen if I got lost. With the wet suit, it is strange, if you have never experienced one before, especially in British seas. You get the initial freezing water, making you hyperventilate. Then the trapped water starts to warm up. It wasn't pleasant at all.

I went to the pool a few days before and did a mile and a half front crawl to prepare me, as I intended to do the swim with front crawl. I was prepared and now just worried about the weather. In the last few days, the wind had picked up and two days before, it was calm. Then the wind picked up to potentially worrying large waves, yet it was dry. After all, I didn't want to get wet if it rained.

I said to the boys that I wanted them to see me finish the event at the marina in Largs. Marathon athletes on television, when they crossed over the finish, or just before, they were met by their kids. I imagined the pleasure of seeing their pride as their dad accomplished something like this, so enlightening, it almost brought a tear to my eye. For me, this was the ultimate motivation. I felt I wasn't there for them in my recovery, so I wanted to make them even more proud of me. My mother, Madeleine, our son, and my boys all agreed to see me finishing.

From Phoenix and Carers, where I worked, I got sponsors from the staff and from friends, plus my family. That side was looking healthy. I was getting used to doing something for charities. This gave you added motivation for doing the swim, and it made training more purposeful.

The night before, I got my swimming gear organised. On the actual day, I walked to the taxi rank and got a taxi to the marina. I was ready. Again, I had visualised myself doing the swim many times, even with different weather. The weather for the big day was dry, but it was windy. On the way, I could see the waves making 'white horses', which isn't a good sign at all. The wind was blowing offshore towards Cumbrae. My thoughts were on swimming face forward into the wind and the big waves. That would be tiring and would produce anxiety for me.

Meeting the people there, the organisers said it was too windy, but the route had changed. We were to go along the coast from the marina to Mackerson, putting green in Largs seafront before the pier and return. This was the same distance as doing the swim from Cumbrae to the marina, only a different route.

I got suited up and was ready with others to start. Most swimmers just plunged in the sea, so I did the same. Going into the water, I hyperventilated trying to keep up. To start off, I did the breast stroke then tried to speed it up by using the front crawl. Putting my face in the cold water produced more hyperventilation and it was difficult, so I carried on with the breast stroke and found a rhythm, although my legs protested movement and only kept it to a minimum, thus I was slow in comparison to others. My leg kicks were poor and it was all on my arm movements to give me motion in the sea. It was temporarily good, as the wind was behind us. This meant we swam with the waves, but this meant we would be going against them on the way back, which was grim thinking.

Folk overtook me. As per usual, I was alone in what I presumed was deep water with jellyfish somewhere lurking in its depths. It was great to go part the pencil from this view and the sandy island I grew up playing on, and even when I was older, I camped there. A long way down the route passed boats that were moored. It was amusing seeing the boats so close – a reminder that it was such deep water that you couldn't put your feet on the bottom.

All the way along, there were people in kayaks as support. I knew one of them and kept my eye out, looking for her. I couldn't see her. I thought I had passed them all and where we had to change direction to go back, I saw her. I said jokingly, "Well hello, fancy meeting you here. Do you come here often?" This gained a needed laugh to prepare me for swimming against the waves. There were gusts of wind, which produced inconsistent waves of different sizes. For only a short while, I was getting into a rhythm of breathing at the tip of waves, but so erratic they were, waves swashed over me and instead of breathing, I took in a lot of sea water. I kept doing this and couldn't find a pattern of assessing the peak of waves to breathe. Being swamped by the waves, I kept taking in sea water. Often I would choke and to catch my breath, I lay on my back. This was good, yet to make it worse, I kept getting swamped by waves crashing into me. I was bloody going to do it. I was one of the last by now, as it was just my arms doing the work. My legs still did the movements, but only for balance. I had been swimming for what seemed ages and I was on my energy reserves.

Getting hit by inconsistent, big, erratic waves, I just focused on passing certain bits of the land, knowing I was getting closer. After getting swamped so often, one kayaker sailed over to me and asked if

I was okay after coughing so violently. I asked if I could hold onto his kayak for a bit and this helped catch my breath. I could see the end and in theory, it wasn't that far off, except for the choppy waves. I ploughed on, gulping in more water. I kept pushing myself and it wasn't far now. I felt drained. It had to find strength to plough against the waves again and again. To get there, I was on my last legs. The will would have got me there and under other circumstances I would have just ploughed on with my last leg of energy. My concern was Madeleine and Luca. If I didn't, it would leave her waiting for me for ages to find out I had drowned. My sons made me want to complete it, knowing how positive I was, and I didn't want to let them down. Being swamped again and on my back, I made the decision of asking one of the boats to drag me closer to the end.

It was only a short distance and the slip and the boat let me swim the last bit. There were lots of people on the slip. My mother and Michelle were relieved to see me after it being such a long time I had been away for. It was fabulous to see my boys. Not exactly as I had planned, but I had finished.

I had been swimming for two and a half hours in choppy sea conditions. I was obviously shaky on my feet and one of the organisers helped me along to the showers at the sailing club. They assumed I had hypothermia, although because I was tired, my speaking was affected by slurring and my balance wasn't at its best. These were the symptoms of hypothermia as well and I was peeled out of my wet suit, to reveal the sleeves of my special t-shirt to stop the wet suit from rubbing against my body had ridden up and I had two big grazes from repeated arm movements.

In the warm shower, I was handed soup. Having soup and a shower at the same time is a good thing. I started to shiver. It was hard to peel off my wet suit, as my stomach was so swollen with sea water; someone helped me. At this point, I wasn't caring.

I got my clothes back on and relaxed with sighs of relief. Then rapidly progressing, was the need for me to visit a toilet.

I met up with everyone and we went to the main hall to hear how fast the person who was finished first was. Just over an hour. Whoa! Then the urgency to go to the toilet was an utmost priority. I speedily went in and locked the door. This feeling was not a good sign. I had never experienced stomach cramps like this before. I sat on the toilet and waited. My thoughts wandered away from my stomach cramps and then I heard noises that sounded like a broken pipe flowing which I thought was outside. It wasn't a broken pipe, it was me. It just went on and on and on. Where the hell did all this water come from that was leaving my body? It seemed impossible, the amount of water that I had taken in and now wanted to leave my presence. I guess that is to be expected after continually being swamped and swallowing tons of sea water. It was remarkable. It was my body's way of getting the sea water out. I was so glad I wasn't projecting sea water out my mouth. I would look like an image from an old horror film of a demon vomiting, spraying volumes of an unknown amount. For once, of only very few times, I had the urge for a sugary drink of Coke. I then drank lots and ate the food that was in the finishing buffet.

I got a lift from my mother, myself and Luca. We eventually got home. I fell asleep quickly and slept for a long time. I needed it. I achieved this, but it was extreme for me under these conditions. With the variance of the weather, it caught me by surprise how much it would affect me with my 'wee car bump wounds'. It was good to feel that extreme, and the energy that would get you through it. This was worth its weight in gold. For years I had read books of expeditions where an extreme was encountered. I didn't experience anything that would have made it impossible for me to go to such mountains, although I found this experience at home. With cuts and possible hypothermia, it was extreme for me, yet this was what it was all about – something that would hold you back. It's having the drive I had read of so much. A very monumental experience and best of all, I got something free. I got what may have been mild hypothermia.

Still, all in the learning I had gained from this, I picked up an excellent tool for avoiding hyperventilation, which I used on holiday daily with one of my sons, Alex, near Oban. After a long period of thought, I came up with the solution strategy.

Each day at Tralee, near Oban, we would go for a swim in the sea. We would walk in to just below our waists then splash water over the front of our bodies. After about four times, our breathing eased. When this happens, you quickly squat down to go into the water fully. Again a few times till your breathing calms, then you are ready for swimming with smooth breathing.

There was one time we swam out a distance, and then a boat with an outboard engine came to us. It was a fisherman saying that we shouldn't swim to the buoys, as those were his fishing nets, in case we got caught up in them. "That's fine," we said back, and thanked him. It may have been to protect his nets from damage, but drowning is such a hassle, we swam back to the beach.

It was a fantastic sandy beach surrounded by its natural beauty. We had a caravan at Tralee and we went there a few times. A wonderful part of Scotland, its beauty doesn't involve mountains: this was a first for me, not involving hills of any kind.

Open University Psychology: The Academic Challenge

Over time, I was given placements, being self-employed with stress management. There was a big cutback of government funding, so I lost them. What I trained for in stress management seemed like a dead end to an extent, so I thought of another angle of training – my new direction. I was sick of going into the old routine of applying for jobs. Because I lacked qualifications in the area I wanted to go into, I faced the old problem of not enough experience, and not enough qualifications. I thought I had done my bit in both of these fields, so I went to use my trump card – I needed to study from another angle to gain high qualifications that weren't practically assessed. They would be academic. I had found out that going to university at this point was not the way I seemed to learn, with other people in the class distracting me. I had furthered my skill with NLP. I wanted to further my education with psychology.

I went to an introductory part-time course covering thought and personality. The content, I knew, and it was good to get it in another form, yet being the only guy in the class and being part-time, isolation came back to haunt me again. I found the layout and instructions of the work confusing and at times almost Double Dutch. The next thing I knew, learning support got in touch with me again.

I was embarrassed as I didn't want them to think I was thick. One thing about this university evening course was there were no qualifications needed to sit it. Meeting with learning support, it gave the impression that I wasn't capable of the university style of studying. I didn't know where they were going, nor was it obvious what help they would give. It just confused me with unseen obstacles, so after a few months and one exam, I left and gave up that ghost. This left me confused about my capability. I wanted to learn at this academic level, I knew the basis of the course, yet I could not work out where I was going wrong.

Talking to a person I was a colleague with as a therapist, I found out from him he did counselling at a particular website. This appealed to me, so I went for a look at what was available. I saw some interesting ones in cognitive and behavioural and coaching and mentoring diplomas, so I applied for them. It came out of my pocket and I was sailing tightly into the wind, although it was an investment for my future. I took the money from my business account for this training.

I got the work and it looked good from the work books given. The work was to be done online and I was sure I could do it this way. Instantly with the first bit of work I did, it was so refreshingly peaceful. This made me focus on what I was doing, with nobody breathing down my neck and getting me stressed. There was not a particular time to finish the work. This helped me develop a structure to work with. I also phoned my tutor who marked my work and told him about myself. Now there was a connection I felt comfortable with, in having an understanding that if there was something that didn't read right, just to get in touch with me.

This was comfortable for me and the stress that stopped me before wasn't there. I read and did my homework, to then hand in my first completed exam paper and I passed. Overall with this particular course/folder, there were five assessments. This gained me a certificate in cognitive and behavioural counselling. I read the book faithfully and underlined the most important parts for notes for me, and used it in different contexts. The theory was similar to NLP and I could take it in and write about it clearly.

I passed another assessment to eventually pass the course at level one. This felt much better and I was actually getting results. Going on to level two, the game got more complicated and I started to struggle. There was so much to focus on. On completion of this part of the course, they offered me a discount in another diploma course that contained the certificate course on cognitive and behavioural therapy. It was addiction counselling. I jumped at the chance, despite it majorly denting my business account, although I just had one folder to complete this diploma.

The coaching one was similar to the cognitive and behavioural therapy certificate, and I could do this one. With my training delivery from hairdressing materials and learning about coaching with NLP, my answers were clear. I passed that folder too. I was lucky that the materials were fresh in my mind from certain NLP training. This helped. I spent days and nights studying this material. It was probably too much even with my condition, but I loved the material and this put pressure on me to pass these.

I carried on with the cognitive and behavioural one after this. It was more specific, with an angle that was totally cognitive and behavioural. Understandably, that was the course and that's what content they were looking for, but in later therapy work with clients, I never solely used one process by itself. I worked holistically with the person. This in itself taught me a valuable lesson that if I was learning a course, to deliver the work suited exactly to the material I was studying.

The knowledge I got from this was more than I ever expected and it worked well with what I was doing. This was a good choice and direction for me. Again, I passed this through more work than I expected, but with more knowledge gained.

Now, the mentoring folder I confidently took on board. This was unexpectedly not so straight forward. My first exam, I just passed. The second one was sent back and that scar was cut open again, just as my confidence academically was being built. I wasn't unsure of what they were looking for in this course, therefore this built-up confidence took a tumble. I eventually got that one completed through painful slog. My writing was all over the place. My mind was racing ahead and my writing was slower, so there may have been a few things explained at once. I lost clarity.

At my worst, I felt downtrodden, but under no circumstances will the consequences from my injury get the better of me.

No way. So, I pushed that folder into a bag and started with the addiction counselling one.

Having given myself the determination to complete this, I let go of feeling sorry for myself. These lessons were brilliant and relevant to the work I was doing with addictions. I could relate to the content well. Going through this course, I could relate it to experiences I knew that people and clients actually had.

Studying as I was used to, I put in my assessment, only to have it marked as an 'A'. This was my very first 'A' ever. I saw my boys and told them about this, giving them the notion that as a family, there's nothing stopping us getting the highest marks. It is possible.

I got another 'A' and finished the folder. This in itself was another hurdle in life's adventurous game. It gave me such an energy boost and I was on top of the world.

I realised that the one I put away in a bag had been there for ages. I was going to give it another go. I was clearer in thinking and submitted the assessment. A few days later, I got a reply from my tutor saying it had been a while and the work was much improved from the last time. I got a pass. It was only a 'B', but I didn't mind. I was on a roll and finished the folder with relief.

Overall, I got the qualifications and had ran out of material from that company that would have been useful to me. This led me on a quest to find more.

After days and days of searching, I came across something I would have never given a second thought to and that was Open University. There were a lot of people I knew that got qualified this way and there was a lot of very interesting courses. I hoped I could study with them. Going to a university didn't work, so this may be a better option from my own home.

There were introduction units, level one, two and three. I was drawn to the psychology section. This degree was an honours degree and what drew me particularly to this, was that you were registered with the British Psychological Society BPS as a psychologist on completing the degree. That motivated me, so I selected a few courses at the introductory level of level one. It would be absolutely amazing if I got a degree after what I had been through. I wasn't earning, so I got them paid for by the government, which was a change. I would gain the qualification I eventually wanted as a degree and there was no cost. I could only guess that the government would get their money back from me later through tax when I was working, never mind broaden the country's abilities.

The first course was an introduction to psychology. I got in contact with the tutor to gain an understanding and that went well.

It was the same set-up as what I was used to with my last courses, only the book was more fascinating. It covered a lot of facts from popular psychology studies. It was good to get to know who and what they were and it brushed over the main concepts of psychology. This time, when you were submitting an exam, there was a part at the end of it that was for you to explain how you found the exam. It was more formal. There was a particular way the Open University wanted their exams done and following this regimentation was an issue. The difference was with this course, you had a list of requirements for a week, and when the exams were due. I got a high mark, as I thought the way I was doing it was suited to my needs with all this information. I wrote clearly and I thought it didn't blend, yet it did, to my favour. The exams were passed well. I got the highest mark for that one too.

I sat another two courses. At this level, I could do them okay, as I had the formula. Both were good marks. Not as high as before, but the bubble had to burst at some point for me with this unusualness.

By this point, it seemed plausible. I had developed a routine in order to help me. I also got my mum to check my exam work before I submitted it. Yes, there were still grammar problems and I just accepted that. It would mean more work for me and I was now used to things increasing the workload. There were a lot of alterations I had to find, to produce what was required.

I noticed from the website that Open University provided help for students with a disability, so I gave them a call about this and explained that it was acquired dyslexia. There was talk of a dyslexia test and I was apprehensive about the cost. They said they would pay for it, as it would give written testimony that I needed help. It was arranged that I was to see an educational psychologist and get some additional tools to help me learn. This, I got organised first. I had to go to a college in the east of Glasgow that was difficult to get to, so it required a lot of route planning. The time had come and I set off, only to find it straight forward. I met with the person I had to meet and we had a good talk about learning with a disability. I was still defensively biased about my disability, as it could mark me as inferior.

We decided on 'read and write' software that was very good. I could highlight the work I wanted to focus on, and then it would read what I wrote back to me. It had many different voices and it sounded natural, only in certain bits the accent differed with commas and full stops. Regional differences are a big factor and this would have made their job very difficult. It also had a spell check that was detailed and even a medical spell check, which appealed to me greatly. I also got digital mind mapping software, that was useful, but I never really used it, as I do lots of mind maps by hand. Lastly, I got a digital audio recorder – a very good one. I had a digital audio recorder, but with this one you could record and send the information to your computer. Then you would see it written out. I quickly realised these would help my learning a lot. I also got the company who supplied them to visit me and explain how they work. This helped and as time went on I forgot about the rest and only used the bare essentials. It's like buying a new mobile phone, it has so many functions and ways of doing things, yet the priority is phoning and text, maybe taking photos.

I then had an appointment with an educational psychologist to test if I was classed as dyslexic. I had to go to Glasgow. Their area was quite close to the town, but around upmarket houses and flats. It was impressive to see. I had never been in this part before, so I found out where his grand flat was.

He was friendly and I began with tests to do with what I hear, write, my coordination, and sums.

After the tests, we had a good talk he asked if there was any particular part of psychology I would like to be in, which was with the educational process. He said there were elements of my ability that were affected from my head injury in terms of processing, and he said my writing was slow. He then said I had no symptoms of dyslexia. I was relieved in a way, but wondered how this would affect help with the Open University.

A week later I got the report emailed to me. It was pages long and I was just looking for black print where my defaults were under this sea of complicated facts and figures from other experiments. The Open University got one too and I phoned them about this. With trained eyes, they explained what it meant and that they would send it off to SAAS to get the go-ahead for learning support. This was accepted and I got letters from them verifying this. In contact with a firm down south, they asked if I could send them a copy of this. There was confusion in what they could offer and I could not locating the letters, so I gave it a miss. Anyway, I had my new toys to use.

With this episode at the university course, I was scared handing work in at this level. The scar of failure was always there – the pitfalls and losses I had recently experienced laid the foundations these failures had amounted to. It was so difficult to work out what they were looking for that I kept getting lost in what material to use. At this pace, my slower processing let me down and there were lots of times where the social embarrassment of getting a low score affected me, although I got passes all the same. Putting large amounts of effort into my whole life finally paid off with a visible result.

Getting low marks and not understanding information that was said too fast for my processing left me looking as if I couldn't be bothered, or that I put in the least possible amount of time. It gave the impression it was something I had to do. That's far from the truth. This was my aim and I loved the challenge. My way of measuring success was different from general society. After what I had been through, this bar was at its peak and I was running at full speed downhill, until the pressures of this academic requirement were over. Academic life is suited to a particular type of people with their way of retaining information. My learning strategy wasn't suited to this method of learning. I was more suited to hands-on learning. I preferred to be shown, not to read alone about the instructions. It was challenging to remember the details explained in writing. I preferred to be shown. There were other senses to pick up what's needed – visual and feeling senses were prominent in my choice to gain information.

This course was a much tougher discipline and covering so much in a short time. This got me flustered. It was an Open University level two and the first course was very interesting, yet covered all the basic formats in detail so fast that I was struggling. The compactness of this course posed a problem to me in knowing what to pay attention to for exams. I got four books to study from the OU. There was a fantastic amount of study that I had never been used to. This aggravated my short-term memory challenges. Then I came across a problem I never knew I had, as this was a very new concept for me. It had to do research. All those formulas and the way it was laid out with quantitative studying, I struggled with. Reading the books, there was a barrage of new language and it wasn't long before my head went numb and I lost the plot.

I got extra help from my tutor. This helped, but because I didn't use it regularly, the learning drifted into the horizon to just fade away. This lowered my marks to just scraping by. I got good marks in level one, to scrape by in level two. This was an unexpected blow to me.

After these low marks, there was a big formal exam at the end of the course in Glasgow. Because of my slower writing and the fact that I could be easily distracted, I was given the okay to use a laptop in another building in quiet room. I had never experienced this formality before to check up on the vast amount of work in the whole course.

By chance, where I was actually working at Phoenix Health, the funding had ended and I had lots of time to spare. This time was taken up by revision. I was so worried that my memory would fail me that I ploughed on, revising night and day.

Out of the four books, they said we were only to study two intensely. I didn't fancy my luck, so I intensely studied them all. This was a mammoth task, but I wasn't going to let my memory fail me. I feared picking the wrong topic to study and wasting all that time. I used all the techniques I had learned to help with memory. I learned new ways of remembering. Coming up to the exam, I was impressed with what I could remember like names, dates and contents, although I had no experience of remembering this amount before. Whether it was my injury demanding attention, or that I simply had never experienced this, was just about impossible to work out. Whatever the cause, it was immense, hard work that was extreme to me. I relaxed using trance and that helped a lot.

The exam came and I soared through it using my added extra time with breaks. What a relief. After all those months, the exam was over. I had learned an immense amount and I was very lucky I was off work then. How would I be with other exams? I was sure I had done it well and it faded into past as you have to wait for the results.

Six weeks later I got a text from a student buddy saying the marks were out. I looked and I hadn't passed. I plummeted after thinking I had done well. This drew the onset of a dark looming cloud around me.

I had to resit the exam and was thinking this would be the way for every exam. This was going to take ages. I had a week of intense revision, only this time it wasn't that intense. I had forcibly learned the material and went over how to present it. I seemed to know the material, only this time I could focus on detail of the coursework. The time came again and I was the only person in the room. I finished ahead of time and this time I didn't commit myself to success as before, I'd wait and see. If it was a fail, I would have to resit the course again. At this rate, it would take me decades to complete, but I was going to finish. It would have to be a big thing and not passing the exams was one of them. Eventually, I got a pass this time, only I was ready for the worst. Was this the right way to learn a lot of information myself, with big formal exams?

I started the next course, which I was dreading. It was solely based on research. I did the project online with a group and we worked on university chat lines on the website. I chose a qualitative research project to learn this better this time. We all got along well and in the beginning, I mentioned my disability after not really getting any help about this particular course. There was one woman who said she would help explain difficult areas for me. I thanked her for her help.

Being a people person, I bonded well with the group and encouraged those who had strengths in certain areas, to play their part. It was getting marked as to how we all worked together. My thing was designing question sheets for the experiment. Overall, it went well and we brought our skills together and used them as one. This ended with a pass and I was glad to move on.

Talking to my study buddy, Debbie, we worked out with the other courses, we had to gain more points to get the honours degree. In the free time we had, we selected courses to get the points up. My choice was a counselling one, which was at level one. It suited me, as I knew what was involved. It was passed okay.

Now the next was the main course of child psychology. With this one, I went out of my way for learning support, so I didn't get into so much bother as with the last courses I did. The help seemed unnecessary at first. It seemed too simplistic, although the main help I got was in writing for exams. The effort was painfully hard, having to dissect details of every sentence, but after six months it paid off. Also, while processing lots of information, it put priorities into action and I was aware of what was needed for the work.

I saw my help once a week and this was beneficial to me and personally, it sorted my grammar out in sentence writing. I also found out different point of views that made my life difficult. Everyone at university rewrites what they do a good few times. It's not just me that rewrites work, everyone does. This was a cross that I bore, assuming folk only did it the once and then checked over their work. This was a relief to find out and was emphasised many times by our tutor for this course. She explained how to submit work, as the standards were higher now. This also helped. It was coaching on a different level.

I scraped past the exams; although the work wasn't hard, it was the presentation that was the big learning curve for me. The course work at times, was very interesting and I would have not have gone into these topics in detail otherwise.

It came to the formal exam again and this time, I was to have it at home. Because I was the only one in a hall, they would need someone to oversee that I was doing it correctly. This would have cost them, and I suspect it was more cost effective at my home with an adjudicator.

I was prepared differently in my revision for the exam. This time I just focused on two parts and had to research dyslexia and dysphasia. Also, this time I was fitting the content into other questions, so I learned the material intensely, and that was different from before.

The exam came and I completed it just on time. I covered the material well, but under no circumstances was I going to say I had done well after the last episode. A strange depressive entity was present with me from that moment on. I thought about being positive and my answer was that it wouldn't change the person marking my work, so that didn't help. Once this course was out of the way, the course's back would be broken. There were only two courses left. These were level three and both difficult. They were the hardest yet to come, but the worst was over, as far as volume of work went.

My results were in and I passed it the first time. With the learning help, this taught me how to pass exams.

So I got books from the university on how to study the Open University way and a recommended book on what the next course was about: cognitive psychology.

I talked to a career advisor about furthering this degree when completed to do a PhD in educational psychology or occupational psychology. To earn a doctorate has always been a distant dream from the beginning, now it was a dream that could come true. The taste was getting clearer now.

If I got an honours degree in psychology, then a doctorate in psychology, it would be a magnificent, triumphant stand-up from a person with an acquired brain injury, to get onto this plateau of mastery. I was feeling worthwhile and psychology went perfectly with what I was working as. This gave me greater opportunity to take clients on, and eventually gave back the identity I lost, only this time it was greater than before after my development. I had used what had happened to me as an advantage. Instead of ignoring it, I took the differences head on and came out the other side.

I got my results in from one of the big level three course of cognitive therapy. It was a fail. I was shocked. This popped the bubble of earning a doctorate. My legs were unbelievably kicked away again. It crashed me to the bottom again, and I lost my direction. In my last hope, I contacted a friend who I know just got a doctorate in sports psychology. She got an interview to be taken onto the paid course to get her PhD in research. I asked her what her grade was when finishing her degree. She said first class honours. I was under the impression that she got a lower mark due to her dyslexia. Bang went that theory. My dream for years had been knocked off the wall.

This wasn't going to get me down. I had put so much effort into getting this far, in no way was I going to let my injury win. If it took longer due to resits, then fine. I was going to bloody get this. I had to change this drive I had of getting to a specific academic level to have achieved what I wanted. I went back to the trail of passing for self-improvement and drew out plans for my stress management business ideas to flourish. This was hard going, to lose my footing and always have my face to the wind, sometimes blowing at gale force. It wasn't going to win. I survived for a reason and maybe this wasn't going to be the primary direction for me to help change people's lives. Maybe it would be in a different way. Studying very hard, week after week, I now had two major exams to come and I would be prepared for them. Maybe my business was the way to go after the studying.

You don't know how you will deal with traumatic situations until you are actually experience them. Self-survival turns its head and you adapt to how your personality, life learnings and experiences take on form. This form can vary depending on the person, on their motivation levels. It's like having an athletic outlook. Forget everything else that takes up space in your mind. Know what you want to achieve and make it clear and inviting inside your mind. Having a clear picture in your mind, gives you motivation to achieve. I solely worked on this, not expecting to deal with lots of things at once. You can only process one thing at a time, so why make it more complicated? It has no benefits. What motivation I had came from Chen Man-Ch'ing. He had a head injury, then created Tai Chi Yang style and was a calligraphy master. I could achieve what I wanted in life, it was just a matter of finding the right strategy. Through NLP and psychology, your body is always transforming and renewing. With the right frame of mind, you can achieve just about anything. The limitations faded. It is unwritten social restrictions and expectations that dictate how you should be. How you should be, depends solely on yourself. I had discovered this basic key of life that is at the core of survival. The main aspect is social expectations and presumed limitations to your potential —they influence your development. That is important.

CHAPTER 10

The New Me Part 2:

I'm starting to win. (I'll never let it win.)

All our dreams can come true if we have the courage to pursue them.

– Walt Disney

Knowing the other, know thyself and the victory will not be at risk: Know the ground, know the natural conditions, and the victory will be total.

– Lao Tzu

After the loss of work, apart from my studying challenge, I was so keen to work again and this was taken away during my attempt to scrape a living helping others. I had a lot of time spare in the week now and was in a panic about how to fill it. The thought of being stuck at home was cabin fever for me. I had great urgency to fill my time. I had spent time becoming self-employed and learned book keeping at the same time. I didn't want to fail when what had been my rescue was not acceptable, so I went to a volunteer centre in Greenock.

In an interview, there were some good ideas for placements, but I got the impression I was just filling a hole. Then she mentioned a place called Phoenix Health Initiative. We were in the same building as Stepwell, even when I was there at a placement from college. I knew the team leader. He was in the army at one point and was the only person I knew who had done an Iron Man triathlon. What an achievement. I had a lot of respect for him. Then, he gave me advice on eating good quality brown bread for fast energy needs.

They had moved around the corner from the volunteer centre and arranged for me to meet with Steve. I went around and the place looked brilliant. It was jumping. There was a room used by the National Lottery people, so there was folk coming and going. There was a woman from Children First, who had kids and parents coming and going. Then there were two nurses who did health checks, two development workers, Jackie who was a nurse and knew me from an old folks' home I was placed in for a while during college, and a male who was once a doctor. They belonged to Phoenix and it was Adam who did the administrative section. There were two rooms used for meetings. One was a very large, long room and the other just a large room. This was the room I was going to use.

Talking to Steve, this arrangement seemed perfect for the nurses doing health checks; if they came across folk who needed therapy or counselling, they would refer them to me. I was very pleased to work in such a medical environment and wore my medical tunic all the time, to look like a follow-on from them. It seemed this was what I was looking to do, holding my wishes and aims.

I was to start twice a week volunteering. They paid my bus fares, which helped. I made the room I was in relaxed, yet clinical to suit the company. They were to paint the room a relaxing colour and got some lamps to go with the relaxing chairs, a low table, a massage bed and a computer desk with a computer I eventually got.

I was starting to build a reputation locally with people's carers. This was a good example of word of mouth getting you established.

At times, the nurses doing health checks, Ryan and Jill, came with me as we went to different companies offering health checks. This was a new angle for me and I enjoyed it, making me feel important by getting referrals on the day and also back at the centre from the other staff's patients.

In starting, if there was a quiet moment, I saw each staff member and gave them a treatment, depending on their own needs. Sometimes it was a relaxation massage like an Indian head massage that is not invasive – this treatment is one of my specialities. I take people into complete relaxation. I flow the moves with varying pressure, so they get caught up in my movements and forget about their worries. Slowing down the pace deeply relaxed them also. I gave the nurses this along with remedial massage for a sore back, painful necks and leg strains. This paid itself well, as they knew what their patient would be getting when they referred them to me. I started to keep records of every visit I got.

What helped was that Steven knew what I could do from working at Step Well. I delivered training one time to staff, clients and other health professionals. This was a training class on stress control with NLP, in Step Well's building. He knew I could do this from seeing me do it before.

Adam, the administrator, asked me if I could bring in my qualifications to get them photocopied. I brought them in and my qualifications were like a mini book with all my studying. I had six therapy diplomas, five diplomas in counselling, a COSCA counselling award, training and developing qualification, and the same for being a practitioner/master practitioner, coach, hypnosis coach, life coach in NLP, hypnosis, hairdressing, swimming coach and more. Needless to say, it looked like I don't like television much. That kept Adam busy photocopying for a long time. My two days were busy there and I really enjoyed it.

There was a time when I was down in Largs and I got a call from Steven, saying a suicidal man came in for help and with my certificate in dealing with these situations, he asked me to come to the centre as soon as possible and he would pay me the conventional price I charged. So I went up. He was with one of the nurses and I came in, showing I was intently listening professionally to give guidance and direction.

I understood the problem that was causing him so much unrest and he said he was going to jump off the Erskine road bridge, which was infamous for suicides. I created a pattern break for him to get out of that stuck thinking. What he enjoyed the most and focused on was his desire up for doing up cars. I asked him for what cars he could do up and gave him another focus.

I showed him coping skills that he showed me he could use when things get tough and he feels a lot of social pressure again. I produced more self-control and he was okay after this. I saw him weekly to coach him on problems he had. This was putting my skills to good use. I thoroughly enjoyed working there voluntarily. I signed up with the Job Centre to help me look for full-time work and this was good for gaining experience.

I wanted to work at Phoenix on an employee basis. They had tried to get funding for me on three occasions and on the last attempt, they eventually got funding for my service. After spending almost two years doing voluntary work, they made me the highest paid in the centre. This made me the highest paid person in the company, yet this left the pressure of high expectations the staff may have of me.

I was to work three days. This left me one day to work at Carers Inverclyde and I had worked there for years. This let me carry on doing this.

Through this employment I provided many health services to the local community: a service to groups for SAMH; routes from prison for people released back into society, to help them get on track; school relaxation for health weeks; a clinical centre for the elderly who had dementia; seeing clients on a one-to-one basis, referred by our nurses, community nurses, doctors, NHS psychiatrists, psychologists and other health professionals.

I also dealt with palliative care clients and conditions that were permanent in terms of how they could be better with more balance, and coping skills taught through life coaching.

It wasn't long before I was made up to four days a week and was tightly booked with appointments, which I loved. It was like being busy as I was once before, in my position of hairdressing. I was lucky I could use my skills to help people. It seemed a lot, yet it all had one thing in common – helping people. Only their limitations were blocking their progress and development. Showing other opportunities to clients opened doors to new ways of achieving.

This was what I aimed for – to be giving health care, counselling and life coaching with other health professionals. I was very happy with this secondary health care role.

My therapy room looked good; I was left to do my own thing and the activity sheets were completed by me. This was perfect. I didn't have to struggle working out where the person was coming from with the particular topic they required, I planned out summary figures covering all the work I did to prove its worth. I had no one looking over my shoulder about what was done and what wasn't done. I guess I acquired this from the Rainbow Room, having been left alone to do my own and salon's figures. In achieving this, this position overall gave me inner peace with no distractions that made me perform at my best. I felt so alive now.

Another person who worked in the building was Karen from Children First. We got along so well. I loved the way she worked and as time went on, we had a great arrangement where while she sees a kid, I could see their parent about their difficulties. We were a good team and we had fun. I haven't laughed and enjoyed working with others like that for years.

She planned some very funny staff jokes for me. There was one time I had got an angry, red spot on the tip of my nose and I couldn't hide it, so I brought it up first thing when I went into my work. I was dealing with some paperwork in the main office area, when she called my name. I looked up, only to witness all the staff had comedy red noses on. I roared with laughter. We all had red noses.

There was another time I discreetly told her about an experience I had never come across before with a private client. I was giving her a back massage at her house. That was fine. Going there, I discovered she had two cats. She apologised and made a huge effort to move them into another room. I love cats and said it didn't bother me at all. She instantly relaxed.

I first saw her shoulder blade for remedial help. Then I gave her a relaxing back massage after the work I did on her shoulder and back areas to deal with her complaints. I used just carrier oil to help me work out her tightness.

When I was working on her back, one cat came up and lay down at the bottom of the massage bed. She got worked up and I said it was no problem.

After her shoulders, I went down the spine to her lower back, where she was having pain. In assessing the area of the iliac bone, I came across two gigantic medial muscle knots.

I said, "These are rock firm on both sides. This was interesting to discover."

With her head in the massage bed hole for faces, Eileen's tensed up, as if this was unfamiliar ground she was in and she wasn't too sure what I said. She thought I was talking about her bum. Reassuringly I addressed the situation and explained that I meant her lower back and this was one of the largest build-ups of knots I had seen before. That eased her and I saw her relax again.

I wanted to make her relaxed, so I spent much effort providing a relaxing back massage. This was working and such a relief for the misunderstanding.

I have NEVER known a cat to like oil before. While doing the relaxing movements, the cat arose and moved up slowly towards her back. It began to sniff, as cats do, gently, and I thought this was cute. I carried on with my massage. Then out of the blue, the cat started licking her back. The cat was not leaning on her at all. She just felt the tongue on her lower back as my hands massaged her.

She froze again with tenseness and puzzlement and I had to react quickly by saying the first thing that came to mind. "It isn't me who licked your back, it was your cat." This didn't help at all. After a few more licks when I was talking, she relaxed and burst into laughter.

I told her I have never known cats to like this oil before and we both had a full-blown laugh. "Anyway," I said, "my tongue is not jaggy." What an experience, and I managed to steer the service away from what could have been an embarrassing moment.

My colleague and I laughed about this. Then the next day, I was taking a group in the big conference room. Once I had finished, I was walking back to my room to sort this out again. She said to me, "That's your client in." I looked puzzled, as I knew I had a half hour to catch up. She said she was early and waiting in my room. Normally, clients wait for me seated in the hall before we begin, so I hurried around thinking there must be a particular issue. There was nobody in my room... except a toy cat that was sitting on my massage bed.

After my pause, I said, "Ha, ha," sarcastically, only then to be drowned out by hysterical laughter in the background. I joined in. I really enjoyed our sense of humour and we were on the same wavelength.

As well as working with her at times, I also taught massage at schools for relaxation as part of health week. There were also transport police, firemen, Karen from Children's First, internet security, myself and more.

We all had classes through the day at scheduled times and then we met up with the others at breaks and lunch.

During my school classes, I told them about relaxation and the benefits of this, to help them. I also made it fun and the kids enjoyed it, having a laugh. I then showed the basic three moves to the Indian head massage. I used their teacher and explained the slow pace, the flow of movements and how it relaxes them, as well as them working on their neighbour in the class. I taught them to use the correct stance and hand positions.

After showing them the moves, I would go around the class giving positive help. It went very well. The class was energised with the same level. I suggested to the teachers doing something like that promotes a pattern break and gets them to focus on something different, rather than cause trouble. The secret was creating unity, so they were all thinking in a similar fashion.

At the end of the day, it was exhausting, yet it was absolutely brilliant. I showed the kids how to relax and have fun. They thought highly of me, as my delivery was nothing they had experienced before.

I also started doing group work for the alcohol unit. This was difficult at first, as my delivery was like nothing any of them had experienced, so my flow was broken often. I began to notice health problems that may cause folk to drink, due to their circumstances. After doing regular sessions every few weeks, I got to know a lot of them and some came in to me for one-to-one coaching. With my dad having a so-called liking for alcohol, I could relate to what they were saying and experiencing.

It moved to a new location and incorporated health care into social care, offering a detox of alcohol and counselling for the social effect. I offered life coaching to give a positive approach for direction. Anne, who ran the section I worked with, was an absolute saint. She left me to get on with what I do and I gave her results. This was a great working partnership. I had a lot of respect for her.

About this time I managed to get a centre-page spread about me in the local paper, with a big photo of me with my tunic on pointing in a motivating way. It got me noticed.

At the old peoples' drop-in centre I provided gentle massage on a set-up chair that was non-invasive and less complicated, as dementia was a common condition. To get in, I buzzed the outside door and a nurse let me in. The nurse opened the door and was so enthusiastic about my story in the paper that was published in the *Greenock Telegraph*. She took my hand, led me into the room and went to the doorway where the elderly people were. She said, "Listen everyone, we have a celebrity here. This is Tom and he is in the paper centre pages." She showed them the paper.

Then I noticed one lady who looked sort of intuitively puzzled by me and kept this same look for ages. It made me uneasy, the way she looked at me, even though she was a patient. The nurse said I was here to provide some relaxing shoulder or hand massages, if anyone wanted one. She still kept looking at me in that certain way. I eventually said to her, "Is there something you want to ask me?"

She paused, then she said, "Are you a stripper?"

Instantly, the old woman who sat next to her said, "I want a full body massage."

Inside I said, *I'm a celebrity, get me out of here!* (The famous British television programme.)

Back at the centre, I laughed so much about this. It was the questionable look on the woman's face, never mind her neighbour's request.

This was a funny side of my role and I was doing a job I created – secondary care from the medical model. I was changing people's lives by positively showing them ways they can cope and change with their problems. It is up to them to give themselves the control to change. After all, from their perception, they created this to such an extent, which commonly has health-related side effects. They created this. Knowing they created it, they were able create another version. This was the career I wished for so much, that gave me strength to push on, especially in hard times. I believed in myself and I got there.

Madeleine from Paris: Another Son

Now knowing a lot of people from Europe who presumed I was another foreigner, I was invited for a European gathering where we had a meal. There was a new face, and I got the chance to talk to this Parisian girl. I found her attractive with eyes I just melted into and we got along well together. She had a very hard time working out my Scottish accent, never mind my foreign accent, yet we got along well together. My relaxed, slower speech that I had learned made it easier for her to understand.

We ended up swapping email addresses and we wrote a lot to each other. I gained a friend (and someone French too).

It took a few phone calls for her to get used to my Scottish accent that I thought I had diminished, as she had never come across this dialect of the English language before. I have no doubt my accent sounded more like the Scottish islands with its roll of words, giving softness to expected, typical tones.

It was almost a daily event, speaking on the phone or online. She wanted to visit me in Scotland. I agreed and we met as friends at Prestwick airport.

On seeing her, she looked even better than when I first saw her. Her skin colour looked prettily tanned which I found attractive next to my pale Scottish skin tone. Her eyes were of such a beautiful shade of brown that I couldn't help getting lost in them.

The trip in the car, I felt a nervous bonding between us. Two people who work primarily on feelings and sensations pulled together from the beginning in a non-verbal way.

She had a thing about red hair and I was overjoyed about this, with what I call my 'titian locks'.

From then on, I was to fly back to France often; only this time to Paris, and the plane trips were regular and less expensive at times from Prestwick.

Being over there often, to pass the time when she was working, I ran and swam at the public swimming baths right next to the Eiffel Tower. Swimming past the window, you were greeted with the sight of the tower looking supremely majestic. This was an unexpected pleasure.

We felt both comfortable with each other. It just felt right. Our personalities intertwined.

Even with our families, there were many compliments to show they were pleased for us. That was surely a sign of their approval. Even one of her brothers, his wife and their young kid came over for the Viking festival in Largs with Madeleine. They stayed at a bed and breakfast and Michelle stayed with me as usual when she came over here.

It rained most of the week, which showed Scotland as it really is. I have a saying that rain was invented in Greenock, just up the road from me. This is due to its geographical disposition. It's often raining there. When rain has its money's worth, Scotland will be a very rich country.

We visited Arran, which she loved, and went there a good few times during her other visits. We went to Edinburgh with its castle, Glen Coe and of course Loch Ness, but we didn't see any monster. It must have been his day off, or he was working on a different shift that day.

There was talk of us starting a family and due to her age, she said her chances of becoming pregnant were limited. She even saw a French doctor about this and he confirmed she only had a limited chance.

Going by my own experience in family planning, it would take months and months for this to happen and it may be too late for her, with the little time we saw each other. I said that if it does or doesn't happen, that's okay. This helped her not to get anxious about this. Little did I know that she amazingly would fall pregnant the next month.

I was delighted to have another child, only crowded by how suddenly it happened. We were both surprised at how quickly it happened, and had an on-going joke about how good my sperm swam, and I said it is because I am a swimming coach on Thursday evenings.

With the sperm count of 1,000,000 that go swimming, only one gets through. The rest aren't even given certificates of attempted achievement.

In asking me what I had done one day, I said I was making consolation certificates for my sperm, only I have a few million left to make.

Both of us nearing forty, it would be a great new start to life again. Some folk only get one child. This was going into my third. I looked into moving to Paris, a complete new start for me. Not going into things half-heartedly, I was to begin again on new territory.

At school, I did poorly at French and was in the remedial class. I was going to be a mechanic then and didn't see much need for a mechanic to speak fluent French in the West of Scotland. This time I was relearning it with CDs, books and classes. It was a very hard struggle learning this language and I found out vital bits of information that I probably picked up at school.

A foreign language holds a different way of explaining events from a different part of the world. I came across this for the first time when I went to the Pyrenees: don't try to learn French logically. This didn't work for me. I learned it with an open holistic approach, with the *want* of learning this language. My theme was to get into the French way of thinking and mimic it. The best way to learn is being flung in at the deep end and going to France where you have to use it. This was always my approach, to learn from experience and not waste time trying to perfect it. Having to use the language all the time is my key. If it is just learned, it can be forgotten. 'If you don't use it, you lose it,' is a saying that's particularly true in this case. Get as much information about it as possible and tailor the importance of learning this to suit you. This gives me motivation.

With me struggling to learn French during my frequent visits to Paris, she was getting big now, and when she went to see a midwife, she asked what size the baby was. The nurse said it was about the size of a little chicken. At that point, I called the baby was 'petit poulet Paterson', soon to become grand poulet. During a scan we found out the baby was a boy. I was slowly making the Paterson football team with Adam being the striker. An overall nickname we had for the baby was 'Poulet Paterson'.

Life is a mystery; whatever comes your way, it's what you make of it that's the difference. Accept everything openly as an opportunity and then decide how much of an opportunity it can be for you. If it's not important, just let it go. Finally, just do it, by taking action. Don't be dragged into analysing, just put it into action. This was my way that I learned from my big change. The results may not be exactly what you wanted, it's a result bringing you closer to your aim compared with being stuck in 'paralysis by analysis'. You are getting a result. Very few things are accomplished the first time, remember that.

Confronting the fear of a situation is only as bad as how it is represented to you. You are simply confronting it in another way, to get the results you want, making it your opportunity. The more you confront these, the easier it becomes and develops into a second nature, giving you an abundance of energy and control and knowledge that you've mastered it. I did it and so can you, any time. It just takes a will, practice and knowledge that gives you purpose.

Time was getting close and we still hadn't chosen a name. It got more and more complicated with the haunting theme of this baby of ours having an international name.

There was a continual joke on my behalf with one name that I kept suggesting – Thomas. Whenever we were stuck in the invention of new names, I introduced Thomas funnily and this standing joke was born.

The only particular thing I wanted, was the name to be French. Looking through the more popular names, I came across a category of names. I narrowed it down to Jean-Francois. This name just rang bells for me. Madeline wanted my surname, bringing a sense of pride, knowing I would grow my family name.

The first name was to be a dually settled name and we had three good options, so we could see what name suits the baby better when he was born.

On Saturday morning, I got a call from Madeleine, saying she was suffering contractions. I launched into a panic. Having my boys for the weekend, this brought up worrying complications. Just earlier, Tania phoned and said that they were away for the weekend in Edinburgh, so taking them back home was not an option unfortunately.

Going on the last hope my mum would help, I tried frantically in vain to get a flight booked for that day. It wasn't possible. I told my mum that I couldn't get a flight that day, but got one for Sunday, so could she look after the boys for me that day? Missing the birth was a devastating blow to me. The odds of being in another country, made the odds slimmer and slimmer to be actually present the birth. The pain kept returning when my mind wandered back to not being there.

I went at a hundred miles an hour, getting organised, and ensuring tasks were done before I went. My car that needed a new battery after failing to start. With the help of the breakdown company, it got started, yet it was a weak battery. It couldn't be left till I got back, then it would be completely flat.

I was nervous on the flight and was wound up. I just had the name of the hospital she was at and the metro station. I needed to find my way, as well as been so keen the new boy and Madeleine.

After getting to Beauvais airport, it was a long bus journey to Paris.

When I got to Porte Maillot, I went on my usual walk to the Arc de Triomphe, then followed the road to Trocadéro near to where she lived.

At the flat, her sister and brother were there to take me to see them. Changing the metro line to the correct stop, it was a long walk in an area I was completely lost in. I was greatly thankful to them for being there. I would have undoubtedly got lost if it wasn't for them.

Going into the modern hospital to the fourth floor where their room was, the cleanliness smell of a ward brought back memories that instilled tight etching inside my stomach. That was calmed down by the excitement of seeing them.

We went into the single bedroom where they both were. I went over to Madeleine and gave her an extended embrace followed by a heartfelt kiss. Her sister brought our baby from the cot he was in.

He looked so delicate and small. About five pounds in weight, he seemed so fragile. He was the most beautiful baby, born with amazing deep brown eyes. He was young and handsome. His eyes were so pure that you could see his loving soul. Maybe that was just from his parents' point of view, yet I felt it was far more than my opinion. Seeing the reactions from others justified this, giving me proof that it wasn't just me. He had such a serene aura about him. So peaceful, he was like some all-knowing mentor who was reborn into another life.

I held him and felt so much love for him. There was no sign of my Celtic skin colouring (in Scottish terminology, peely wally) He got tones from the wondrously beautiful, healthy, sun-kissed colouring of Madeleine's Caribbean mother. This worked perfectly with his gorgeous deep brown eyes. The suggestion of hair projected there was darker hair, not red, although it was early days, maybe later as the hair strengthens up, a hint of redness.

I expressed to Madeleine how bad I felt about not being there at the birth. I know the odds were so slim. There was not an actual date that she would go into labour, never mind taking time off my work. The birth was just four days earlier than my pre-booked flight. I was taking off a week before and two weeks after to plan for being at the birth. That wasn't to be, no matter how much I planned. One part of me knew it was slim chance that I would be there due to distance and other things. The other part of me felt so bad, ridden with guilt.

I stayed at her flat alone and was to see her every day. I knew what metro station to go to now and how to get to the hospital from there. I thought of one time running to the hospital although it wasn't a good idea, being so sweaty in there. The metro was always good fun for people watching. On the metro, I kept thinking back to one time with the impression that English was not commonly used; four girls got on the train and the girls all had Nordic long blonde hair and also similarities in looks. I said to Madeleine that they look like sisters. The look I got back was piercingly funny. They kept staring at me with that disgusted look. Madeleine told me to just watch speaking English, as a good percentage of people speak it or know the basics of it. That was on the same line and passing the station where they got on, it kept flooding back to me.

The flat needed tidying up because Madeleine was caught unaware, that's completely understandable. I didn't have a lot of money and just got survival rations to last me until they got out of hospital. I was always drawn to struggle, and always coped. Possibly through what happened to me and the effort I had to put in. Maybe it has always been 'me' to push myself, 'going against the tide' to just get by under the most conditions.

Four days later, eventually they were to get out of the hospital. On the same day, I was asked to go to a new parents' talk by the medical staff, about looking after your baby at home. A woman head nurse talked and I didn't know what she was saying. I was drawn in, listening for medical words I knew of and that helped me guess what she was talking about. Seeing things she was using and how she was using them helped in its own little way.

When they talked to Madeleine about leaving the hospital, she mentioned about not talking French and the nurse was surprised. With the way I was listening intently and giving her more attention than the others, she didn't even question that.

I had a car seat we could use, taking us back by cab.

The excitement of having a new child in a place where I didn't really know French was full and scary. Me being me, I got energy from this.

We got home and made sure the basics were there for the three of us to get along and start up a routine.

Going by how we felt while choosing a name, we had decided on not picking one beforehand, in case it didn't suit him.

Now we decided on a name for him: Luca.

When Madeleine was in hospital, I had to register his birth with a certain department. Jean-Michelle came with me for help and we got his birth registered. Now it was to get him an ID card. To register him for this, we went to the government building. It was busy and it wasn't long before Luca started crying. We didn't have a dummy with us for some reason, so I said I would run home and get one, which I did. It was a long way away and because of my mind was racing with thoughts of him, I nearly got knocked down by a car. I reacted quickly, thankfully, to avoid injury. Still a shock though. In Paris, as with any city, driving becomes a quest for self-survival at such a fast pace. There are a few that don't like to take prisoners. They are out for the kill.

Eventually, I found it in the flat and ran back to the council buildings. I had to take a few routes, as I wasn't too clear of its location. What makes it worse, I was under pressure.

Eventually finding it again, I went inside. It was busy and I couldn't see them anywhere. After a mixture of sitting, standing and looking in different rooms for them, I waited, and after nearly forty minutes, Michelle came out and took me into the furthest point where I could not see where I was. She was having an interview with a woman who spoke a bit of English. She asked me about my profession on Luca's birth certificate. I explained I was a therapist working holistically, mainly with stress, where she went into the usual tale about needing one in this place. Having so many people they see and are involved with, I put my hands up and agreed without a doubt.

All done, and now we had to wait for it to be posted.

On the same subject, I went to the British embassy to get Luca registered and travelled there on my own. I took the metro to Madeleine station and worked out my route from there. As normal, I got a bit lost. My usual method of getting directions worked well now. I sort of knew who to ask. Eventually I found it with a French policeman outside. I had to pass through a metal detector. It was just like the airport again. I even had my passport with me in case they asked. Entering the far-away room, there were a lot of different people with a vast array of problems that brought them there. When it was my turn, it was such a relief to have such a light subject for them to work with. They kept asking me if there was anything else, as if expecting problems like stolen passports or deaths.

With this done, he could now get a British passport when applied for. That was another box ticked.

Getting back to changing, brought back the first experience of cleaning up a filled nappy. It was like riding a bike, you just don't forget.

I found it more of a difficulty making up bottles of milk with a special device for heating baby bottles. What was different from Paris to Scotland was that in Scotland, the water being better, the milk was just made from water from the tap. In Paris, they used special bottled water. With limited space, this was a hassle for me, and time consuming. I got there. I loved feeding Luca and winding him afterwards was a chore to remember how it was done; what I remembered was for older kids and a more boisterous way.

The district midwife came and said she was like Mary Poppins, which instantly likened me to her and her sense of humour. This was a big help and refreshed my winding.

She mentioned baby massage and I was in my form.

I did this regularly with Luca and it proved calming for him:

another huge benefit of touch. It was done at a slow, relaxing pace, that was gentle. This worked so well. I also kept singing to him my favourite Scottish songs: The Dark Isle and A Scottish Soldier. Singing these songs in a soft, slow, relaxing voice worked so well. With what I had learned about conditioning, when I started singing, he very quickly relaxed and calmed down. His company was so relaxing and comforting. I had never experienced this with any baby before. This was so special. Going by the lesson that everybody is different, this was a difference on its own. He radiantly glowed.

Taking him anywhere, he caught people's attention and they melted with his charm. In a supermarché, waiting in the queue, a woman behind me gave him so much attention. She said to me that he seduced her. I was taken aback: seduction seemed only plausible with adults, yet the French descriptive version was so different and used in everyday situations. After finding out its meaning in French, I found it amusing.

This led to more interesting things I became aware of after having Luca: from babies and from the French. With me using massage and having the new understanding of touch with communication, he was very receptive. Being so young, it was my way of communicating with him. I used what I had learned by touch to slow it down to enhance sensations, even pick up what reactions his body was showing. How the mind works with this embodiment, is a way of picking up communications that have no words. The touch being so even and smooth followed a certain pattern of relaxed sensations, creating even more relaxation. When he got upset, I just calmed him down by gentle touch, giving him a new interest to fill his mind. From his mum and myself, sensitivity was high and he picked this up; whether it was somehow genetic, he picked this up very quickly from us. I had never experienced this in a child to this degree before. Maybe I was more receptive to this difference now, which made it stand out. This led to thoughts of intelligence. Maybe being more attuned, he could instantly pick up on what's needed with his senses, or he was just a clever boy. I guess only time will tell.

Having had babies before, I was grey in remembering how to change nappies again. Failing to remember details, I questioned my memory difficulties again. Time had just about removed nappy changing memory now. Being in a different country and having her first child, it was important for Madeleine to look after Luca well. This increased pressure on by myself to give the image of experience to help her. Having to study the process in detail helped, only I was lost with how to mix up milk. I remembered how to burp after feeding, but I had to be careful.

As the old saying goes, it is just like riding a bike, you never forget, and thankfully it didn't take long for it all to come flooding back.

I felt Madeleine was going out of her way for me. I was giving something back to her and Luca, with his dark brown eyes that captured your soul, and I so loved him. He had his mum's eye colour and the energetic drive in them from me. This gave him a special combination.

As time gathered great haste, Madeleine felt the summons of having to return to work, which seemed a lot quicker than back home in Britain. This was a worrying time for her and she needed to get Luca taken care of when she was at work. Her mother offered, which would have been a blessing, yet her health wasn't good and giving her this much constant pressure would have not been good for her, never mind this making Madeleine feel guilty of endangering her mum's health. There is a shortage of childcare in Paris that was witnessed through our experience of looking. The overall verdict was, yes, there is childcare, yet it's very expensive. The understanding that someone is making a living out of this, that's acceptable, yet there's a limit in expense we could afford. Then she got an interview to a local crèche/nursery. Selling her story of basically working full-time and living alone, only with help from me at the cheap expense of Ryanair, she eventually got a placement.

She was so excited when she phoned me, it was similar to when you pass your driving test the first time.

He settled in at nursery well. All the other children favoured Luca for company. This was such a preference, to see the response from the other children to Luca. This brought me great pleasure and proudness, with him showing signs of being an extrovert.

On my visits, I looked after Luca and did lots of household work, as housework was not Madeleine's forte. I made dinner also, yet the reactions I got from her over time constantly were like I was staff. You could still pick it up if nothing was said; the deeper meaning of togetherness would come through. I kept picking this up. There was no change. Warning bells were going off inside me. This wasn't right. If things picked up I would be nothing but a home help for her and Luca. That would be no problem in a relationship where both work as a team, but it didn't seem like that. I was like an employee who was never acknowledged for anything I did, as if I should be doing it. It didn't feel right in one bit at all. Me moving over to Paris to become a second-hand person with nobody to talk to, except Madeleine when she was there, was worrying. Discussing this with her, she didn't recognise it and found it unsettling that I felt like this. Her employee was outspoken. This wasn't working. For me to give up all the hard work I had put into building myself back up again, to be lost and I have nothing, I would lose my newfound identity.

When I came over, it was fantastic picking him up at nursery and see him develop. Ryanair stopped their flights to Paris from Prestwick. I couldn't afford normal rates for flying to Paris. This brought attention to the fact that I was going extremely out my way regularly; the relationship with Madeleine had its problems. These increased and I could not bear our relationship anymore, having nowhere to turn. We were arguing all the time. It was painful for us both and I couldn't handle it anymore. The biggest pain was to separate and cease contact with Luca. This was crushing. I kept it going for his sake, but after a while, it wasn't worth it for him.

This was the end of four years' worth of regular flying every other weekend, to six weeks with cheap flights. This was too much alongside having to scrape money together even though I couldn't afford to fly now that the cheap flights from Prestwick had stopped. The relationship had holes and they got bigger as time went on. I never moved over to Paris, as there was something not right. I didn't have a good feeling about it. It just wasn't right. I would be so isolated with no one to talk to except Madeleine. It wasn't right, as with other parts of it. I felt alone again. There was a lot she didn't tell me and broadened the truth. The loss of trust is a core of any relationship. If it's not there, continuation becomes more difficult over time and this was the end of this path.

It hurt so much, not seeing Luca on a regular basis. When I was there, we argued and it wasn't fair on him. We even argued when we were on the phone daily. This had to end. This chapter had come to a conclusion. Phoning him and seeing him on Skype weekly helped, but not physically seeing him, I missed him with all my heart. Conversation lessened with his little knowledge of English and Madeleine wanted me to speak only English with him. This proved very difficult and increased the ache in my heart from not seeing him. It was weekly pain, yet I still called him every week to see him. I eventually arranged a few visits a year to see him. It would cut my heart not seeing him grow up and missing his development. By now I was used to pulling my chin up and getting on with life, only the blows were getting bigger. This chapter had parts that ended and parts that will always be with Luca.

I am looking forward to the future with Luca.

Life Coaching (Alcohol Unit)

All men dream, but not equally, those that dream by night in the dusty recesses of their minds, wake in the day to find that it was vanity; but the dreamers of the day are dangerous men, for they may act upon their dreams with open eyes, to make it possible.

– T. E. Lawrence, *Seven Pillars of Wisdom*

I had been working at the alcohol unit when I was with Phoenix. I kept this going and added another day voluntarily. I was paid for a session and then did the other weekly visit. Eventually when the need for me was recognised, I got paid for both sessions weekly.

I recorded every visit with a summary of the visit's intention against the original goal, when we had shown progress and they were ready to move on. This gave me proof of progress my team leader could show the council, who were paying for my progress. It was the council who paid me and that was reviewed every year. I showed what psychological processes I was using to help people get balance and control back in their life. I would devise a programme with all the elements of control they needed to get on form again, only better this time. It covered all aspects of life, to gain balance and not aim to have all their eggs in one basket. I added life coaching skills to this as techniques to use. This worked well with the phenomenological and person-centred approach, along with my holistic health basis, and gave a personal service specifically for the clients/patients/service users. This seems all over the place with so many different skills, yet I am able get into their world and whatever they need, I use one of my skills to suit them.

Being classed as a holistic health practitioner, I decided to call myself a life coach, after a visit from a male client during which his friend phoned him, and he said he couldn't talk now as he was with his life coach. That was so much more positive and focused on progress, rather than having to go to counselling to state there is something wrong with them. Changing my name proved very successful. With the holistic approach, I helped with relaxation in the form of Indian head massage, reiki, or aromatherapy. A big part of this was remedial massage. This took away the concept of the nice little massage that really has not much purpose. The combination of life coaching and therapies provided help for the person, covering the whole of them. Being secondary healthcare, this focused on techniques of self-improvement and self-healing.

With the use of NLP, I worked by knowing what would convince them to change and put the ball in their court to take responsibility for their own progress, rather than being told how good or bad they were doing. They saw the end result that was ecologically suited to them and owned it. Being a life coach and a therapist was the way for me to go. It felt just right. This was the niche I was looking for. I was part of what's called 'moving on run' by a woman called Alison. She was great, just letting me get on with my own thing. I got on well by doing this. That's the basis of previous work where I got on with what I had to do and gave more back for being given my own space. Alison is the best as what she does. Her heart and soul goes into her section. It's as if she owns it and I own my section of it.

I listen to them and never give personal judgement on what they're saying. I never show personal opinions, only information to work out what is the best way for them to deal with it within in their lifestyles. With one-to-one sessions, I planned to further this with group life coaching sessions, which involved information that was easily understood that could be put into play. Simplistic and useful were the themes. Working with a group requires simplicity, as it is more easily understood with so many different views of the world in one room. I taught something that they understood and could use. After all, there were similar topics with alcoholics and me. There were different settings, but the same core was met in pushing things beyond their limit, experiencing a disaster, experiencing loss and bereavement, following a new way that's uncomfortable, the adjustment, letting go of the past and working through the barriers all leading to a new way of life. This brought my interests to a communal theme for people coming up against an obstacle in life. Yes, different circumstances with different results that can be caused by implicit or explicit reasons for the imbalance. They could be factors from within like beliefs and attitudes, or factors outside like circumstances, etc. I was contemplating writing a book with my findings to help specific folk with alcohol addictions. I felt the most comfortable working here. I was giving all I could to others in an area I knew from my upbringing. This also made me see from my father's point of view in terms of what he had been experiencing. It was his way of coping.

The Completion of My Honours Psychology Degree

To do exams was like the build-up and competition of an athletic event. I was pushed to the most extreme: studying 24/7 with such intensity put me off balance and my life was out of context. What was important to me before was up in the air and parts of me were neglected. I found out through the course on memory about amnesia with head injuries that my conscious memory was affected and I lost the ability at times to recall newly learned information. Instead of learning for recall, I had to repeatedly go over the study materials so often on different levels that it was ingrained deeper. This depth became recalled knowledge unconsciously. I knew it from different angles and this showed its practicality. By going over the material so much, it became ingrained in my mind, although this took so much more time and energy, but I was getting there. As I learned from my injury: if you can't do it this way, find another that is more suited to you.

The study for the second to last major exam seemed straight forward, maybe from experience or maybe I wasn't taking in the fullness of the topic of cognition. Through NLP, I had learned a massive amount about cognition, although with my acquired difficulties, I had a challenge dealing with this factual approach to a grand amount of knowledge. The materials to learn for the exam were lots of names and detailed facts. My conscious memory was failing with this task.

A month before the exam I went to an all-day tutorial. I picked up the importance of setting up the contents in the introduction to make it much clearer for the marker. I learned a technique to cover all the topics needed. This made it so much easier. Going blind into studying to this degree of university work, I was working from trial and error. This was not the best method of academic studying. I had no other way of studying that I could pick up from other people. This was a big difference for me. I sat the exam at home as usual. I needed a quiet space with extra time and breaks. This worked out best for me and for financial reasons to the Open University. An adjudicator came to mine to oversee that I was doing the exam to the standards of Open University.

After finishing the exam, it felt like this was the best exam work I had ever done, even on a higher course. Six weeks passed and I got the results. This was absolutely crushing. Instead of getting a high grade, I had actually failed. This was a complete shock. I was stunned, under complete confusion. How could this be? This brought my confusion to the whole university requirements. I thought I had it, only to be thrown off. I didn't know what way to go. It was back to guesswork and I had got it wrong.

I started my new course of social psychology and found out the date for a cognitive resit. With the dates of exams of social psychology, this presented a clash of times. I had to produce a qualitative research project, then a few more assessments, my cognitive resit exam, then four weeks till my social psychology exam. The timing involved very tight and intense studying. I found old study material from cognitive psychology and found a section of writing introductions for every chapter. Looking over the contents, I mentioned I was covering too much. Going over the chapters I used, I knew I missed so much content that I had mentioned in my introductions. No wonder I failed. The contents mentioned in the introduction would set you up for a very high mark. I had lost my aim for passing the degree, not getting a very high mark. It's like learning how to walk, then expecting you to represent Britain for gold in the Olympics. I had heightened my expectations and they were unrealistic to me. With 'my wee car bump' and no real university study experience, or academic friends at this level in psychology, I had lost touch with reality.

I would use the same introduction process, yet tailor it to my ability to cover the material I was going to use in the exam. Through trial and error, I found it clearer to work with. There was a reality in what I was studying. This built confidence within me. I was aware that the information on the course material was very effective. Maybe it was me doing the course exam again, the material was ingrained more. I sat the exam and it went very well. At first I thought it was 'in the bag' having studied the material so intensely in comparison to the other subjects. It must be a good mark this time. I would find out the result when I sat the social psychology exam.

Studying for social psychology was done so differently to the other degree subjects. This produced such high anxiety. Overall, I had to cover the chapter contents to show I had an understanding of the material. I had to use the four different perspectives from research projects that covered the chapter contents. I had to mention the themes where it was used. I looked at previous questions to give me different angles on what would be asked or what would be covered. I would compare and contrast different versions to create an argument.

I loved this social psychology. I could relate to this and it covered dealing with people in life coaching who had alcohol problems. It seemed to be more social situational problems that occurred, as well as re-addressing their strategies. Yet the subject was so vast it could go down many paths at different angles. This was different than the course work for assuming qualitative responses, as opposed to the quantitative measures of detail found in cognitive. It was the opposite. This was the side of psychology that brought me to do a degree in the subject. It made you rely on thinking through the responses, rather than remembering specific material, yet this was still required for remembering the details of the chapters. It brought on such anxiety in me having to rely on thought memory, as opposed to factual information which I had got the hang of by now. What was worrying was recall that seemed to vary if you were in a different mood, or there were other elements that could influence your performance. There was a strong need to trust yourself. I used essential oil sniffed up my nose every time I studied so to set the same mood for recalling the information. It is classed as mood, congruency and memory. The oil I used was rosemary. This suits clarity in thinking and is good for memory recall. It seemed perfect for what I needed.

When the exam came, I put in my best effort. It was based on a psychologist thinking from different angles, who was disassociated and not emotionally involved. To argue the concept from different angles, due to my way of studying, this new way of thinking was with me all the time. I was prepared for the test and gave it my best shot. It just depended if it was up to scratch of what the Open University required for examinations. The worry I had was that the next day I would find out if I had passed cognitive psychology or not. The worst thing was, I found out I was twenty points short of getting my honours degree. This wasn't my last exam. I thought I worked it out three years ago and adjusted for doing extra courses to save time and complete it quicker. At one point I was doing three courses at once. I thought this was covered. I had done this with my study buddy in the course to cover the points so we would finish at the same time.

Being short of points, we decided to do the same course to finish at the same time and end it enjoying doing the last course. It was a counselling one. After the six months of complete heavy studying, this seemed a relaxed way to end things, doing a course at a level two, which was hard, yet less difficult than the level three courses that posed the main problem. The main problem was, it meant I had to do another year. Instead of doing five years of hard work, it changed to six years, although it gave me a more relaxed way to finish this degree.

I worked out the worst-case scenario of not passing the exams and next year seemed even worse than this year in terms of studying. The stress of this was deflating; it was so close, yet I could be doing even more work. I found out I had passed cognitive psychology. That enriched me with motivation to finish this course and achieve my honours degree.

This was a major accomplishment after having a head injury. It worked with all the other aspects: I refused to accept the fact that I couldn't do things like public talking, walking, running and open swimming. I could do it under my own steam and not succumb to what is socially expected after a head injury. I refused to be limited in my life and these things were very hard to complete. Even if I had to learn my own way of doing them, I did. My drive proved itself, not letting this head injury win. Under no circumstances was this head injury going to win. I had to find out if I was successful with social psychology. Then it was a straight forward ending to content I knew. At worst, I would have to do a resit, but that would be okay.

I was given my results from the course. It was a fail, although I was just over a pass by my marks. Questioning this result, I was told that with my exam scores, I may have got one question higher than the others and that would make me just pass. They were looking for more even-ness with the answered questions. So, resit it was again. In a way it gave me a better opportunity to dissect the material I love the best out of psychology. The day of the passing out parade was getting very close, after years of hard effort and putting my ability at 100 miles an hour all the time, sometimes 120.

I was finally going to achieve what I only dreamed about as a way of getting past other people's and my own view that I couldn't make it anymore. My inner self was helped by this motivation, yet it seemed like a fallible dream. Going beyond that fear of failure, I went for it, thinking if I wasn't successful, at least it would get me closer to a better way of being. This dream was becoming real.

Everything is possible. Get rid of your expectations and what could be perceived as limitations and 'just do it'. Everything has a way. It's finding that way that suits you and just making it happen. There may be knocks and blows, but keep with it by experiencing that energy of you achieving it. Keep the thought fresh, as this will give you motivation when needed and keep you on track. It doesn't matter what you were before, if it 'rocks your boat', experience the energy this gives and go for it to keep you on track. Don't let it win!

I sat the social psychology exam. This was indeed my favourite. I studied intensely both the subject and what the university were looking for in the answers. I had been given a lot of advice before, but it wasn't till this point that it all clicked together, like any aspect of your life.

After this, I was lined up to do a counselling course to finish. What a good way to end, not being so intense in a subject I knew and already use. This learning experience would end when this course was complete, only to see if I move onto another chapter of my journey, or continue on with this theme to masters in the same topic, if allowed in with my low scores, or perhaps in development of people or companies.

With a head injury, I had a lot to prove. I excelled with my physical improvements. Also, I intended to gain an honours degree. Instead of being the worst point in my life, acquiring this injury, I have turned it around to make it my advantage, whether away from pain of failure, or towards pleasure in achieving. With all the ways a head injury can affect you, I wanted to prove to others and myself that I could overcome this looming shadow of academic education limitations. There was a personal interest to show I could do this particular one. There were the social implications of me passing this qualification: I had lost my social identity and psychology was getting me back there. Lastly, there was the survival point, of the importance of a new career that hurried its completion. I was sick of being on the bread line. It was very tough at times, but I kept focus and used the coping skills I had gained to put me back on track to achieve this. At times coming up to exams, it was like a professional athlete doing a competition and putting his maximum into the event. This was me. I experienced going at maximum pace to overcome my difficulties that surfaced in academic education. More importantly, I had learned about me. This was a very valuable life lesson for me.

CHAPTER 11

Lulu was looking, I was looking:
Our paths crossed.
We were on the same path.

The most beautiful things in the world cannot be seen, they must be felt from the heart.

– Helen Keller

There was one girl who I bumped into occasionally that I was attracted to. We seemed to get on well together. Although it didn't seem right to push to a relationship, the aim for us was just to get along. That was a lot easier and not complicated, yet there was something there. I couldn't explain it. Words failed me, but I kept drawing myself to be with her more. It was unexplainable. There was something about her. Not knowing her fully, I didn't know what it was that attracted me to her. Deep down, I was picking up some amazing sensation that left me with an intensity of feeling I've never experienced before. There was something there I couldn't explain, but I wanted to take it further. Consciously I knew it wasn't the right time and I needed to get myself sorted after the knocks I'd experienced. To make things more complicated, I picked up that she was attracted to me. We got on so well, so relaxed with each other's company, yet there was that attraction between us both that kept getting in the way and demanding attention. I got her phone number and our contact went on.

At times, there was an amazing amount of flirting going on and we met for walks. On every walk I was hoping for the opportunity to kiss her. Something kept me from kissing her in case I picked it up wrong, because she was important to me for some reason. I guess I was worried that I just assumed she was attracted to me: There were no words spoken about togetherness. There were many times I would beat myself up by not taking the chance to kiss her and poorly justify why I hadn't. There was one time where I was determined to kiss her. We met and went for a coffee. All the way through the day, I justified that this was the right time and got side tracked.

Our company was so relaxed and felt just right with this underlying attraction I had for her, and maybe it was the same for her with me. I could only hope she had the same attraction to me. If she didn't, the loss would be tremendous. Opportunities came up — possible chances I had to kiss her — but I didn't want to give the impression of it being second nature in to get intimately involved with females. The pressure of kissing her was a scary crescendo of missing the chance again and if it was missed, it would eventually be too late. One time we met and I drove her home. Before she went away, I grasped my confidence, leaned over and said, "Come here," and I kissed her. The kiss was so gentle, with feeling. It was amazing. Thankfully, it was evident that our kiss was due to mutual attraction. I got that from our reactions to each other. There was no evident tension over a difficult situation. I picked this up with no words mentioned; the way she kissed and cuddled, is what I was looking for.

As time went on and I found out more about her, we had so many similarities. This felt so right between us. We both had an attraction to each other and we had similar life histories, like our dads having a big liking for alcohol, previous relationship similarities, and losing things in life: they were different items of belonging but they were similar in terms of emotional reaction in dealing with them.

We saw each other once a week, leading to overnight at mine, making it a weekend event. I would also see her on Wednesday after work and get my dinner up there also. Her step-dad prepared magnificent food that was all home-made, sauces and all. It was always absolutely brilliant. His engineering background led to his precision in cooking. Her mum was like me, keeping busy all the time. They were both great to be around. The family dog was acquired at the dog rescue centre in Glasgow. He was a presumed Staffordshire bull terrier. He had the strongest legs I've ever known in a dog. He was renowned for going for other dogs and defensive about other people being around Louise and her mum. They loved the dog, but were at the end of their tether. How the dog behaved annoyed me, and I wanted to know what would change that. After a long time of taking him out for walks, he got to know me and built up trust and knew my boundaries. When he walked, he was always pulling so hard. It would take you off balance if he moved about. After nearly falling a few times, I learned quickly and brought the leads in to lessen his momentum. If he got upset by another dog, I would just lift him up by his harness, leaving his back legs on the ground. This dramatically took his power away. I used an authoritarian approach to calm him down when this was happening. I was the leader of the pack.

Months later, I discovered his aggressive stance for other dogs was his defence. He learned that it was not called for with the strong support from me, and it disappeared months later. He didn't need to be the leader of the pack anymore. I was doing it and he built up trust in my stance. There was constant pulling that needed to be addressed, so I took him out jogging with me. This was the first time his lead slackened. Running kept him focused, rather than seeing things that would normally get him worked up. I also made a noise accented as: "Heyyy up," that I constantly used in the same way so he knew exactly what it meant. Dogs don't know English, but work on tones and body language. I used this always when I was displeased with something. I used operant conditioning to get him behaving in a more suitable way. When he heard the same voice tone of, "Heyyy up," he automatically changed what he was doing. The same noise worked for Louise when she used it with him. I became close to this dog and he was my six o'clock shadow every time I went to their house. I was his 'precious', as Louise's mum said.

Louise's family were very close. The closest I had ever seen. The whole family accepted me so well. Her sister, brother, mum and dad, on her mum's side: her aunts, her cousin and her gran. Her gran was 96 years old and wasn't well.

I cut her hair a few times. It was me attempting to be one of the family and they were one step ahead of me with their acknowledgements of my nature. They were so pleased Louise had found someone who cared for her so much and was a 'worker'. If anybody needed help, I was there, especially for walking Tucker as often as I could. This gave him a routine and helped balance him out with working to a schedule. We all need some form of structure to get by. Tucker gave me full trust and doted on me. I've only ever experienced this twice in my life with dogs. It's a unique, close unity that words fail; such a strong bonding between man and animal.

I was welcomed into her family. I could see it was genuine and that firmed our togetherness even more.

We used to meet every week and we got on so comfortably well together. Inside I wanted to take our relationship closer, so one time I bought her a single red rose. We met and I gave her the rose. She seemed delighted, yet later, she behaved as if she was following a routine. It sounded process-based. I thought I had overstepped the mark and this was it, on the downhill. I phoned her and instead of ignoring it, I brought it straight on and mentioned to her about her reaction. She said when she went in she cried the minute the door was closed. I thought, Here we go. At least going downhill I'd ski down instead of dragging my feet through the snow to the bottom of the mountain. Then she said that nobody had ever given her a red rose before. She was touched so much. Whaow, this meant so much to me, showing me her affections as a result of me getting her a red rose.

On the next meeting, I told her that I loved her. She said she was in love with me. My heart exploded with joy. I had never experienced meeting with someone I was hugely attracted to, we got on the best I have ever experienced and we just seemed to click together. We were on the same line, of the same page, of the same chapter, of the same book. This was a million to one. This was my soulmate. I had spent a lifetime looking for such companionship and eventually I had found her. She was the same in finding me. You don't know how love is going to work its magic with whom and where, yet it does out of the blue. The small part of the surface you are aware of shines so bright and the deepest part of you tells you that it just knows she is the one. This was the start of our shared adventure, supporting and loving each other like I have never experienced before. It was love on a different level.

As time went on, she was the only one I trusted with thoughts of myself. I had brought up such vulnerable things with her that I had always kept quiet about, relying only on trust. This was the biggest step I took with anybody in letting them into my very personal ground. It seemed natural to her and she was so pleased I had opened up to her in this way. After giving her this, she opened up to me, talking about her vulnerabilities and secrets. This cemented our togetherness. I recognised our unique similarities. She was the one for me. My life was important with her in it. I had eventually found that person to share my life.

Every day I love her even more. From past relationships, we know the pain of being in unwanted areas. We share this similarity and turned this into one of the strengths of being so close together. This was, in my view, one in a million. It was so rare that we had similar physical attraction to each other, different life events, yet we experienced similar themes and were products of the aftermath of alcohol on families that only those who have experienced it can understand. We both were on the lookout for close love. The one thing my accident gave me was her. Finally, I had found my soulmate. We had the same path and life was never to be ventured alone. We had support and love for each other.

This was it. I trusted her fully. I told her things about me that I've never told anyone because I wanted to. Never had I experienced the need or want to share such closeness with anyone before. Only in the past, I've shared that which made me feel vulnerable and defensive – being presumed as a burden and me not being up to scratch. Instead of making their life better, they attributed being tied down to my presumed needs, therefore I never showed anyone my full persona, ever. Years of going out my way, only to have my openness and trust thrown back at me. This being the response I always got, whether it was true or not, it formed a pattern that I would never verge across the boundary line, therefore I wouldn't get any more penalties, until now. One last chance and I scored a goal. Going through this brought back major anxiety of never being so open to someone before. It was completely new and scary: the fear of the unknown.

Yes, I lost so much through this accident and ventured into areas of unknown territory. The constant fear of the unknown became second nature. I was always prepared for the best and worst outcomes. This could be compared to someone in the army who was trained for extreme survival conditions. There is no way he can let his guard down. It is always up ready. Over the years, this may lessen, but the core is always there. This is like me, having lost something so personally valuable in delicate times, I'm always on guard, instinctively working on how to solve things with my motivation as my friend. Louise was let into my world of gold and crutches. I have never felt this strongly about anyone before. We weren't with each other for better standing in society, friends or family, it was about true love. I had spent my whole life looking for closeness like this and against all odds, our paths met. We seemed so in tune with each other, giving plenty of support and love. 'We were fighting against the world' is a phrase I love.

You don't know who that person will be, what they will really look like, you just know. We all have lists in our mind of the ideal partners. Their job, their hair colour, body shape, humour, and so on. That's in the realms of lottery to find someone as perfect as this. Would you really want someone as perfect as this? Someone that has no faults compared to your world? How they deal with this is another realm of questions.

I had won one of the biggest parts of my worldly experience and I wouldn't let my injury win again. This injury had ended my life as I had known it. All material and social standings were lost. I was left with nothing, yet with this clean slate, I could construct what I wanted out of life, not having the cultural restraints of growing up in a certain community dictating what you can or can't do. I was turning the next blank page and could put anything in it. Through my experience I learned to listen to myself and not what society expects. I learned that we all act in different ways to do different tasks. To get different results, you change the way you deal with things and act differently. Starting with a blank page to construct my new life – Life Part 2 – the acquired injuries gave me limitations that became 'my cross to bear'. I painfully learned to change how these burdens were represented to me. After losing control based on what society predicts and you experiencing not fitting in, I gained control of the choice of how I was going to deal with situations. I could change anything I wasn't happy with. See it from a different angle, adapt, or choose to not get annoyed by it – to do something different, or stop doing it altogether. It's your life. You have the control to change anything. You can be with people who are important to you. This control gives you the power to live your life the way you want to.

We went to a lot of family gatherings together and the feedback I got from family was that Louise and me worked well together. We were an item. As time went by, being together, we talked about really being together – buying a house and getting married. This went on for a while, talking of being together, and it looked we matched and both wanted the lifetime commitment to each other. Talk of getting engaged a few years after our studies was a prominent discussion. We went around jewellers to see if anything caught her eye. This was important, as she would be wearing it all the time and it had to match her idea of an engagement ring. We also talked about the most special place I would propose to her. It was summed up that it should be in a place special to both of us. The place that kept coming up was up the Cloak road where we used to take the dog up at least once a week. It was so peaceful, so scenic and quiet. Eventually we decided on a ring in which the stone was raised so the marriage ring would go next to the engagement ring smoothly. This was the ring. The jewellers said they would fit it. Louise's fingers were so thin that it was a shock, the actual size it was to be altered to. It was sent away and they would phone me when the newly sized ring was ready to be picked up.

It was my day off when I was to pick it up. I was also to pick Louise up from her university course in Paisley. When picking up the ring, I bought a single red rose and hid them both in the back of the car away from her sight. Driving home, I took a detour to the Cloak road. I stopped the car and went into the back of the car. I said we could go for a wee walk to stretch our legs. There was a point where the single-tracked road went downhill past a lock, an isolated farm, with the backdrop of Ben Lomond in the distance: this gave the most beautiful view in this whole area. We stopped to look at such a vista, that changes every time with different weather. I said I got the ring back and brought it out. With the ring in my hand, I kneeled down and asked her if she would marry me. Smiling profusely, she quickly said yes. This was a milestone in my life that I will always treasure. The path had changed upon finding a person to share my life with. We were both so pleased that we were to be together always. It was more of a commitment to be acknowledged by others as being together, rather than to ourselves. We knew we would be together always. It was so unique to genuinely find someone who held the same beliefs about being together always. We both looked for a soulmate, as time went on, and we eventually found each other. It was amazing how we actually found each other. When I got to know her, I just knew she was the one and it was the same for Louise about me.

Our families were so pleased for us. We both got on well with both sides of families and the support was there.

As time went by, I got the email saying I had eventually completed the honours psychology course. It was a completion that didn't seem real to me. I phoned the head office and yes, I had. A flow of success after all this hard work, I was electrically alive. I was to get my qualifications in the post and they enquired if I wanted to go to the graduation ceremony. What a way to end it. Of course I did. I had dreamed of this graduation in dark times to keep me going, to complete this challenge of making my mind work to a high level. A higher level than it was before. I stepped aside from the obstacles my injury presented me with, and got results that suited me. As time moved on, my qualifications came through the door: it was such a finalisation to see them, but not ecstatic. I put them in my qualifications folder and focused on my next step. With me finishing this course after six years of work, it left a huge hole that needed filling. Anxiety arose at the thought of filling this hole.

Being involved in swimming teaching, I had work with the local council as well as coaching at the swimming club. I seemed to be very good with kids. I could get attention and enthusiasm from them. Going back into training and now with a focus on kids, I aimed to go for a postgraduate in primary teaching, or a master's in educational psychology. I had a direction again. Going for teaching, I had to go back to college for higher English and maths life skills 5. My honours degree would get me in, but I needed these qualifications too.

I applied for three universities in primary teaching and one for educational psychology, which was my ultimate directional choice. I would apply for as much as I could cover all my options. 'Belts and braces' – I was as double sure of getting in to some form of education. I also booked my gown and photos for my graduation. There were two graduation ceremonies, one in the morning and the other in the afternoon. Coming from the other side of Scotland to an area I didn't know, was not appealing, so I went for the afternoon. I asked Louise if she would see me getting my award and she gladly said yes. It was brilliant sharing a very prominent part of our lives together. My sister said she would be there. She had seen me grow up, hospitalised, recovering, and turning things around for myself. It would be so valuable for her to see it, and finally my sons. Euan would be away on holiday and Adam said yes. This was going to be an amazing experience. After many years of hardship of going against the grain, I was finally ending this journey. My 'study buddy' Debbie was going to the morning session. It was a shame that after all what we had been through we couldn't end it together. That was a sore bit of this occasion.

I got my suit organised and sorted out my things for the day. We were taking my car through to Edinburgh and getting the tram in to the centre. Louise was driving. Before my graduation from counselling, I went myself and I organised every level well. Relying on Louise driving was a load off my mind with all that was happening that day. It made her feel she was contributing to my day. I cringed inside because she went by what she remembered going to the 'park and ride' once before a few months ago. I Googled it and memorised the driving procedure in case she forgot at any point. Time was tight and we couldn't really afford time wasting. Adam had an important football match on. I wanted him to see me graduating as he was so important to me. Being with older women, to see me graduate and having to go hours through the ceremony and hours of clapping may have been too much for him, especially the age he was at. He went to his football game instead. Well, he got the 'player of the year' award. He could see my photos of the event. I was disappointed, yet I understood why he didn't go.

I was up doing my exercises as normal. We got ready and double checked we had all forms, wallets and purses, and phones to keep in contact if we were separated. We went to the car and smiled with anticipation of the day. Driving up the coast from Largs, we stopped off for my sister, Margaret. Then we headed on to Edinburgh. The weather was low clouds, so it was a bit foggy. This faded away after Glasgow. It wasn't sunny, but it was dry. At times, the sun came out through the day, which was okay to good, plus the temperature was good to slightly fresh.

The 'park and ride' was easy to find. It was next to the airport.

There were lots of places to park and we waited for the new tram system to Edinburgh centre. We waited and it came. My sister was so pleased with its 'ding, ding' noise before it stopped. The journey was good. Then we got off at the west end of Princes Street, Then a short walk down Lothian Road to the Usher Hall. We were in good time, so I went into register and made sure we had a contact by phone. I got registered easy and quick. I got my tickets and their tickets. I went out and handed the tickets to them. I was to go upstairs and get my gown. Just like registering, there was no queue, so I got one straight away, and the coloured tabard. I went downstairs to meet them again, then we went next door for professional photos of me. Margaret said we had been to the hall when I was a wee boy. I had dreams of sitting in the gallery in the exact place Margaret pointed out. That was amazing. Again, no queue so it was quick. The photos were taken easily. I had to stand on taped footprints on the floor, so it was no hassle. It was over just like that. I had anxiety about these processes; if my family weren't allowed to be there in the supposed queues, I was concerned how they would fill in their time.

Back down outside the hall, we decided to go for a coffee. Louise was hungry so we looked for a place to eat instead. Walking up the busy street for a while, I was gowned up for the graduation. I looked out of place. It was as if I should be giving out fliers to the general public. We found a good place. Margaret found her burger was the best she'd had for ages. I just had a cappuccino. I wasn't hungry. I looked out of place in the restaurant too. It was designed well. It looked modern, yet relaxed. It looked well planned and was run well. We were in there for a while. Still early, we went back to the hall to go to our seats. I was in the stalls and they were in the first floor. After I got seated, it was quiet and I got a text from Louise asking to go down to the start of the stage and I would see them. I went down and turned around. They were on the right side away up front just above me. They were so close. I was so chuffed. I went back to my seat and talked to my neighbouring graduates. We were in the last row and there were hundreds of graduates. When it started, it was with a wonderous routine of dressage, bringing in staffs and people high up in education. The speaker talked about the honorary degrees given to people like Sir David Attenborough. Then we watched a video of the Open University. Its main aim was to let folk achieve further education like degrees who couldn't in the conventional way.

This applied to me, for not passing the educational requirements from school and the traumas of my head injury from my accident. Instead of being written off, I had the opportunity to change it. The Open University was perfect for me. It focused on your potential. Yes, it addressed areas which challenged me and my disability couldn't permit me to do that in a certain way. I got the opportunity to find my alternative way of learning and mastering memory problems I had acquired. Then there followed another video of people getting their awards and all the different extreme reactions like dancing. To me, it lost the appeal of graduating by making a silly entrance that catches attention. The ideas came into mind of the different ones I could use, yet my conscience disallowed it due to any embarrassment it might cause. This went on for over an hour.

The ceremony began. It started with the few who received master's and doctorates. Then it was us with honours, then degree and higher awards. When asked, we were to line up the side in a big line to go on the stage when your name was called. I was impressed by their organisation of the order with the names. With every person, they got an clap for their achievement. There were so many people and the clapping became difficult in keeping up momentum. I just thought of the effort I gave to do this course; they deserve a big clap. I'm sure they would do it for me.

Eventually my line was called up to stand in the queue at the side. I was bursting with excitement, yet worried if I was to make a mistake. Everybody must be going through this. I had come to an idea in what I would do on stage. I'd stop, look at Louise and Margaret and say thanks with my arms open. Eventually my turn came. My name was called. It happened so fast. I stopped with open arms and lip spoke thanks, only it was very quick. Then I had a wee conversation with the scroll deliverer. I went to the other side of the stage and joined another queue to go back to my seat again. The tube with my scroll was like a large tube of Smarties sweets. It was a long haul for a tube of Smarties.

Then the speaker spoke again about belonging to this group always. This greatly appealed to me. Yes, to belong to a group of people that have similar quests for knowledge in psychology, but also a united sharing of people who put so much effort in and sacrificed many things for this achievement. Since my childhood, in hindsight, I missed entering the army. 'Me being me' would be in the SAS. They have a similar drive for finishing your training and they always belong in a group. That has always appealed to me. That path didn't materialise, yet psychology did. I belonged to this group and felt very proud.

We met just outside and I went upstairs to hand in my gown. I had to put the gown on a big pile and that was it. I went downstairs to meet up with them again and we left to get the tram. It went so quickly, yet so much specific detail will always stay with me. I was determined now to get my master's and go up again. I guess it is a form of addiction. That could explain my thirst for knowledge, but this is more about being recognised for all the hard slog I made.

This was a perfect way to end six years of hard slog, dealing with the difficulties I acquired, but I achieved it. Physically training myself to avoid the pain of immobilisation I experienced: I wasn't returning to that. It was a fear I had that always haunted me, jangling its chains. This gave me motivation to further what had been just a vivid dream of graduating, maybe not with a doctorate, but maybe a master's. It's so powerful, going towards your dream. In theory there's nothing holding you back, only what you allow to hold you back. There may be times when holding back on one thing would benefit another thing and that choice is yours.

We returned by tram and the 'ding, ding' noise still impressed Margaret. I'll need to see if I can get the tram bell app for her phone. She would be so chuffed.

It was the ultimate honour to share my day with them, especially Louise. I wanted to share something that meant so much to me, that touched me the most. It felt so real between us. We both had communal aims to be together always. I wanted this to last forever. After all, love is the best healer.

CHAPTER 12

Conclusion of My Journey: Overcoming My Obstacles and Discovering Myself!

Good character is not given – we have to build it by thought, choice, courage and determination.

– Mahatma Gandhi.

These are my personal findings from my journey. This journey itinerary is unique and everyone is unique, yet these findings have a similar theme to big events in your life. I am sharing this path's discoveries, showing experience of great change and loss. It's not a lonely journey. The most important alterations I had to make to my journey gave me the direction to make changes. Head injuries are all different with their 'shape, formation and effects'. I found the keys that make the core difference in the life changes we experience. Some of these keys may not apply to you and that's okay because everyone is individual. In mentioning them, I have highlighted action or knowledge at the end of the category for homework to put them into action and use in your world, if needed.

The keys I found that made a difference to the quality and direction of life after a disaster were:

• Relaxation.

This is fundamental in keeping your cool and balance. It's a way of letting go of things that bother you, whether big or small. Meditation is so good for this. Meditation gives you ways of controlling your mind and the way you do things. It can alter priorities, if needed, to promote better balance and therefore results. Meditation is a way of clearing your head of unnecessary complications. Clearing the complications out of your head, it gives you a clear opportunity to create a solution and not have parts conflicting with your new ideas. This makes it easier and successful to promote a oneness within, which improves your well-being.

• Change your breathing.

When stressed in thought, your body responds ready for action with a 'fight or flight' scenario. Your thinking affects your breathing, therefore your body responds to the signals from the brain. You just flip it around: you change your breathing. Your attention is on your breathing. You can only think of one thing at a time, thus changing your thinking. (Magicians use this to distract your mind. Counteract this by taking control of your breathing: if your breathing is slower, deeper and relaxed, then your mind becomes relaxed.) You find more solutions being relaxed and will not show bias to an area which confuses your choice. This way you have control over external events or even inside thinking.

Action – practice and use relaxation through every angle of your life, plus master your breathing to give you control.

• Linguistic change, language control: it's not defeating you.

Language is something we don't give much justice. It's affected by culture, social situations and what environment you are in. These frame your thinking. What is spoken and the way it's said, your body finds its meaning, thus responding to it. Also, what you say to yourself enhances meaning over the conversation. It makes things worse or better by re-framing its meaning. For example, if you say, 'I can't do this,' your mind looks up the meanings from stored information, then the behaviour follows with the body reacting and it becomes tedious and boring.

Another version of this is instead of using extreme phrases, if you normalise it, you will get a normal result instead of an extreme result. For example, change: 'This is absolutely the worst ever,' to, 'This has been better.' Your body minimises how it responds. This can also work if you want to enhance a topic. Instead of normalising, you exaggerate, thus enhancing your drive and your behaviour, and your body follows.

Please note and be aware of conversations in the future to see this in action.

• Coping skills – NLP (neurolinguistic programming): swish, pattern interrupts pattern changes.

These tools are very important to me. They helped me by convincing me that this injury is not winning. They use communication language to work for you. I'm going to succeed, not just survive and get through life. Learning NLP for me was the difference between using tools for surviving and succeeding. NLP brought control back into my life. Having control in your life at any time is one of the biggest keys. There might have been something I could have used instead of NLP, but NLP was fast and very effective, so I chose NLP.

Rather than taking years to correct a psychological problem, I changed old pictures in my head to new ones repeatedly. They reformed the pattern to one I wanted, with the effect being rapid change. I pictured this old image with its exact location, its size, colour and clarity, then I make a new picture of what I want with its location difference noted also with its size, colour and clarity. 'Swoosh', the old picture to the new, replacing its location, size, colour and clarity with the new one. Your mind changes how this old picture is represented to you to the new one. For swish to be effective, location change is the key. Do this at least six times so it becomes regular and replaces the old picture to become automatic. Practice in different situations so you'll know it'll work.

Another one was breaking up the pattern by hard blinking, saying 'blah' loudly and closing my eyes when I wasn't in company. Blinking could be done in public. It interrupts the un-useful pattern and its strength, and eases out the frame of what you want to get rid of that isn't working for you. These do it right in the middle of the pattern. Then you can decide what you want to replace it with. The most suitable thing I found was the opposite thought to show contrast, and it can be amusing too.

Another useful tip is reframing the event by making what it means to you more intense or less. Change what you are saying to yourself, as with the linguistics of NLP. For instance, at a busy food store going towards the checkout: instead of saying to yourself, 'This queue is moving too slow. I'm getting even more frustrated,' say, 'The queue has given me time, now I can spend time breathing to relax and make this work for me. I didn't have time to relax before. I'm taking advantage of this to make events work for me.'

Action – practice what you would say to yourself in negative situations so it becomes natural to use words that change the results. Be in control of what affects you. You hold your own reins. Allow yourself to build the solutions you want.

• Pattern interrupt.

Being caught in thoughts and feeling can make you feel stuck. You just can't seem to change them or their behaviours. This can deflate your confidence. Your mind can only hold six bits of information, either plus or minus two bits. If you change what is a priority to you, your body reactions change to the most prominent thoughts automatically. Think of something completely different that you have interest in. Make the new thought stand out with fascination and this thinking takes prominence. It's advised to have different forms of attention to push away those prominent previous thoughts, i.e. doing exercise where you are consciously aware of your performance. It's being preoccupied with your attention on the safety and benefits of this physical improvement. This takes over your thinking and breaks that problem. Do anything that takes your attention away from your stuck thinking, to give you a newer thought that has benefit for you.

There is ways NLP to use; making a distinct noise or action to break the pattern of thought before it can return is fast and effective.

Think of something different to your benefit, like doing another task that will benefit you far more by doing it. This works well and is an important part of mastering your thoughts.

Action – practice and use swish, pattern interrupts and pattern changes to give you control over your situations and change bad results to better ones for you.

• I found role models that helped me on my way and broke that lonely feeling.

Even with family, I was still alone in this world. I would now see life events differently, yet others would only see what was socially accepted. That had its plus and minus points and I succumbed to my enhanced sensitivity.

My reaction would be different from others, showing we weren't on the same page, as if we were looking at different books. Apart from the social loneliness, this could be an acquired gift.

Increase knowledge and understanding of how you observe things are done by other people, and use this to your advantage. Learning swimming is a prime example of this.

• Self-hypnosis.

This method of relaxation works very well for me and was a personal key to gaining control by showing strategies of how to deal with situations better. I get relaxed and my mind's focus is on something different, to feel comfortable. By relaxing, you switch off the barriers you have to give you another view of achieving what you want, and it takes away the protocols of anxiety. By constantly listening to self-hypnosis CDs, the relaxation suggestions are taken on board by you and it slows down the fast pace inside yourself. With repeated listening, you mind knows no difference between actual and repeat visual contents, so it thinks you've done it many times and takes away the anxiety. It also helps clear out the unwanted clutter in your mind surrounding events which affects how your mind performs. With my processing difficulties, this made a huge difference to me. It's like when I had to go for exams, I had to go to a quiet room with no distractions that would affect my attention. This gave me clarity of thinking and direction. Cut out anything you don't need in your mind.

Action – practice and use self-hypnosis to give you another view via relaxation, to get the best results for you.

- Studying new material.

Studying made me focus on content I found interesting. Seeing things in a new way gave me so much drive and energy.

It improves your learning. It's something different to focus on, something else to talk about, new friends and different content for organising which is another way of learning more skills. You can get courses free online, or indulge in the nearest college or university. Gaining new information and beliefs helps you to move on in this ever-changing world and not be stuck in the past. You constantly update yourself and that leads to changes, big or small, in your development. At first with my acquired learning challenges, slower processing and my writing being slow, this was a fabulous catalyst for recovery that led to new skills by giving me different motivation. I found my alternate physical and mental exercises a way of being for me. This level of studying takes up a lot of time and discipline with work to be done on time. Studying worked for me. It directed my attention to something different that I am interested in, thus making my production in life a positive one. I was making a result for myself.

Action – find a course of a subject you're interested in; start with an easy course if you haven't had much use with computers and learn the process for other courses if this is for you. Make it work for you and have a 'want' to finish it.

- Tai Chi daily.

This holistic martial art gives you so many life skills and a way of living to get you prepared for the day. After learning the Tai Chi form, I do 'the short form' to keep me in the right frame of mind and focused so I can react automatically if I ever need to defend myself in any life experience. Far more importantly, it makes me stronger, and able to adapt to events in life while keeping control. After doing the form, I am ready to take on the day and prepared for it. I would change up how I did it for variation, and to see it in different settings. Having to relax in a different way, you become aware of different energies and sounds all around you. You can pinpoint them precisely. It's using your peripheral vision like a can, relaxing to hear and sense all around you. This is a perfect example of a pattern interrupt. With this, and remembering the moves in different modes with your body position and your intent, it is perfect for blocking out negative thoughts. Also, it makes you aware of energy all around us, and you don't feel alone.

Tai Chi minimises what's in your head. This is another benefit when you're trying to keep only what you need in your mind, not wasting time and energy. Doing Tai Chi movements and following its way of living makes it pure, simplistic and crystal clear. It cuts out confusing detail and keeps to the primary basics. This worked very well for me; instead of having lots in my mind that's irrelevant, which has a major impact on my performance, I performed as best as I could with my energy and focus only on what's needed. I lived for the 'here and now'. Tai Chi has been around for a long time and is beneficial to me in helping to clear my mind of useless stuff, which was key in my future being. It works so well for clearing your mind and achieving balance in your life. After all, it's another form of meditation.

Action – you can learn Tai Chi from the beginning and practice daily to give you focus so it becomes second nature. This is a great example of a pattern interrupt and is very useful.

• Regular exercise: swimming and running worked for me.

Exercise is a perfect way of destressing. First of all, it changes your focus onto something different, like meditation. This is a universal core for controlling yourself and it is essential. Exercise is great for improvement, and for your body functions to work as they should do with all the natural chemicals like adrenalin, serotonin, and dopamine and so on.

These chemicals put balance back and put you in a better mood, giving you a natural high and drive. It's how you are supposed to function. It also gives you achievements that you can relate to other aspects in your life. This can be said for any hobbies or interests. It gives you more strength, enabling you to cope with situations better physically and emotionally. Different forms of exercise produce different results. For example, swimming pushes physical achievements to improve my ability for achieving goals; whereas running lets you solve both the world's and your own problems. It also makes you achieve small goals to push yourself.

Problems are caused by different parts of you conflicting with each other, producing unrest. I summarised lots of research by going over a few key areas. In exercise, you can see things from another point of view that doesn't bother or upset you, to forgive others for making you feel bad. Then let it go. Hanging on to the intensity of the problem keeps up the intensity of these bad feelings. Making it less relevant, makes the emotions less severe. Some things are easier than others to let go of and this is holding you back. Is it worth the hassle it causes? Afterwards you feel physically and emotionally fitter. Your body is working the way it should and exercise increases energy.

Knowledge – find a physical activity you like and build on it to get results, and experience the change in chemicals within yourself for balancing and giving you more energy.

• I always do exercises first thing in the morning to set me up for the day.

My morning exercise is for flexibility, stretching, building up strength, swimming movements, and to help focus, to improve my posture and clear my mind. This sets me up for the day and makes me ready for its wonders. I would highly recommend this. It takes away any feelings of being run-down to make me fighting fit and gets me in tune for the day ahead. It speeds up my vibrations inside which makes me savour challenges, knowing I can cope with situations. It's like training at a job, for the way to handle and deal with situations. I was doing the same. It also stretched my mental ability, because I would push myself not to give in with all exercises. This gave me self-discipline.

After the exercises, I would do the tai chi short form. Yes, 45 minutes a day before I washed, got clothed and ate. Then I was prepared to tackle the day. Sometimes it seems like a hassle, yet it is worth doing. It makes your body work as it should be that with focus, and improves your posture. I love it and still do. It was a valuable way to help me feel physically better, look healthier, improve my health and get set up for handling things that the day could bring. I was focused. The mind needs exercise like the body. Puzzles are good, but the most effective learning is from subjects that make you think of other parts of your life and how this integrates with it, or not. This keeps your mind working. You only have one life, so live it!

Action – exercise is key. Practice and put into practice exercise suited to you. This has so many benefits for you physically, and inner chemicals for balance.

• Dealing with isolation.

There are times when you feel alone and the whole world is against you. For me, when there was a lot happening, I lost control and felt different to what was going on. I felt a social difference and became alone. It was hard to get a good sleep then. What worked for me was every night reading a page of a book called *365 Day Tao* I got from my work in the Rainbow room. There was a topic for every day to do with life that focused on energy or not being trapped by society's expectations. Tao gave me a unity in life and a sense of belonging. Knowledge gives power to replace the power loss. The topics would also work in your mind later to put this into perspective in terms of other aspects of life. It takes attention away from your stressful focus, and since you can only focus on one thing at a time, it helps to not to keep you awake or feeling isolated. At the end of the day, it comes down to what you think. What you focus on. Change your focus to change your thinking.

Also exercises when running – expanding energy to fill the house, to fill the street, town, county, country, Europe, the world, other planets and the whole universe. This meditation works well when feeling insular.

Knowledge – this increases your understanding and makes you feel less alone.

- Get up at regular times.

Our body has a natural clock. It knows our sleep routine, when to be hungry, fluid intake, peaks and troughs of energy at different times, and it knows when to issue the needed biological chemicals you and when, which improves your functioning and so on. There are sayings that show these body clock patterns: a saying like 'an early lark or an evening owl'. You may be more suited to getting up early and function your best in the morning, or you may get up later and are best in the evening. It's having a regular time to get up which balances your biological functioning, thus evening out erratic energy and behaviour that affects your life. I always set the alarm early in the morning and always get up. I don't put the snooze on. I just instantly get up. Your body reacts to the sound of the alarm like conditioning and I had a set routine of exercises to do. This woke me up and by that point, I was awake fully and had done more things.

Action – put it into action and just do it. It can be a change for your body, yet this is the path to better function and works with the whole of you, giving you more understanding.

- Structure to the week.

Get a diary in which you can see the whole week on two pages. From one look, this gives you a clear picture of your week. It takes initial discipline to plan your week, but it's taking control of your week. You put in your regular tasks, exercise, relaxation, hobbies, etc. that you plan to do. If there are any gaps, this gives you a chance to productively fill the spaces. This gives you a productive week and you can see what's happening. You also see what you have achieved in the week. Oh, the benefits of planning. This generates a sense of achievement and you can be more aware of how to fill your time, instead of following daily life as a lost sheep in a panic.

Action – buy a weekly diary and use it from now on to experience the benefits of organisation on your productivity. We all need planning.

• No matter what happens to anybody, they may feel a loss to some degree, of something they had or could do, and now they can't due to its loss.

It's important to understand it in relation to the big picture of your life's journey, and get rid of the rigid unspoken thinking that society presumes you will act in a certain way, that's not needed anymore. You have the chance to make your own direction in life. The most important changes you can make are what you want and ways to achieve it.

With the unknown reality of my injuries and brain function, will things improve over time or not? How will I fit back into society again? This is the biggest fear. The loss of who I was before and having to make a new life, only this time I had more knowledge and experience. I saw things in a different light and in a different way. I didn't want to make the same mistakes again. I would use this as 'my life part two'. My life was totally upturned, as with so many other people that I wasn't aware of before. With this, apart from many other side-effects, my sensory awareness became very high, so things may not go back the same way but life is never the same. It's always changing. It's like days. A day happens continually, but no two days are the same. If you look for sameness, you'll find sameness. If you look for change, you'll find change. That's how we develop, to continually improve. We change and adapt; sometimes we are not aware of the changes or adaptations, yet they are there. Who wants to go back? It leads nowhere, whereas moving forward gives development as a person.

Knowledge – this will increase your understanding of loss to give you more control.

These are the main points. I'll now mention other important parts that give you further understanding. This no doubt makes an important difference too.

• The actual trauma that occurs that can dramatically change your life. In my case, it was my 'wee car bump'.

With possible injuries to your physical or emotional self, there is loss of your old way of life. That life has died. To some degree, if not all at once, loss comes to you.

I started from the beginning again: I commenced with new ways. You have the opportunity to live the life you want to. These new ways are different and require adjustment to achieve the same thing, only in a different way. It's the new way you begin your life again.

These new ways promote difference. Yes, you behave differently. You have been through a major upheaval, whether physical or emotional, of course you are different: you are a wiser self that has developed and grown from these challenges.

• The power of laughter and flexibility has immense qualities.

I love a laugh and it makes me think of things in a different way, not such a big deal.

Flexibility is very useful with the vastness of life. This life is not rigid. At times it needs to adapt.

Having the outcome in mind of different methods increases the chance of them matching greatly. These two are very important.

Laughing will increase the effect of your coping strategies.

• Not letting society's expectations control you. You control yourself.

A classic NLP statement says, 'Who drives your bus? Who

controls you?' You can't control external events, but you can control yourself inside and not allow things to get to you. Let them go. With all that's happening, or changing, it cannot change you: the real you. Your behaviour CAN change, but who you are WON'T change. Don't succumb to letting events change how you view things if you know it has no benefits for you. Reframe to suit yourself and what you want to achieve.

- I have learned from education and experience.

It comes down to perception. The event or situation has constructed in their world what's right or wrong to suit them. They may be not aware of it, yet this influence can give you the perception that it is black-and-white truth. It is mainly truth for them so that they belong to a group of social understanding. They don't really question it. On picking up their perception, I step back and refocus on my aim and what I am good at. Their version may be an important view which offers me an opportunity to adjust my perception to get the results I aim for. It's suiting the conversation to match their version of their world. It's just changing my priority and my aim comes first. Other influences can help, but it is not important, nor will it ruin what I am about.

- Food intake (nutrition).

It is important that you eat for nutrition and not just for that feel-good factor. The food you eat gives you the energy, performance enhancement and nutrition for your body. I kept food basic and natural relying on water mostly and eating regularly. It is best for my system. This boosted my energy. With exercise, and correct food intake that boosts performance, this made me function better. Study what foods are good for you and keep away from processed foods. If the food you eat is more natural, the better the results it gives.

- Appearance.

How you look is very important. It makes you feel good about yourself and that adds to your ability to perform. This also enhances your self-esteem. Getting your clothes sorted out the night before gives you time to think about what you are doing tomorrow that will make you look the part. Preparing can be a hassle, but not as bad as a morning panic and having a bad day while not feeling right or that you don't look the part and 'chase your tail' all day. The same can be said for your hygiene, cleanliness and hair. Aftershave too conditions you into a successful state. The same applies to your appearance. When spraying aftershave, imagine great things happening where you feel so good. Each time you spray it, those feelings come back even stronger. The fewer situations that can mess up your day, the more quality time you can spend on the important things.

- Ways of coping with short-term memory problems.

Short-term memory is a major problem for head injuries. Make life simplistic so knowledge of where items are can be found automatically with no conscious thought. Position things like wallet, phone, keys always in certain pockets when out and I always keep the keys on the door handle when I'm inside. This process works well. Have a strategy in place to adapt to a better way of remembering that's easier for you to work with.

To remember events, look at the theoretical process of memory. When we gain information of the event, it becomes encoded. It gets stored, and then can be retrieved. Conscious coding is needed. Exaggerate the subject to make it stand out when you look for it in storage. If you don't consciously store it in your mind, distinctly and fully, its recall will be hard. Exaggerate it and constant repetition in different circumstances makes a difference.

An effective method is to make an exaggerated story in your mind relating to other things it reminds you of.

An understanding of this process helped me greatly. Most importantly, let go of the thought of not having a 'perfect memory'. Even using techniques to help memory difficulties, there will be times when memory lets you down. Nobody can remember everything 100% of the time. Accept and let this annoyance go to improve other aspects of your life.

- Striving for what I need to improve.

Initially striving to master life events is a core of living that make you develop quicker. Learning how to overcome events is a major part of your life development. This added to my drive – I wasn't succumbing to the injury and reacting the way that society expects you to. Life is always changing and nothing stays the same. It is always changing, so all things need alteration. You have to keep ahead of events. It's like maintaining a house. It constantly needs attention, some rooms more than others. Maybe something broken, maybe something new, or rooms just freshened up by painting. It's constant. That's the way I look at life. It was reinforced by tai chi – life is always changing and requires discipline in keeping your standards up for control and being prepared. Failing this, you are under the control of situations and not being prepared for events. Succeeding lessens the amount you have to process and leaves you with less to worry about in case it goes wrong. It's been checked and sorted earlier. This is a good example of time management and being in control.

One of the big breakthroughs for me on this journey was recognising the fluency of speech.

My problem, called dysarthria, or as some call it 'foreign accent syndrome', was playing its game. This altered my speech by what's called the porosity, volume, pace, tempo, pitch and speed and could change the words spoken to a different meaning. Breaking down conversation to different levels helped greatly. I had difficulty with the speed of words. By adjusting the tempo, pace and pitch and importantly, coming away from how things are said normally, I was able to accent different areas to create interest and a different meaning with the subliminal part of a conversation.

I also found hypnosis, which fitted me like a glove. This made life seem much easier and in my control. It creates a different way of thinking and relaxation. You can only focus on one thing at a time, so if you are stuck in how terrible things are, change your focus to something else like relaxation, and the body follows the thoughts.

All the achievements I made gave me the strength through day-to-day repetition of 'I can do it'. This injury was not winning.

This strengthened up my determination. I had a will not to conform to what is presumed you should suffer and be limited to by a traumatic accident or disability. With NLP, there is future pacing. I went over and over events till it felt fully right inside. This might have taken a while, yet by the end of it, I know I am fully committed and have covered the events of things not working out. Even preparing your body, chemicals assist you with the needed changes that will keep you at your best, not in a panic situation when faced with the unknown. This strengthened my ability to do what I aimed for. Anything is possible. Everything has a strategy of how it's done. You find out that strategy, adapt it to you, and you have a drive to achieve this. IT gives you motivation to accomplish what you want in life.

Life is too short. Instead of waiting for things to happen, you can make them happen. Sometimes they will happen, sometimes they won't happen, and that's okay. An old saying that my grandma always used is so relevant: 'What's for you, will not go by you.' It's more worth trying than doing nothing instead, waiting for something to turn up, if it does. Seize the opportunities. Be in control of your life and make your life as close as you want it, if not all the way.

With NLP I had discovered later on the deeper aspects of what communication levels and psychology entails.

In hindsight, I wish I knew about this angle to understand communication, although it's got to be learned through different perspectives and understanding of other topics relating to this. In a way, this knowledge of communication enhanced my sensitivity. Communication is on multi-levels. The actual content of what's being discussed depends on the delivery from the person and what affects their version of it at that moment, whether the influence is from inside or out. It also depends on your state at the time. The two of you need to be in similar states, to get the communal meaning. There is so much hidden information, such as the power ratio in this content, and whether it is individual or socially based. The underlying intention gives a deeper meaning and sometimes could be different from the original content. This comes from cues from the other that relate to stored information of what this means and how to respond to it. With head injuries, cues can be picked up wrong and therefore people predict a different response. In some people it is major, for some it is minor.

To throw in a spanner in the works, we all are universes within every single person. Your body will make improvements with the constant self-healing it is designed to do. It doesn't mean that everything will be healed either physically or cognitively (cognition is based on social expectations). It means you can see a difference, as long as you work towards an aim. There are some illnesses that can't be self-healed, yet attention to your quality of life is vital. 'All answers lay within' is the best quote from Milton Erickson.

To follow this, I want to address not the trauma of the aftermath of an accident, but the gift it gave me. This too, is within. My sensory acuity was now so sensitive that I could pick up a lot from people that would be missed before. These senses we all have, yet after an incident, we can become more aware of these. The film I saw recently backed this up, where three people acquired a new sense after illness and nearly dying in a tsunami and experiencing the loss of a brother. In this film, these separate tales heightened this theory of mine and I wasn't just assuming. I became attuned to people and situations to do with energy levels. I seemed to acquire a sematic strength and with massage, I could pick up exactly where the injury was. That was just with my hand over the spot. I could pick up the cause of it. That was the same with health concerns. With this gift, the only downside was when there were a lot of people and the atmosphere was bad, I felt I was overloaded and made my excuses to leave.

This got me thinking, was this totally due to my accident? Was it part of my nature, or was it situational in being in the right place at the right time in my life? It could be one thing, or another, or even all together. After years of puzzling thought, it really doesn't matter. It's here now and I am working out what strengths I have. A good description is yin and yang. There were losses I experienced, yet I was given special skills that I wasn't really aware of. In seeing this in a new light, I can put this to use in a new way. Anyway, this adds light to the severity of the losses I experienced. My inspiration, Milton Erickson, had amazing sensory acuity; he could pick up amazing information from his patients. Cheng Man-ch'ing of tai chi founded this martial art based on sensing the other to counteract their actions and put them off balance. I am honoured that the people that were special to me, had similar characteristics of sensory awareness and experiencing health conditions. I seemed to be in the same club, although I never got a free badge and wasn't invited to the Christmas night out.

There are so many people I know who had serious head injuries and by chance they could continue working, which this giving them the motivational pressure to improve or adapt. Motivational pressure isn't something you can instantly put into place: it comes from the whole of you at the right time and the right place. Each part in its way has advantages for you in following this path. There are many parts of you and if they are aligned, your self-survival kicks in for the whole of yourself. It is the same for athletes in training. The constant push forward is driven by motivation, and gets them to their peak performance. This brings me to the story of Roger Bannister's one-minute mile. Before achieving this, it was impossible. When this idea was turned on its head, there were folk achieving this one-minute mile. This so-called rule of what is possible changed.

You set your own rules, not of what's expected by society, mainly from your own thinking. Make your own new rules and be realistic. There's no way you can say, 'I am going to climb Everest in one big leap.' This may be real in your head, but in reality, it's not possible.

Yet, it's seeing outside the box of what you can or can't do, only governed by your limitations.

Being outside the box is always scary and unknown. It's better to be doing something than nothing. Doing something and not achieving, is a step closer to achieving as you gain more knowledge and experience, rather than doing nothing at all and being stuck in the same place. That's what progressing in life is all about. Life is constant learning.

A famous cognitive psychologist named Piaget mentioned that learning through trial and error finds the way that's suited to you. The life lesson from this is to always have an aim, constant meaningful practice, reward for achieving, and a plan to constantly move forward.

Life is constant learning and it's not just for recovery with the case of injury or ill health. I profited through flexible learning to improve and fit in. This vital life skill is needed with the constant changes in these modern times. You are always learning. I learn through academic work to stretch my thinking and constantly improving my walking and physical ability. For me it's through athletics like swimming and running to get the best of my potential. There are so many skills these give you, not just actually running or swimming. It's the quest to master them with physical constraints at this particular stage. I never let my health slide away. I control my fitness physically and mentally with constant studying of the facts of the world. To some extent, I am in control of my physical being and health. With the mastery of academic work, I have learned so much about how to improve my writing style. This in particular, meant my injury was not getting the last laugh – I was laughing. Gaining control is giving ownership to you.

Lastly, society has unwritten expectations of what you should be and therefore do. Now you do things or aim a bit differently than before. It may appear that you are stereotyped to be and act in a certain way. These rules are unwritten. With consistency, you can change these presumed rules and expectations and be yourself. Your will changes these expectations and your determination can win honour in society as you accept the change in yourself. Society can stereotype you. If you change the expectancies of society by chipping away at it, the stereotype can be broken for the new you. Remember this: injury, illness, situations, or events aren't winning. You win!

FURTHER READING

Anthony Robbins, (1992), *Awaken the Giant Within*, Simon and Schuster Ltd., Sidney, Australia.

Betty Lou Leaver, (2001), Bouquets of Bitterroots, iUniverse.com, Inc., Lincoln, USA.

Rosen S. (1982) *My Voice Will Go With You. The teaching tales of Milton H. Erickson*, W. W. Norton and Company, Inc. New York, U.S.A.

Rhodes, R. H., (1952), *Therapy Through Hypnosis*, Hal Leighton Printing Company, California, U.S.A.

Shelle Rose Charvet, (1997), *Words That Change Minds*, Kendal/Hunt publishing company, Iowa, U.S.A.

Whitsett, D A., Dolgner, F A., Kole, T. M. (1998), *The Non-runner's Marathon Trainer*, McGraw-Hill books, New York.

Myself climbing on the Buachaille Etive Mor, Glen Coe

At home at last, visiting my mum with Adam

At the Astley Ainslie

UNIVERSAL hero: Tommy Paterson of Largs receives his award in London for Headway Achiever of the Year from Louise Lakin, Great Britain Miss Universe, on left, and Katrina Hendon of the sponsors.

Recently we told the story of how Tommy has fought back from brain damage after a serious road accident to regain his speech and movement. (ps)

Pyrenees in the Gavarnie region

Pyrenees

Gavarnie

Famous gap between France and Spain in Gavarnie

On my way home

Delivering my life coaching classes

Printed in Poland
by Amazon Fulfillment
Poland Sp. z o.o., Wrocław